If I Had a
Hammer

If I Had a Hammer

More Than 100 Easy Fixes and Weekend Projects

Andrea Ridout

Collins

An Imprint of HarperCollinsPublishers

This book makes every effort to present accurate and reliable information. It is not a substitute for professional electrical, plumbing, and other home building and repair services. If you are not completely confident in proceeding with any of the projects outlined in this book, you should call a professional. The author and the publisher are not responsible for any damages or losses resulting from reliance on the information contained in this book.

The images on pp. 2, 3 (hammers, screwdriver, interchangeable tips), 4 (hacksaw, measuring tape, balance), 5, 6, 9, 11 are courtesy of Great Neck Tools, Mineola, NY. The images on pp. 3 (drill), 4 (Cordless Circular Saw, Reciprocating Saw), 5 (staple gun), 38, 128 are courtesy of iStockphoto. The images on pp. 29, 105, 121, 122, 140 (chair illustration), 144, 145 are courtesy of Bill Strode. The image on p. 45 is courtesy of Insinkerator, the leading manufacturer of food waste disposers and instant hot water dispensers. The image on p. 48 is courtesy of ACP. The images on p. 59 are courtesy of Stanley Segel. The image on p. 62 is courtesy of wallies.com. The image on p. 68 is courtesy of Jody Davis. The images on pp. 92, 93 are courtesy of Mark Clement, author of The Carpenter's Notebook and The Kid's Carpenter's Notebook, www.thecarpentersnotebook.com. The images on p. 168 are courtesy of M-D Building Products, Inc. The images on pp. 193, 194 are courtesy of Saint-Gobain Technical Fabrics. The images on p. 220 are courtesy of Thompson's Water Seal. The images on pp. 233, 234 are courtesy of Amerimax Home Products. The images on pp. 239, 246 are courtesy of The Quikrete Companies. Andrea Ridout supplied the remainder of the images.

HarperCollins books may be purchased for educational, business, or sales promotional use. For information, please write: Special Markets Department, HarperCollins Publishers, 10 East 53rd Street, New York, NY 10022.

FIRST EDITION

Designed by Jaime Putorti

Library of Congress Cataloging-in-Publication Data
Ridout, Andrea.
If I had a hammer : more than 100 easy fixes and weekend projects / Andrea Ridout. —
1st ed.
p. cm.
ISBN 978-0-06-135318-5
1. Dwellings—Maintenance and repair—Amateurs' manuals. I. Title.
TH4817.3.R53 2008
643'.7—dc22   2007041948

08 09 10 11 12 ID/RRD 10 9 8 7 6 5 4 3 2 1

Dedicated to my family and friends—
most of whom helped with this book.
Without them, I would not be here.

contents

foreword

by Ed Del Grande, Host of _Ed the Plumber_ on the DIY Network

I always say that first impressions are the best guide to know what a person is really like. So far, Andrea has made two very good impressions on me since we've known each other. Andrea and I met a few years ago over the phone, and to this day we have maintained a close friendship. At our first meeting, she was kind enough to invite me to be on her radio show, and I was expecting the interview to be like a standard radio interview. Usually the guest stands by while the host does a lot of talking, and every now and then the host will ask the guest a question. Boy was I wrong! Andrea welcomed me like part of her family and was well informed about our subject. Then she practically turned the show over to me, letting me talk one-on-one with her audience, becoming a listener herself. It is very uncommon to work with a host who is so giving, and my first impression was "what a kind and confident person this is." In our many radio interviews since then, I realized my first impression was right on the money!

The second very good impression that Andrea made was when she recently sent me an unpublished copy of this book to read. What follows is my actual e-mail that I sent her after I started to read the book. I think this letter says it all:

> Hi Andrea, I already started to skim through your book and my first impression is, "Hey, this is Andrea talking to me." I know we have been friends for a few years now and we have a mutual respect and admiration for each other. Because of that, I always expect the very best from you. However, this is a

breath of fresh air to see that you write as you speak and your wonderful per-
sonality comes through with words as it does when we talk over the phone.
This is a gift that many people in our business cannot achieve: the ability to
mix good information with a real down-to-earth personality. I look forward to
continued reading and seeing what other surprises you have in store for me!

Sincerely, Ed.

After I wrote the e-mail, I continued to read Andrea's book. The more I absorbed, the more I appreciated the technical aspects of the projects. For instance,
when Andrea tells us how to change a faucet, she not only goes over the installation instructions, she also teaches us how to choose the right faucet for the job.
From a Master Plumber's point of view, this is key information that most "How-to"
books overlook. Another example is the simple but very effective tips contained
throughout the manuscript—such as the little known tip about pressure treated
wood. Andrea tells us that most pressure treated wood is not really waterproof,
and a wood sealer or stain should be applied for proper waterproofing protection.
This is all valuable information that every homeowner needs, and Andrea tells it
like it is.

This is how I feel about Andrea, and I want to add something very special to
what I've told you so far. As of yet, Andrea and I have never met in person. Eventually our travel paths will cross and when that happens, I know I'm going to get a
very good third impression from Andrea!

Ed Del Grande / Master Contractor / eddelgrande.com
Author of *Ed Del Grande's House Call*
Spokesperson: Kohler Co.
Columnist: Scripps Howard News Service
TV Personality: Scripps Networks

introduction

As I sit in my office typing this, I look around at the myriad of unopened boxes of brass hinges, wrenches, toilet seats, window film, a sack of paint rollers, and a pile of cordless drills. The pockets of my overalls bulge with the usual: leftover washers, cabinet knobs, and screwdriver tips. My overalls are my standard uniform—I have more pairs of them than I have blue jeans! Not that I'm complaining. In truth, I love it. I host a home improvement radio show, you see, so I live and breathe this stuff 24/7.

How did I ever get so hooked on the "do-it-yourself" bug? How can I explain a lifetime obsession with home improvement products and processes and the people who make and use them? I think the addiction can be blamed on my parents. They restored a Victorian house in Connersville, Indiana, during the mid 1960s when I was just a wee lassie. Well, I say that *they* restored the house, but that's not really the truth . . . all of us kids were expected to help, too. From my brother Jim and my sisters, Kate and Christy, who were in high school, to Phil, who was in junior high, and finally down to me, just a grade-schooler at the time—we all learned how to use hammers, drills, and other tools with aplomb. Through all the smashed fingers and spilled paint, my parents were reasonably patient teachers. They must have been, because I do not think Valium was invented yet. Though we children might have contributed to some of our parent's gray hairs, I look back on those days with fondness. I could drive a nail long before I could drive a car. It was great fun.

Just as many people do, after we fully restored the house and got it just perfect . . . we moved. And not just around the block—but all the way to Texas. But we brought the do-it-yourself legacy with us. By the time we were able to say "Howdy, ya'll," my folks had bought another house and we all helped to fix it up, too, sometimes with a bit too much enthusiasm. One weekend when my parents were on a trip, my sister and I painted all of my mom's Duncan Phyfe mahogany furniture bright orange. Are you cringing yet? Well, believe it or not, she loved it. It was the 1970s, after all.

As an adult, I ended up owning a hardware store that specialized in products for antiques and old houses. The more I learned about history and hardware, the more of a purist I became. So eventually the orange paint had to go and my mom's furniture was refinished back to its original mahogany red. This is just a small example of how tastes change and why one should always think before buying orange paint.

In my hardware store, I developed a love of gizmos, gauges, and gadgets. And as I became more proficient at using them, I wanted to help my friends and family enjoy these wonders of the modern world, too. When my inner circle got tired of listening to me, I began a home improvement radio show. I love to pass on what I have learned to anyone who asks for help. That's why the show is called *Ask Andrea*. So be careful what you ask me. I may give you an earful.

For instance, I went to a friend's 1950s home not too long ago and noticed that many of her glass doorknobs were loose. She was frustrated that they kept falling off and some had even been broken. In no time, I scooted from door to door, adjusting each knob and tightening all of the setscrews. An easy job for anyone who has done it before, but she thought I had worked a miracle. Before leaving, I gave her a quick lesson on what to do if the knobs ever fell off again. My friend was so excited that she suggested I write a book full of tips for fellow homeowners on making simple home repairs. She may have just been trying to get rid of me, but in any case, *If I Had a Hammer* was born. As the sixties song by Peter, Paul and Mary implies, if I had a hammer (or a screwdriver) I could accomplish quite a bit, and it's really true.

So here it is: this book is my advice to you as one friend to another. In it, I've assembled many of my favorite do-it-yourself projects—some that can be accomplished in short bursts, many in one hour or less. You'll find an assortment of preventative measures that can keep small problems from becoming bigger ones. For larger issues, I'll walk you through how to resolve them as quickly and as comfortably (on you and your pocketbook) as possible. You'll also find many fun decorative projects, too. So whether you're fixing or updating your home, you'll find plenty of ideas to suit your needs.

While I have been a do-it-yourselfer since I was young, I am constantly learning new ideas and techniques. That is why I invited many of my friends—the experts who visit on my radio show each week—to contribute their suggestions here, too. I've also highlighted some of my favorite tools and products throughout each chapter. To help you decide which projects you'll want to take on yourself, I've applied a rating system of one to five hammers, with one being the easiest and five the most challenging. If you are a newcomer to home improvement, you might want to start with one- or two-hammer projects and then gradually tackle more complicated tasks. In truth, there's no rhyme or reason to the selection of projects included here. It's much like my radio show in that it is a potpourri of ideas. But I hope that you'll find a few to suit your needs and maybe have some fun along the way.

Doing your own home repairs, maintenance, and improvements is not rocket science (or brain surgery, for all of you rocket scientists out there). Simple instructions coupled with the right tools can save you hundreds, even thousands, of dollars and lots of hassle. Plus, you'll be building memories with your family and friends that can last a lifetime, like I have done for years. So grab your hammer, keep reading, and let the repairs begin.

1

the right tool for the right job

Tips, Tools, and Techniques to Get the Job Done Right

> The big secret in life is that there is no big secret. Whatever your goal, you can get there if you're willing to work.
>
> —OPRAH WINFREY

Whether you are replacing a broken tile, regluing a wobbly chair frame, or waterproofing a deck, to complete any home maintenance project correctly and efficiently, you need the right tools. Half the fun of working around the house is learning to use the gizmos and gadgets that help you achieve your goal.

We'll begin this chapter with my picks for the top-ten household tools that everyone should have, then we'll pull together a basic home repair kit that all do-it-yourselfers need. We'll also go over a few safety suggestions and troubleshooting ideas. For all you old-home restorers, we'll discuss some of the do's and don'ts of getting the most out of your historical location. And while you may want to conquer many home improvement projects yourself, we'll address when, why, and how to hire a contractor—just in case you need some professional help along the way.

▶ Household Tools 101

▶ Project: Assembling an Everyday Home Repair Kit

Household Tools 101

Buying the right tools can be a daunting experience. Walking into one of the many huge home improvement stores with brand names blaring their messages at you can alarm even the most experienced tool owner. I myself have collected a huge assortment of gadgets over the years, some of which I have never used. I even have a few hand-me-down items that look more like torture devices than practical tools. So don't fret if you're sometimes baffled by a tool's appearance or function. I've compiled a list of the top-ten must-have tools every household should have, whether you are a newcomer to doing it yourself or an old hand.

1. Hammer

If I had a hammer, I'd hammer in the morning, at noon, and at night. In fact, the hammer is one of the most used tools in any home. Abraham Maslow, the great psychologist, said, "If the only tool you have is a hammer, you tend to see every problem as a nail." Perhaps that's true, but it would sure be hard to accomplish much around the house without this basic tool. For everyday tasks, I keep a small 7- to 10-ounce household model in my kitchen tool drawer and a midsized, 14- to 16-ounce version in the garage tool kit. Depending on your needs, you

---

may also want a large carpenter's hammer for jobs like deck building or wall framing. Though hammers are simplistic in theory, there are many new hammer technologies on the market, ranging from those with tuning forks in the handle, which cut down the reverberation on your arm, to $200 contractor models made with titanium heads.

Before you buy, visit your local hardware store or home center and try out several types of hammers until you find one that's a good fit for you, especially if you will be using it frequently. If you're going to be hammering above your head or in a strange position, look for a hammer with a magnetic nail-holder in the tip that makes a hard-to-reach place much more accessible. Specialty hammers such as a rubber mallet and sledgehammer can also be useful for certain projects. Rubber mallets should be used on materials that are easily damaged or broken, such as a brass faucet handle or a tile backsplash. And a sledge-hammer is just the ticket when extreme muscle is needed for jobs such as breaking apart a sidewalk or tearing down a wall.

2. Screwdriver

Probably the second most-used tools in the home, good quality screwdrivers can be lifesavers. To save money, instead of buying several versions, choose models that have a center shaft with four interchangeable tips (including a smaller and larger size of both flathead and Phillipshead tips) to accommodate a wide variety of jobs. You may also want some mini screwdrivers for use on toys and computers or even your glasses. Battery-powered versions can make repetitive jobs a snap. A cordless drill can also double as a power screwdriver if you have the screw tips to go along with it.

3. Cordless Drill

A cordless drill with a variety of drill bits can help you complete many jobs more quickly and easily. Look for a drill that fits your hand comfortably and feels well balanced. If you have room, keep a small drill (under 10 volts) in the kitchen and a larger model (18 volts or more) in the garage. A fast-charging battery (one hour or less) is also convenient. If you use your drill a lot, you may want to keep a spare battery or two

in reserve. Some manufacturers now make batteries that can fit several tools interchangeably, going from a drill to a sander or a circular saw, thereby saving you money on duplicate power packs.

4. Saws

A small hacksaw and a cordless circulating saw can be extremely useful. Hacksaws are just right for cutting small tubing or wood projects. I keep a small cordless power saw in the garage for cutting plywood, paneling, and other thin materials. I save my larger corded model for projects like deck building and wall framing. Another handy tool is a reciprocating saw. This bad boy is like an alligator, cutting through almost any material with no discrimination. They are very handy for hard-to-reach spots and demolition. Just be sure to follow all safety instructions carefully and keep all saws out of reach of kids. Another tip: before sawing, spread a drop cloth out under your work area to make cleanup easier.

5. Measuring Tape or Yardstick

Measuring tapes come in many different lengths and widths. You'll want to keep a 16-foot tape in the kitchen and a 25-foot tape in the garage tool kit. It's handy to have both inch and metric measurement scales, which are usually found on the same tape. Choose a tape measure that is strong enough to support its own weight when extended at least 3 to 4 feet away from your body. A stiff tape can be useful when you're measuring across a room, since it basically guides itself. Check out the new electric versions that extend and retract automatically, which are especially useful when you need an extra hand. A yardstick can double as a tape measure, plus it makes a good straightedge for hanging wallpaper and other decor.

6. Level

Whether you choose a laser level or the old-fashioned bubble variety, a good level is essential for hanging pictures, bookshelves, wallpaper, and curtains. Laser levels which use a beam of light to form an absolutely straight line can also be used in place of a chalk line to set tile, carpet squares and other flat materials that must stay along a straight path.

7. Pliers and Wrenches

Every home needs a pair of slip-joint and needle-nose pliers. Needle-nosed pliers feature a long nose that can reach into tight spaces. Most versions also sport a handy wire cutter. Standard slip-joint pliers are made to grip nuts and other objects to tighten or loosen them. Another handy plier is a groove-joint plier, which has wide jaws that can grip larger items.

As for wrenches, the grip-type wrench, featuring a rubber belt or strap that wraps around an object, is quite handy for jobs such as opening a jar or loosening faucet handles. The straps and grips can be used on delicate surfaces, without scratching. New versions of wrenches that have multiple pins inside of a socket or "head" can adjust to fit various nuts and bolts and other irregular shapes. Since they are infinitely changeable, you can use them on multiple sizes of jobs, particularly if a bolt head has been stripped or is hard to reach, such as in a tight corner. However, if you only have room for one wrench in your home, make it an adjustable spanner, also known as a Crescent wrench, just like your grandpa had in his toolbox. They are still quite handy for a wide variety of jobs.

8. Staple/Nail Gun

A cordless or manual staple or nail gun is very useful for upholstery, curtains, and even home crafts. Choose a small model that is rated for household use and be sure that you can operate it, especially if your hands are not very strong. More than once, I've had to use someone else's staple gun, and it has left me with an aching hand and wrist. Cordless, powered guns are extremely helpful, as they can usually dispense staples and small nails, and have become quite affordable. I also recommend keeping a hammer around when using any type of nail or staple gun, to pound in those stubborn holdouts that need to be shown who's boss.

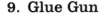

9. Glue Gun

Any crafter will tell you that a glue gun is indispensable for hobbies and many home repairs. Choose a model that uses ½-inch glue sticks, because they're suitable for both small and large jobs. I admit, the newer cordless glue guns are quite convenient, but they may not be able to keep up with high-capacity usage, so for all of you serious hobbyists out there, I'd stick with the traditional version. Pay attention to the types of glue sticks that you purchase, too, because they are rated for various types of projects. You don't want to use wood-rated glue sticks on a scrapbooking project.

10. Utility Knife

A utility knife is a must for trimming vinyl floor tile, wallpaper, leather, and carpeting. There are many great versions on the market, some with a light to help guide your cuts and several with built-in blade storage. Modern blade technology has produced versions that can last up to ten times longer than older models. When laying carpet or vinyl flooring or doing other repetitive cutting jobs, you will want the blades to last as long as possible. Break-off-blade models are less expensive and will work quite well on thinner materials. Just remember, when handling any kind of utility knife, always stroke the knife away from your body.

While you're tool shopping, pick up an assortment of protective gear, such as goggles, glasses, earplugs, gloves, an apron, kneepads, and a sun-shading hat to keep your head properly covered and ventilated while working outdoors. You might also want to invest in a tool belt to keep things close at hand while you work.

PROJECT: ASSEMBLING AN EVERYDAY HOME REPAIR KIT

Level of difficulty: T

When a repair is required, nothing is more frustrating than searching in vain for the proper screwdriver or wrench. Giving tools a proper place in the home can be a real time-saver when a problem arises. Most of us hide our tools in the garage or basement, but I recommend keeping an everyday tool kit in a drawer in your kitchen or laundry room for problems that arise on a regular basis.

You will need:
- ✓ A drawer in the kitchen or laundry room
- ✓ An assortment of essential tools
- ✓ Labels and a permanent marker

1. ORGANIZE THE DRAWER SPACE. Make a list of tools and tidbits you use frequently (each of us has our own needs, but many items are universal: see my suggested checklist in step 2), then divide the drawer into segments accordingly. If you don't want to spend money on organizers, just look around the house. An old plastic silverware tray can find new life as a tool holder and a discarded plastic egg tray makes the perfect nut and screw sorter. Select a square cookie tin or large margarine tub for bottles of glue and other liquids.

2. GATHER ALL YOUR ESSENTIAL TOOLS. Set aside the items you already have from the list you made in step 1 and then go shopping for the remainder. Here's a suggested checklist for what you might keep in a kitchen or laundry room kit.
- ▶ Small, 7- to 10-ounce hammer
- ▶ Multitip screwdriver
- ▶ Cordless screwdriver or mini cordless drill
- ▶ Mini screwdriver set—for toys, eyeglasses, and computers
- ▶ 16-foot measuring tape
- ▶ Ruler
- ▶ Superglue

What tool can be your best friend? The humble flashlight. Although it is one of the most overlooked gadgets in the toolbox, don't take it for granted: it may save your life, or at least your sanity, during a power failure. Locate the flashlight in a place where you can easily find it in the dark. Every few months, make sure its batteries are fresh and your bulb is good. Keep a spare bulb and extra batteries on hand as well. Ask yourself if the light is bright enough to help you find those extra blankets stored in the basement on cold nights. It's also wise to keep a rechargeable flashlight or two plugged in at key areas in the home, such as in the kitchen and near the breaker box. For homes with kids or older folks, choose models that light up automatically during a power failure. Some flashlights can even be shaken to recharge the batteries in an emergency. These are great for situations in which you might not think about changing the batteries often or where recharging is difficult. I store one in my car glove compartment, and it has proven to be invaluable several times.
(Resource: Paul and Kerri Elders, WordPros Publications)

- ▶ White glue
- ▶ Glue gun and glue sticks
- ▶ Assorted pliers
- ▶ Adjustable wrench
- ▶ Grip-type wrench
- ▶ Picture hangers and cup hooks
- ▶ Various nails and screws
- ▶ Duct tape
- ▶ Carpenter's pencil or marker
- ▶ Bubble level and small laser level
- ▶ Heavy, good-quality scissors
- ▶ Safety glasses or goggles
- ▶ Goo Gone or other adhesive remover
- ▶ Small flashlight
- ▶ Light-duty extension cord
- ▶ Assorted spring clamps and spring clothespins
- ▶ Velcro strips and/or other items that you use frequently

3. LABEL EACH TOOL. Be sure to label everything with a permanent marker or labels that say "Kitchen Tool Drawer" or other location to help each item find its way back after use. Another idea is to paint the household tools a bright color, such as fire engine red, and be sure that everyone in the household knows that the red tools always go back into the kitchen drawer (or whatever the location). Yet another idea is to label the inside of the drawer itself or trace around each tool's location with a permanent marker so it is obvious when it has been left out of the drawer: like a crime scene and you have to find the culprit! ■

CREATE AN INSTRUCTIONAL-BOOKLET BINDER

If you're one of those people who can never find the instruction sheets or booklets when you need them for appliances, tools, and toys, you're not alone. We all seem to keep them in the wrong place or optimistically throw them away, assuming the item will never break. To avoid future frustration, create an instructional binder for storing them all in one place. Buy a brightly colored three-ring binder and fill it with clear plastic sheet protectors. Then simply place each booklet and assembly instructions in its own protector. Keep warranty cards and original store receipts there as well to make repair claims easier. Label the edge, front, and back of the binder so that it's obvious what's inside. Find a centralized spot to store it and you'll always have the info that you need when you need it. I keep mine with my cookbooks in the kitchen. ■

Quick Tip:
Handy Multitools

Keep a few all-in-one multitools in strategic locations around the house for quick fixes. A multitool usually consists of a screwdriver, a knife, a corkscrew, and other tools in a handy gadget that often looks like a large pocketknife. One version even has a small hammer on the end. I stash one in the glove box of my car for those on-the-go problems. Multitools can be a real time-saver when a simple repair is needed. Just be sure to keep them out of reach of children.

Safety First

Any time you are doing any kind of home improvement, safety must be your primary concern. Invincibility and manual labor do not go together. My friends from DoItYourself.com offer the following advice for avoiding accidents when working with tools.

1. Wear protective glasses or goggles when using power tools, and when chiseling, sanding, scraping, or hammering, especially if you wear contact lenses.

2. Wear ear protectors when using power tools, since many operate at noise levels that damage hearing.

3. Tie long hair back and do not wear loose clothing or long necklaces or scarves that might get caught in tools.

4. Wear the proper respirator or face mask when sanding, sawing, or using substances with toxic fumes. Try to do all of these projects outside or in a well-ventilated area.

5. Keep blades sharp. A dull blade requires excessive force and is therefore more likely to slip and cause accidents.

6. Always use the appropriate tool for the job.

7. Repair or discard tools with cracks in the wooden handles or chips in the metal parts, as they may fail and cause injury.

8. Don't drill, shape, or saw anything that isn't firmly and properly secured.

9. Take care when storing oily rags, which can spontaneously combust (I am completely serious—it's not as cool as it sounds).

10. Don't abuse your tools. They have feelings, too.

11. Keep a first-aid kit on hand.

12. Don't work with tools if you are tired or under the influence of drugs or alcohol. Power tools are like cars in this way, except you generally escape with your life from tool accidents.

13. Read the owner's manual for all tools and know the proper use of each.

14. Keep all tools out of reach of small children.

15. Unplug all power tools when changing settings or parts.

Ladder Safety

According to the American Ladder Institute, close to two hundred thousand ladder accidents occur in the United States each year. Don't become a statistic. Follow these simple tips and stay safe.

1. Whether you are cleaning your gutters or repairing a roof leak, if you feel uncomfortable or unsafe going up or down a ladder, no matter how new or sturdy the ladder may be, hire a professional. The money spent may save you a trip to the emergency room.

2. Wear flexible, closed-toed shoes, not sandals or high heels, when climbing a ladder. Tennis shoes are ideal.

3. Set up the ladder on a flat, level surface. If possible, have someone spot you from below, keeping one foot on the ground and the other on the ladder.

4. When working on gutters or roofing, use an adjustable ladder stabilizer that attaches to the ladder and braces against the roof. This helps keep the ladder from slipping and allows you to work on the gutters directly in front of you. It is also important to brace the feet of the ladder by putting them on blocks (to make them level) and then driving stakes into the ground right behind them.

5. A ladder's base should rest approximately one-quarter its vertical height from the wall. In other words, an 8-foot ladder's base should stand 2 feet from the wall, a 16-foot ladder's base should stand 4 feet from the wall, and so forth.

6. Choose the correct ladder for the job. Ladders are rated according to its type of use and weight limit. Follow the manufacturer's recommendations.

7. Select a ladder made of the proper materials for a specific usage. For example, do not use a metal ladder for electrical work.

8. Use a stepladder or A-frame ladder for most interior jobs. Extension ladders are normally best for outdoor use.

9. Never stand on the top two steps of a ladder! Never!

10. Don't be sentimental about using Grandpa's old ladder if it is ready for retirement. Only use a ladder that you're sure is strong and in good shape.

11. Buy a special ladder tool bag to hold your equipment within easy reach, or wear a tool belt. Overreaching is one of the most common causes of accidents.

cool, dry spot, out of the reach of small children. Avoid moisture, which can cause surface rust and damage to motorized equipment, as well as excessive heat, which can deteriorate rubber and plastic parts over time. It's best to keep your tools as close to a normal room temperature as is possible. Tall, roll-around tool cabinets are a convenient way to hold everything you need. I purchased one recently that features a removable top portion that is a small toolbox itself. When you just need a few tools or want to tote them around, you just snap it apart and take the top with you. You might also select a smaller model on casters or just a conventional toolbox with a sturdy handle. Some folks prefer to hang their tools on Peg-Board or other wall units. The inside of a door can even be used for this purpose; just be careful when opening it.

Learning to Use Glues and Adhesives

Do you get stuck when choosing the right glue for jobs around the house? Aliphatic resin, polyurethane, or ethyl cyanoacrylate? Huh? Don't fret—you just need to bond with your inner glue karma. Of course, there are many specialty glues designed for particular uses such as joining PVC pipe, which can be a wobbly mess, but most household stickums fall into the following main categories. If you're still confused after reading about the following types of glue, just conduct a little online research to find the best type of adhesive for the job.

White and Yellow Glue

America's most popular adhesive is standard white glue, which is perfect for kids' crafts and sticking paper to paper. You probably already have a bottle or two around the house. White glue's cousin, carpenter's yellow glue (aliphatic resin), is normally recommended for bonding wood to wood. Yellow is also more water resistant and sets up faster than white glue, so make sure you set it right the first time you stick.

Polyurethane Glue

Polyurethane adhesives such as Gorilla Glue have become popular in recent years. They will stick to almost anything and are a great choice for many applications, especially adhering unlike materials to each other, such as metal to wood. But remember, less is more. Some polyurethanes tend to expand, so be careful not to squeeze that bottle too hard or you'll end up with too much of a good thing.

Superglue

I can still remember the first time I used superglue. It was like magic. No more hopelessly broken toys or soccer trophies. Superglue and other similar ethyl cyanoacrylates work great on glass, metal, most plastics, ceramic figurines, crystal bowls, eyeglasses, and acrylic fingernails. But again, just use a little bit, as these products will not bond properly if you apply too much. For greater control of application, pick up a tube of superglue in a pinpoint dispenser. Superglue is also offered in a gel form that works well on porous materials. Make sure you keep it out of reach of your child who may have ideas of gluing his younger sibling to the toilet seat. (Yes, I speak from experience!) Do not use ethyl cyanoacrylates to repair an item that will hold water, such as a broken teacup. For maximum water resistance, choose the next category: epoxy.

Epoxy

When you need a bond that will never break, especially between dissimilar surfaces such as wood and metal or glass and stone, epoxy is a terrific choice. Epoxy can also be used on most plastics. Using a two-part product may seem a bit confusing, but mixing is relatively simple: just blend equal parts from each tube. Look for brands that are sold in a double syringe. Dispense what you need and thoroughly stir the two parts together. Apply it quickly and wipe off the excess. Once epoxy sets up, it is almost impossible to break the bond without the risk of breaking whatever it is you've glued.

Epoxy technology has expanded to include other products such as a formula that will bond copper pipe, even when wet, for small plumbing repairs. Epoxy fillers are also often recommended to repair large gaps in wood and fiberglass.

Construction Adhesive

Originally, construction adhesives such as Liquid Nails and other brands were just a mainstay with professional builders and remodelers, but they are gaining popularity on the home front. An excellent value for decks, moldings, paneling, flooring, and other construction projects, these superstrong adhesives are normally dispensed with a caulk gun. Since most construction glues are waterproof, you can use them inside or out. I like them because I can often use a construction adhesive instead of nails for simple projects.

Hot-Melt Glue

Hot-melt glue is often the choice for hobbies and crafts. It is a quick solution for most porous surfaces. I use it for furniture repair, too. Even though hot-melt glue is water-resistant once it has cooled, make sure your surfaces are dry before you apply it. Trying to hot glue a wet surface is like using a curling iron on damp hair: it just doesn't work well. If your project is going be continuously wet, choose a polyurethane glue, epoxy, or construction adhesive instead.

Stain-Removing Solutions

All good do-it-yourselfers know that home improvement comes at a cost—often in the form of stubborn stains left behind after the hard work is finished. Since I host a national radio show, companies often send me products to test for them. Below are some stain removers that have worked for me, plus a few home remedies that I have discovered along the way. (If you have a favorite product or idea not mentioned below, please let me know about it at andrea@askandrea.com and I'll pass it along!)

One of my favorite groupings of products is Mötsenböcker's Lift Off. The folks at Mötsenböcker's have created different removers for different problems. Got house paint on your best shirt or jeans? Lift Off 5 is the solution. They also have a formula for food, beverages, or proteins and another for pen, markers, or crayon. Mötsenböcker's Lift Off solutions are great not only for clothes, but for your upholstery and carpets, too. Visit their Web site at www.liftoffinc.com.

Some General Tips

▶ Your results may vary. Test all products and remedies on a hidden area first for colorfastness and durability.

▶ A black light can help to show up certain kinds of stains, such as pet urine. Also great for finding scorpions.

▶ Blot. Never rub a stain, as rubbing can strip a garment's color, leaving your clothes stain-free but also color-free in that area.

▶ Pretreat reminder. Find a way to remind yourself of when an item needs to be treated for a stain. Put it in a special bin or tie a knot into the article of clothing.

▶ Beware the dryer. Make sure any stain has been completely removed before you dry it. Once it goes into the dryer, stains are typically baked in for good.

Home Remedies for Oil, Grease, and Lipstick on Clothes

▶ Sprinkle cornstarch or baking soda on the stain. Place the garment stain side down on a large rag on top of an ironing board. Iron with a hot iron on the wrong side of the stain and most of the oil and the grease will come right out.

▶ Dishwashing detergent also works well on grease and lipstick. Lipstick is one of the hardest things to remove, unless you use this technique: Gently rub on liquid dishwashing detergent. Let it sit for about an hour and rinse with cool water. That should remove most of the stain and can be repeated as needed. Also, try rinsing with vinegar and water, then flush with clear, cool water.

▶ Soak stains in a solution of 3 parts detergent and 1 part ammonia. Swab greasy stains with a little shampoo and then run through the wash as usual.

Products for Removing Grease, Tar, Lipstick, and More

▶ OxiClean Laundry Stain Remover works better than ever, especially for grease and grass stains. Simply spray on, gently rub into the fabric, let sit for 5 to 10 minutes, and then wash as normal. The results are amazing. Visit www.oxiclean.com.

▶ Lift Off 2 Adhesives, Grease & Oily Stains Tape Remover removes stains of a natural oil, petroleum, or solvent-based nature,

Andrea's Choice: Managing Mold

Mold is such a nasty problem. Not only does the odor seem to linger forever but the stains that it leaves behind can cause irreparable damage to all sorts of materials. In searching for a solution to mold in my own home, I discovered a unique product with an unusual name–Concrobium Mold Control. It's simple to use; you just spray it on the afflicted surface and let it do its work. Not only does it eliminate the stains and odors, but it does so with a nontoxic formula that is completely safe for most surfaces as well as pets and people. Visit www. Concrobium.com for more info.

such as tapes, adhesives, chewing gum, grease, tar, crayons, motor oil, salad dressing, and lipstick. I love it.
Visit www.liftoffinc.com.

▶ Go Spot Go, made by the folks at Superglue, comes in an easy-to-use dispenser. Very handy! Visit. www.supergluecorp.com.

Home Remedies for Grass Stains

▶ Wipe the fabric with alcohol (but test a corner first to make sure the material isn't damaged by the alcohol). Then apply mild chlorine bleach to any remaining stain.

▶ Rub the stain with liquid detergent or naphtha soap. Then rinse thoroughly.

▶ For stubborn stains, try rubbing with vinegar or hydrogen peroxide (test fabric first).

▶ Mix 6 tablespoons of baking soda and a cup of warm water into a paste and rub onto stained clothing before laundering. Be sure to check for colorfastness first.

Home Remedy for Paint Stains

▶ For latex paint, soak in a solution of warm water and detergent for about 2 hours. Then brush gently with a toothbrush. Repeat if necessary, then wash the garment as usual.

Products for Removing Paint Stains

▶ Lift Off 4 Spray Paint Graffiti Remover works miracles on oil-based paint and spray paint. It saved the carpet in my car when I accidentally spilled oil-based paint on it. I couldn't believe the results! Visit www.liftoffinc.com.

▶ Lift Off 5 Latex Based Paint Remover is a patented break-through formula that removes fresh latex paint as well as dried old paint from all surfaces. Visit www.liftoffinc.com.

▶ Briwax removes paint and other residues from finished wood surfaces, plus leaves a beautiful wax shine. It's an antique collector's dream come true. Choose the correct color to match the wood finish. (Caution: Be sure to test a hidden area, as it can remove color from the surface. Also use a drop cloth to avoid staining clothing and flooring.) (Visit www.briwax.com.)

Home Remedies and Products for Rust

▶ Soak fabric in a solution of 1 part lemon juice and 1 part water. (Never use chlorine bleach on rust stains.)

▶ Lime-A-Way is my favorite product for removing rust and oxidation on household surfaces. I have also used it on clothes, but very carefully!

▶ CLR is another product that works great on rust.
Visit www.jelmar.com.

Home Remedies for Bloodstains

▶ Soak in cold water so the stain doesn't set.

▶ Rub Ivory soap on the stain.

▶ If all else fails, try using color-safe bleach.

▶ Hydrogen peroxide works wonders on bloodstains on white clothing.

Product and Home Remedy for Removing Candle Wax from Carpets and Upholstery

▶ Candle Wax Lifter by Goo Gone: Apply wax lifter to clean cloth, blot stain, and then use the lifting tool to push wax up and away. Repeat as needed. Visit www.googone.com.

▶ Use an ice cube to harden the wax. Then use a blunt-bladed knife to scrape up wax.

Products for Removing Fingernail Polish from Carpets and Upholstery

▶ Goof Off is a product that one of my radio listeners recommended. (Visit www.goofoff.com.)

▶ Lift Off 4 Spray Paint Graffiti Remover is also recommended for fingernail polish remover from household fabrics. (Visit www.liftoffinc.com.)

Home Remedies for Fruit Stains

▶ Oddly enough, you use fruit to fight fruit stains.

▶ Always put lemon on the stain first.

▶ If that doesn't work, try a bar of soap.

Products for Removing Pet Stains and Odors

▶ Bac-Out is a nontoxic, biodegradable, natural stain-fighting solution that is made up of live enzyme cultures and lime peel extract for cleaning power. It is great for pet stains, food, drink, and other organic stains. The live enzyme-producing cultures attack the stains until they are gone. Bac-Out also makes laundry detergents, wipes, and other products. I have been impressed with the whole line of products. They smell good, too.
Visit www.bi-o-kleen.com to see more.

▶ Simple Solution is fantastic for removing pet odors from carpets and clothing. We kept a gallon jug nearby when we were housebreaking our Scottie puppy. (Visit www.simplesolution.com.)

▶ Urine Gone is also good for pet stains.
Visit www.urinegone.com. for more information.

I cannot stress enough that all products need to be used according to the manufacturers' directions and tested on an inconspicuous area before treating and using on the whole area or garment.

The Cost vs. the Value
of Home Improvements

If you're considering multiple home improvements, you may want to weigh the cost of those projects against the value the updates will add to your home, especially if you plan to sell within the foreseeable future. If you've been wondering what projects can add the most value to your bottom line, here are a few suggestions.

▶ Real estate agents will tell you that among the key areas that help to grab a potential home buyer are the front door, the entryway, the landscaping, the kitchen, bathrooms, and the master bedroom. If your goal is to raise your home's "sellability," start with those areas. Paint and flooring are also important.

▶ If your home needs major work, particularly projects that will incur substantial expense, such as foundation repairs, roofing, or appliance replacement, it generally makes sense to do these repairs if you plan to stay for three years or more. This is also true if you're trying to sell your home and your equity is limited.

▶ If you plan to sell soon and you have a large amount of equity in the home, you may want to simply lower the price and allow the buyer to shoulder larger repairs. You can still clear a good profit in the sale, and the buyer will feel like he or she got a better deal. The lower price may actually help you sell more quickly, since it will be below that of similar homes in the area.

▶ Room additions present another quandary. Should you add on or just move to a larger home? If you like the neighborhood, a room addition such as an enclosed patio or a bump out on a second story may make sense. But take care not to overbuild for your area, as it may make it difficult to recoup your expenses or the original integrity of the house.

▶ Before you make a firm decision about possible work, write down an estimate of your home's worth. Check your local newspaper or online listings for houses in your immediate neighborhood to help calculate its approximate value. Then make an

⚒ *Quick Tip:*
Vintage Vexes

If your home was built before 1960, use caution before making major changes to its structure or decor. Affecting the character of an old house can dramatically decrease its value. That doesn't mean you must keep using an outhouse if you aren't graced with indoor plumbing, but take care to add that new bathroom in a way that complements the integrity of your vintage structure. If you are unsure, consult a qualified expert on historic homes such as a historic architect.

Restoring an older home can be very rewarding, but it is important to enter into the experience with your eyes open. See the following section for more information on working with classic homes.

educated guess of the costs that you will incur to complete the remodeling project. Also figure your outlay if you decide to have the work done for you. Then weigh whether the total costs will add that amount or more to your home's value. Of course, if you love your home and plan to stay in it for a while, cost may not matter. You and your family will reap the benefit of increased comfort and beauty by having surroundings that better suit your needs and desires.

▶ If in doubt, ask for advice from a local real estate agent. Agents are usually happy to give you their two cents worth, knowing that you may become a customer someday.

Do's and Don'ts for Restoring Older Homes

Nothing helps preserve a historic structure like use. It's a mysterious fact that buildings, like old cars, seem to deteriorate most quickly when they are least used.

—NORM ALSTON

The irony of working on historic buildings for the first time is that they are at once familiar and mysterious. We know them; we've seen them; often we've lived among them; but the proper techniques for caring for them are not commonly understood. Sometimes these techniques seem contrary to what we know about modern homes. They're not harder, just different.

Norm Alston is a top restoration architect in North Texas. He has been involved in projects raging from the renovation of historic courthouses to vintage homes. Norm offers the following advice to those who are getting ready to remodel a home built before 1970.

▶ You can't make good decisions if you do not have good information. Do some research on your home and try to understand what it was truly like when it was new and how it changed over the years. The local public library or heritage society is a good place to start. Try to pick a period in the building's history to restore to and use that as a guide for restoration decisions.

▶ Much of the value of historic structures comes from the fact that it represents the plans and dreams of people long gone. Retain and preserve original historic materials, conditions, and details to the greatest extent possible. It's just like antique furniture: a 2006 replica of an eighteenth-century Shaker table, no matter how exact, is not nearly as valuable on any level as the original.

▶ Repair of a historic structure that includes exact replication of missing historic features is generally okay. What many people don't understand, however, is that new additions or details that did not exist historically should not match the old exactly. They should be compatible, but readily discernible from the original. The concept has been compared to tree rings: they are all part of the same tree, but each occurred at a different period of growth, and the age and development of the tree can be better understood by studying them. Likewise, building additions should be readily understood as products of their own time without subtracting from the historic integrity of the home.

▶ Nothing does more for building preservation for less money than a good coat of paint. When you paint a historic structure, it is not necessary to remove all the old paint down to bare wood. In fact, the opposite is true. Well-adhered existing paint continues to protect the wood and remains as a source for exploration regarding original colors and finishes. I have seen overzealous homeowners try to remove all old paint, resorting to disc sanders and propane torches (yikes!). This removes important historic integrity and often damages the wood and adds significant costs.

▶ Preservation does not really deserve its reputation for being expensive. Proper preservation practice means minimal intervention. Whenever possible, repair instead of replace, and only fix that which is broken. This approach usually means minimal work

Quick Tip: Old or New?

When you are shopping for hardware or plumbing, choose antique originals with care. They are sometimes more trouble than they're worth. For instance, vintage doorsets are usually narrower than their modern counterparts and often won't fit newer doors. And older faucets made with lead can be a health hazard. Fortunately, companies such as Nostalgic Warehouse and American Standard offer excellent hardware and plumbing reproductions with updated mechanisms.

Light fixtures and architectural trims, on the other hand, can often be salvaged from the junk pile. Many salvage yards even offer services to refurbish items or you can do it yourself. Rejuvenation offers vintage originals as well as stunning reproductions. One item that's hard to find from salvage is ceiling fans, but both Hunter and Fanimation offer remakes in a wide range of styles and prices.

and less expense. The idea that preservation is expensive typically comes from efforts to make a house or a building look "like new." This approach requires far more effort and expense and very often results in replacement of important historic fabric, which is contrary to the ideals of preservation.

▶ Check the resources section at the back of the book for more help for old houses.

Tips for Do-It-Yourselfers

Being organized upfront makes your project a good experience. The more prepared you are the more profitable it will be. That goes for family time, too.

—KARL CHAMPLEY

My friend, Karl Champley, has hosted several TV programs on HGTV and DIY (including *DIY to the Rescue*) and is also an experienced contractor and carpenter. I had the good fortune to work side by side with him on a project for Habitat for Humanity and was impressed by his incredible talent. I asked Karl to share some of his ideas for do-it-yourselfers, flavored with his unique Aussie perspective.

Want to save money, time, and perspiration?

▶ Plan it out. Have a clear understanding of what your project entails: time required, tools required, materials required, etc.

▶ Budget everything you can think of. It's simple to do. I recommend this for any size project! A budget estimates the upfront costs and gives you a greater understanding of what tools and materials are needed.

▶ Do yourself and your loved ones a favor and purchase top-quality safety equipment before you start a project. Safety gear is everything. If something happens to your eyes, hands, etc., the fun is over. This is a great lesson to pass on to kiddos, too.

▶ Do your research. If you are not 100 percent sure of what you are doing, read books (like this one), magazines, or surf the Net for necessary information on building techniques, materials required, etc. The more research you do, the smoother, easier, and safer your project, and you will save money, too. You will also make fewer trips to the hardware store and save gasoline. (See the resources section for more information.)

▶ Permits are your responsibility. This is very important! Before starting a project, check with your local municipality for any requirements and restrictions on the type of project that you are doing. If you proceed without your city's approval, all of your hard work may be a total waste of time. They have the power to instruct you to remove everything and reinstate the original. Not good! It may also be a liability when it comes time to sell your house. Getting the permits can be a painful process, but it is worthwhile, and you won't have to worry about your neighbors spilling the beans.

If You Decide to Hire a Contractor

Not only can home improvement be enjoyable, doing your own work can also be a great way to save money. But with today's busy lifestyles, it's important to choose your battles, based on your skills and available time. If you are having trouble keeping up with all of the jobs that you have to do around your home, don't despair. No matter where you live, chances are there are some reputable contractors nearby who can help. Just remember that a proper repair can secure the investment in your home and make it easier to resell in the future. But before you pull out the phone book or credit card, here are some tips to keep in mind.

▶ Act like a big shot. Get at least three bids for your job. Just as municipalities and large companies do when they are bidding out a project, talk to several contractors before making a final choice.

When having any work done around your home or when doing it yourself, save the extra materials. Most contractors will gladly give you leftover tile, roofing material, or paint, so they don't have to deal with throwing it away. Since you've technically already paid for them, tuck these free bonuses into an attic corner or garage shelf for future repairs or additions. Just be sure paint and any other perishable materials are stored where they will not freeze, fade, or overheat. Also be sure to write paint formulas on the paint can in several locations, in case they get wet or rusty.

Also, don't necessarily choose the least expensive bidder; weigh each company's bid against the quality of materials, warranty, and reputation.

▶ Ask for a written quote on company letterhead or forms. Do not accept verbal offers. This goes for every change order, too. Ask for confirmation of any additional fees in writing, especially when a salesman says, "Oh, it won't cost much more to add that!"

▶ Watch out for fly-by-night companies. Avoid contractors whose major references come from out of state. Ask for a list of past customers who live within a 50- to 100-mile radius of your home and then call a few for feedback. Also check to be sure that the company maintains a local office and phone number. A yellow pages ad can be an indication of a company's longevity, since these ads must often be placed up to a year in advance. Ask your neighbors for referrals. If a nearby home has enjoyed satisfactory repairs for five years or more, include that contractor on your bid list.

▶ Be wary of drop-by deals. Busy companies do not usually need to solicit on a door-to-door basis. Especially watch out for a contractor who claims that he is working in a nearby neighborhood and has leftover materials. Although you will sometimes be offered a good price when a company is doing jobs in your neighborhood, this is a red flag to check that company's references more carefully.

▶ Never pay up front. Most reputable companies will not require a down payment until materials have been delivered. When materials arrive, it is common to advance up to a third of the total job cost, with payments made at specified milestones during the job. The final payment should not be disbursed until the job is complete and you are satisfied that the materials, suppliers, and workers have been paid. Also, never pay cash. Use a credit card or check for all payments and save all receipts.

▶ Choose a company with a solid reputation and the longest warranty possible. Make sure they are members of the Better Business

Bureau (www.bbb.org), the National Association of the Remodeling Industry (www.nari.org), or other professional organizations related to their industry.

▶ Contact your local Better Business Bureau to see if the company has numerous or unresolved complaints against them. Remember, every business may have a few disgruntled customers. It's how they handle those situations that can be the mark of a reputable firm.

▶ Make sure the contractor secures all required building permits and liability insurance. You want neither to incur penalties for unpermitted work nor be responsible for on-the-job injuries. If the contractor seems evasive about either of these issues, it should be a red flag that problems may be ahead.

▶ Avoid contractors who pressure you for a quick decision. Take your time.

▶ Remember, every time you make a change, most contractors are going to charge an extra fee. Try to make all selections in advance to avoid change-order costs. Once you have decided on a company, ask for a listing of included costs and materials. Verify all changes and fees in writing from a decision maker in the company, not a helper. Most disputes are based on misunderstandings.

▶ Try to stay calm when a problem does arise. Remember: You can catch more flies with honey than you can with vinegar!

2

kitchen creations

The Heart and Hearth of Your Home

If you want to make an apple pie from scratch, you must
first create the universe.

—CARL SAGAN

If you ask most people which room in their home is most in need of an update, the answer is usually the kitchen. Not only do we spend much of our time there, but updating the kitchen is also important if you are thinking of selling your home. Studies show that attractive and usable kitchens are at the top of the list for prospective homebuyers.

Often, simple changes can transform a poorly arranged space into a flowing masterpiece, ready for family gatherings, entertaining, and haute cuisine. But it takes some thought and preparation to make each project your own. In this chapter, we'll start by planning from the bottom up, looking at some of the best options in flooring, countertops, fixtures, cabinets, appliances, and special considerations for older homes. Then we'll whip up some easy updates that can make a big difference.

▶ Planning a Kitchen Remodel

▶ Options for Older Homes

▶ Choosing New Appliances

Planning a Kitchen Remodel

If your family is like most, the kitchen is the heart of your home. Whether for a holiday party, a family gathering, or time for homework, we tend to congregate where it's warm and cozy. We require so much from this space. It can store our valuable china as well as our Tupperware. It is a place to prepare formal meals as well as daily lunches. It's where we want to work efficiently and comfortably in the company of our friends and family. The kitchen is the most used and enjoyed space in the home. It only makes sense that it should be designed to give us everything we need as well as some luxuries to make dining in just as much fun as dining out. It is a great place to start a remodel. When you're done, you will love your kitchen so much you'll want to tackle the rest of the house.

One reason why kitchen remodeling is so popular these days is the huge variety of quality products that are available. Shopping for them has gotten much easier, too, from decorative centers to online resources. Just a few years ago, it might have taken weeks or even months to find specialty products such as commercial ranges and trout-shaped cabinet knobs. Now it's usually as effortless as driving a few miles or simply logging on to the Internet.

There are many reasons to consider a kitchen makeover, from lack of function to an outdated style. Often, a project is borne out of frustration and then grows into a massive undertaking. You might decide to replace your outdated fridge, only to find that the newer models do not fit into the old space. If you tear out cabinets before planning properly, it may take months to replace them. In the meantime, where do you store your food and dishes? Planning is crucial. Before you grab the crowbar, take some time to think about what you want to accomplish.

The Work Triangle

Remember when you swore you would never use geometry in real life? Once again, your math teacher can delight in an "I told you so." The work triangle brings geometry to the kitchen. A well-designed kitchen, meaning a kitchen planned with the cook in mind, brings the sink, range, and refrigerator together in a work triangle. There should be a comfortable distance between each of these stations. If the distance is too short, the area will feel very cramped. If the distance is too far, the cook will be worn out from dancing all over the kitchen. As a general rule, the three legs of the work triangle should add up to between 12 and 26 feet.

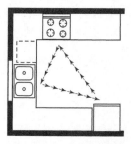

There are three basic layouts for the work triangle: U-shaped, L-shaped, and the galley. The U-shaped kitchen is designed with the sink on one wall, the range on another, and the refrigerator on a third wall. The L-shaped kitchen is designed with one element of the work triangle on one wall and the other two along an adjacent wall. In the smallest of spaces, a galley kitchen is created with all three components arranged along the same wall.

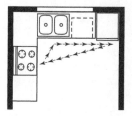

The idea is to keep traffic through the workspace at a minimum. Most cooks can attest to the frustration of pets, children, and, dare I say, spouses interfering with the flow of meal preparations. Many designers incorporate an island into their kitchens on a regular basis as a way to solve this traffic problem. An island is a convenient way station during food prep, allows children or visitors to be a part of kitchen activities without creating traffic hazards, and generally instills a homey character into the area. It is important to place the island where it will neither become an obstruction in the work triangle nor be too far away to be useful as a workstation.

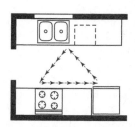

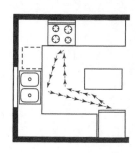

Fantasizing about a new kitchen faucet? Easy quarter-turn valves only require a small motion to turn the faucet on or off. And choose state-of-the-art finishes so that whether your faucets are bright brass, pewter, or green, they'll retain their brightness and color forever. Many companies offer lifetime warranties for even greater peace of mind. Features such as water filtering are a real bonus. See chapter 3 for instructions on how to replace a common faucet.

When designing your work triangle, place the refrigerator on the triangle's outer edge so that people who are not involved in meal preparation can still grab something from it without totally entering the kitchen's core. The sink should also be universally accessible, while the cooking surface should be the most remote point of the work triangle.

Of course, the kitchen is not designed just for the cook. Thoughtful planning should also keep the human dishwasher in mind: be sure to place the dishwasher appliance just to the left or right of the sink. When in doubt or in the interest of resale value, locate the dishwasher for right-handed users. Cabinets for storing glassware and dishes should be near the sink or the fridge. Frequently used pots and pans should be stored near the cooktop from a hanging rack or between the sink and the cooktop for easy access. The silverware drawers should be close to the dishes but out of the way of the primary work triangle so that someone can set the table without interfering with the cook.

One other important area to consider is the sink itself. If you have room for it, opt for a triple sink with the disposal hole in between two full-sized, deep basins. That way, as you are washing dishes, you can scrape food into the disposal. Deep basins are also a boon when washing a large chili pot or salad bowl. If your kitchen is extra busy, consider adding a second sink for food preparation, separate from the dishwasher, perhaps on the island, if you have one.

Whatever the type of sink you choose, make sure that the faucet is the correct size. The spout should extend at least one-third of the distance across each sink basin. Also, consider lever handles instead of knobs, as they are much easier to turn on and off with greasy or wet hands. Single-handle units work well, too. Sprayers are a must. If your old sink will not accommodate one, consider a new sink or purchase a faucet with a pullout spout sprayer. Many faucets also offer built-in water filtration—what a great idea!

When designing your kitchen, keep in mind the length of your countertops. Minimum counter lengths are considered to be 36 inches on one side of the sink and 24 inches on the other. These measurements allow for a staging area for dirty dishes on one side and a drying area on the opposite side. You want to arrange your counter space so that more space is available on the side of the sink closest to the cooking area.

Once your layout is designed, put some careful thought into lighting your kitchen. A combination of overhead wide-angled lights, spotlights, undercounter fixtures, and natural lighting should be used to provide illumination at various times of day and for different tasks. For instance, you may want spotlights to shine on your food prep area when you are slicing vegetables, but you don't need that same lighting when you are eating lunch at the island. I recommend using compact fluorescents as much as possible to save energy and to reduce heat in the kitchen.

Although not part of the work triangle, the everyday dining area needs to be considered, too. It is important to keep in mind some basic parameters for this zone when designing the kitchen. Allow about three feet of clearance all around the dining table for chairs plus adequate space for moving in and out of the area. Although most dining tables are rectangular, a round table is a wonderful option, as it takes up less space and accommodates more seating capacity. It's also easy to add an unexpected guest.

Creating a five-star kitchen is all about customizing. A well-designed space achieves a balance between aesthetic desires and functional needs for everyone in the family. With a new kitchen, dining in will be far more luxurious and fun!

Options for Older Homes

Okay, I admit it: I am a bit of a purist when it comes to old houses. I'm often surprised to see a beautifully restored vintage home with a kitchen that looks completely out of place. If you live in a piece of history, my advice is to employ careful thought when restoring the kitchen. Since it is often the first place that prospective buyers will consider, many of whom are also sticklers for authenticity, you will want it to seem as original as possible while still providing you and your family the modern conveniences that you crave.

Before tearing into your old kitchen or anywhere else in your home, do some research. Several wonderful magazines are available to help you. Homeowners who are creating a classic look in a modern home

One of my favorite "lights" is actually a skylight made by Solatube. It can be installed in almost any area in a kitchen, a bathroom, a closet, or even a basement. The product consists of a dome on the roof that transfers light (but not heat) down a tube into the living area. It is so energy efficient that it carries the ENERGY STAR rating. Solatubes can be installed in most homes with minimal skills and simple power tools. Drop by www. solatube.com to find out more.

will find a plethora of ideas in these publications as well. Among my favorites are *Old House Journal* (www.OldHouseJournal.com), *Old House Interiors* (www.oldhouseinteriors.com), *This Old House* (www.thisoldhouse.com), and *Preservation* (www.nationaltrust.org). Also check your local bookstore and library for titles on the subject.

Although it can be a challenge to keep your home completely authentic, the vast array of reproduction products on the market has made the task much easier. Just a few years ago, nostalgic appliances simply weren't available. Now you can find vintage-looking fridges (with icemakers), stoves, and even microwaves. Flooring and countertop options have gone back to the past, integrating 1950s-era Formica with metal edge-banding and genuine linoleum. And thank goodness faucet technology has improved, along with styling. Just a few years ago, faucet finishes might not last more than a year or two. Now, many classic designs carry lifetime warranties on both the function and the finish.

Although I love to use salvage items when possible in historic homes, there are some things to consider when installing genuine antique plumbing fixtures and fittings. Antique faucets can contain high amounts of lead: bad for kids and grown-ups. Newer faucets won't have that problem. Also, many reproductions are made with quarter-turn valves that are more comfortable for tiny and elderly hands. Many styles are exact duplications of antique originals, just updated so that they work better.

Installing modern reproduction sinks may also be a better choice than refinishing an older sink. Unless you can afford to have an antique sink actually reporcelained (not epoxy-coated), it will not last very long under heavy kitchen use. Epoxy coatings are fine in the bathroom, but will not hold up to the abrasion caused by silverware and dishes.

Choosing New Appliances

Tired of that old refrigerator? Now might be a good time to replace it. A beautiful new fridge can be the ideal focal point for an updated kitchen. The problem is that you will want a stove to match, and then an updated microwave, too. Then that old dishwasher will have to go, plus you'll want to add a trash compactor. Before you know it, you will have spent thousands of dollars when all you really wanted was a new fridge. If your budget is limited, what should you pitch out first and what can you live with?

Often, just a few modifications in appliance layout can make a big difference in meal preparation and everyday convenience. Today's manufacturers are creating new products to make our lives easier with innovative gadgets that truly fit our busy lifestyles. So before you begin a remodeling project, make a few trips to local kitchen retailers. Also visit the Web sites of some of the major appliance manufacturers to see what's new and upcoming. The general rule is to buy the best models that you can afford, but don't be oversold by features that you don't need. If you only cook once or twice per week, you probably don't need a $5,000 commercial-style range.

Appliance Style and Color

Regardless of the decor theme of the kitchen, stainless steel remains the most popular choice in appliances. From country French to contemporary, stainless appliances complement and even enhance most design styles. This material was first introduced on the residential scene in the form of large, industrial-style ranges and refrigerators, but now you can find virtually all kitchen appliances in stainless. The beauty of stainless is that it blends well with almost all styles of cabinetry and countertops.

Black is also popular because it is stylish and easy to clean. It is a lovely contrast to warm wood and laminate cabinetry and provides a natural outline for most color schemes. White appliances can tend to connote "budget" unless careful thought is employed to enhance the white theme. Bold colors such as red or blue can limit future decorating possibilities but also create a strong statement if you don't mind living with them for a long time.

The Refrigerator

The old chiller is often the most critical appliance to replace, especially if it is ten years old or more. Modern ENERGY STAR appliances are much more efficient and can save you money in the long run. New models also offer conveniences that may not have been available in

Andrea's Choice:
Retro Plumbing and Hardware

If you are looking for vintage-styled products for your old house, check out the resources section at the back of this book.

To help decide which appliances you need, check consumer publications for ratings and reliability records. Magazines such as *Consumer Reports* research products for factors such as frequency of breakdown as well as type and cost of repairs. When comparing items, try to find the most reliable model in your price range with the features you want and need. Also look at the warranty terms; this may be a good way to decide between two otherwise comparable units. (Resources: www.doityourself.com and www.homedoctors.com)

your old unit, such as built-in water filtration, wine-cooling trays, a refrigerated drawer where you can store your jug of milk right next to the cereal drawer, and even a computer built into the door.

No two refrigerator models are the same, and there are many factors to think about when shopping for a new one. It is important to consider capacity, exterior size, features, and style as well as reliability. As with any major appliance, different brands vary in their capabilities, cost of service, and repair records.

Before you go to the appliance store, measure the space where the old fridge sits. Make sure that the new unit will have adequate ventilation area, if necessary. If you are trying to create a roomier feel in your kitchen, look at counter-depth fridges (approximately 24 to 30 inches deep) that do not protrude as far into a room as the conventional 34- to 36-inch versions. Because of innovations in design, they can often pack in as much food storage as your old unit in a smaller space.

Double or French doors on fridges are becoming popular because they fit better in galley layouts and kitchens with islands that limit how far a fridge door can swing open. Since twin doors are less wieldy than one large door, they are perfect where space is tight. Bottom freezer drawers are also very handy because it is easier to view their contents and for little ones to reach frozen treats and ice.

Cooktops, Stoves, and Ovens

If you are completely renovating your kitchen, one major question will be, do you want an all-in-one stove with the cooktop and oven combined, or should you opt for separate components? Stoves are offered in two designs: a freestanding range, which can sit alone or can appear to be built-in, and a "slide-in range," which actually fits into a custom cabinet. If you choose separate components, your cooktop can be installed in a kitchen island or countertop and the oven can be located separately. You can even install two ovens, if you bake a lot. Most cooktops are made to sit almost flat or "flush" against the countertop to present a sleek, stylish look and allow for easy cleanup. But if space is limited, a combination stove is the best option.

You have several options when choosing a stove: traditional electric coil, energy-efficient gas, and emerging technologies, such as induction. When choosing between electric surface elements and gas, keep in mind that electric tends to maintain low heat better, but gas flames are easier to adjust to multiple heat levels. Electric stoves are often less expensive, but you may find the greater temperature control of a gas flame is worth the higher price.

If you are an avid cook, gas is probably your best bet. Gas stoves have been preferred by professional chefs for decades because they give instant heat, exceptional temperature control, and the added benefit of visual feedback as the flame is lowered or raised. Gas stoves are fueled by natural gas or propane. In the old days, you had to use a match to light a pilot light, but today's gas stoves feature electronic ignitions—no more nasty fumes or wasted energy.

Emerging technologies, such as induction cooking, can create a safer cooking environment. With induction cooktops, a magnetic-based pot or pan (throw out the old aluminum cookware) interacts with a magnetic field created by the cooking coils, inducing a current in the pot or pan. The pot or pan actually heats up and cooks the food while the surface stays cool. The system is entirely flame-free. Visit a local kitchen showroom to see all of the newest technologies. Many showrooms hold periodic cooking seminars with actual chefs so you can see the stoves in action.

Ovens come in two basic types: convection and conventional. Even conventional ovens are sporting updated features, such as built-in rotisseries and computerized thermostats. Touch-pad oven controls offer more precise heat than knobs, but make sure that computerized elements are under warranty—just in case they are affected by high temperatures. If you bake frequently, consider installing double ovens that can be placed side by side or stacked on top of each other.

Convection ovens can be pricey, as they feature blowers that circulate the heat for faster, even cooking. Innovative combos such as convection microwaves offer convenient cooking options for the busy chef. With roasting, baking, and crisping capabilities, convection microwaves combine all the reheat features of a microwave with the cooking options of a convection oven. They cut the cooking time in half but achieve the same flavor and texture. Check out drawer-fitted convection ovens or combo units. They are a great addition to any kitchen, even if you already have a conventional oven in place.

Andrea's Choice:
Instant Stainless Steel

If your old appliances are in good shape, but simply the wrong color, check out SoftMetal decorative films, which can be applied in minutes to transform the fronts of almost every appliance to the look of stainless steel. See the complete instructions later in this chapter (or visit www.ezfauxdecor.com). Another option is Thomas' Liquid Stainless Steel, a special coating that can be used on almost any surface to create a stainless look. Great for hardware and kitchen accessories, it can also be used on appliances. (Visit www.liquidstainlesssteel.com.)

Microwave Ovens

Microwaves are showing up as drawer units, too, but it may not be the best choice if small children are often in the kitchen. If space is a premium, microwaves are now offered with built-in coffeemakers or toasters.

Any microwave oven that you buy should have a turntable that is removable for safer cooking and easier cleaning. A window is also convenient so you can see the food inside your oven while it's cooking. Microwave ovens vary in power (wattage) and size (cubic feet). Wattage on small, apartment- or dorm-sized units may be inadequate for a busy family.

Dishwasher

Whether your old dishwasher has seen better days or you are looking to get your first one, there are some simple things to keep in mind. Check for the number of spray levels. If the sprayers blast the dishes at several levels, your dishes will be cleaner. Shop for a dishwasher that heats to at least 140 degrees Fahrenheit and features a food grinder or built-in disposal. And don't forget to check the Energy Guide label: lower numbers mean more energy savings.

If space is a premium, check out mini dishwashers or kitchen sinks with a built-in dishwasher on one side, which can be just the right size for a couple. Dishwasher drawers are also gaining in popularity. Most feature two drawers, one on top of the other. If storage is a problem in your kitchen, one drawer can hold dishes while the other washes them. Whatever you choose, consider buying a sound-dampening package if your dishwasher will be operating when the kids are doing their homework nearby or at night when the household is trying to sleep. Or look at "quiet" dishwashers. Some of the newest models are so muted you may not even know they are running.

Trash Compactors

Do you get tired of hauling out your trash every day? Consider installing a trash compactor. This handy gadget uses a ram to flatten trash so that you will be able to accumulate much more debris in a smaller space. There is also the environmental benefit of sending less junk volume to the landfill.

You can put virtually anything in a trash compactor that you put into the wastebasket in your kitchen, even glass—unless, of course, you live in an area where glass is recycled. Just be sure to place the bottles and jars toward the center of the compactor, away from the bottom, to reduce the risk of shards slicing through the compactor bag or cutting you. Avoid placing mushy or rotten food or anything liquid in a compactor, as they can squirt out and make a terrible mess. And never put poisonous, flammable, or explosive chemicals, or empty aerosol cans, in a trash compactor.

Your choice of a trash compactor will depend on its size, ram force, and prospective location in your kitchen. Other options include the means by which you empty the debris once it's compacted as well as the type of bags used; this varies by manufacturer. I prefer disposable plastic-lined paper compactor bags because they hold up better than the all-plastic versions.

ONE-HOUR WONDER: **FAUX STAINLESS STEEL**

Level of difficulty: T

Want the look of stainless on your old appliances and accessories? Now you can peel and stick the appearance of real stainless steel, nickel, or embossed metals on almost any surface with SoftMetal decorative films. They can be applied in minutes to transform the fronts of refrigerators, dishwashers, trash compactors, cabinets, backsplashes, ceilings, garage doors, electronics, and more. SoftMetal decorative films are available online and at many hardware and craft stores. I used them on my own dishwasher and trash compactor to help my old cream-colored appliances blend in with a new stainless fridge.

You will need:

- ✓ Clean rag or tack cloth
- ✓ Fine sandpaper (if necessary)
- ✓ Ruler
- ✓ Pencil
- ✓ Metallic film
- ✓ Scissors
- ✓ Razor knife
- ✓ Ruler or straightedge
- ✓ Soft plastic spatula
- ✓ An iron

1. PREPARE THE SURFACE. If you can remove the appliance panel from its frame, it is easier to install the film. Many dishwasher and compactor panels are reversible, so they can be removed with just a few screws. I recommend installing the metallic film on the least desirable panel area. In other words, if you think you might want to switch back to almond appliances at some point, then apply the stainless film to the white panel side. Once you have removed the panel, lay it on a table or other flat surface to work. Just be sure to protect the underneath surface from unwanted knife cuts. If you cannot remove the front panel, simply install the film directly to the appliance.

Metallic films adhere to almost any smooth area, but it is essential that

⚲ *Quick Tip:*
Silky-Smooth Application Tips

When applying film to larger surface areas, first remove approximately 4 inches of backing paper from the adhesive side of the film and smooth down this initial section. Then, while evenly removing the backing paper with one hand, progressively smooth down the film with the other hand. Always smooth from the center to the edges.

For best results smooth out any air bubbles or creases with a soft cloth. Should air bubbles form, just prick them with a pin and flatten out. If you find you've applied the film crookedly, don't worry: full adhesion takes several hours. Carefully remove the film without stretching it and then reapply.

the surface be clean, dry, and dust-free. Rough surfaces should be sanded smooth and cleaned prior to adhering film. Use a tack cloth to remove even tiny dust particles.

2. MEASURE, CUT, AND APPLY. On flat panels, such as the loose front panel of a dishwasher, cut the film slightly larger (¼ inch) than the panel, and then trim to fit with scissors or a razor knife after application. A ruler or straightedge can be used to ensure a nice, clean cut. If you are fitting the film into a given area, start with a slightly oversized piece, apply it, and then trim into place with the razor knife, carefully peeling away any excess. Make sure that your razor blade is especially sharp and change it often when doing larger projects.

Tips for trimming edges and corners: To apply adhesive film cleanly and exactly on edges and corners, overlap the edge by about ¼ inch. Carefully, using the razor knife, cleanly cut along the edge and lightly rub the cut with a fingernail or soft plastic spatula. To apply film around edges and corners, carefully wrap the film around and press lightly with a warm iron at the lowest setting. To avoid any damage to the film, insert a sheet of paper between it and the iron. The heat will release the tension and the film will adhere firmly to the edge. ■

Quick Tip:
Removing Foil

Most films are just as easy to take off as they are to apply. Normally, they can be peeled away. But if they adhere more firmly, they should be warmed with a hair dryer and then removed. Any adhesive leftovers can be cleaned off with Goo Gone or other adhesive remover. To remove dissolved adhesive, wipe it away with a damp cloth sprinkled with some flour. (Resource: www.ezfauxdecor.com)

Appliance Tune-up Tips

Hate to throw out those old appliances? If you want them to last as long as possible, the experts at www.RepairClinic.com can help you keep your dishwasher washing and your trash compactor packing and offer lots of other free appliance advice. Here are some of their top tips, plus a few of my own.

Manual-Defrost Refrigerator/Freezer

▶ With manual-defrost refrigerators/freezers, check for frost buildup in the freezer. If frost has accumulated on the walls to a thickness of half an inch or more, remove all food, turn off the appliance, and allow all the frost to melt. Then reset the thermostat and resume normal usage. Be sure not to use any utensils or tools to scrape off the frost, because it is very easy to puncture the evaporator and ruin the refrigerator.

Automatic-Defrost Refrigerator/Freezer

▶ With self-defrosting refrigerators/freezers, clean the drain pan underneath the refrigerator that collects water. (Some drain pans are not accessible. Don't worry if you can't find yours.)

▶ Clean the refrigerator cooling fan and the condenser coils periodically. The coils are underneath the refrigerator. They are usually black and look like a series of small tubes and "fins" connecting the tubes. Use a refrigerator condenser brush to make the job easier.

▶ Check the door gaskets to be sure they are sealing properly against the frame of the refrigerator/freezer. If they are torn or don't close tightly, the refrigerator or freezer may not cool properly. This problem is worse when the weather is warmer and more humid. Clean the gaskets and the frame with warm, soapy water so they don't stick together.

▶ Inspect the back wall of the freezer for any frost buildup. It's not normal to have any frost on the back wall or floor of a self-defrosting appliance. The presence of frost is normally an indication that the self-defrosting system has a problem, so it may be time to call in the pros.

Icemaker

▶ If you have a built-in filter that supplies the icemaker, replace the filter approximately every six months.

▶ If you don't have a water filter built into the fridge and you find your ice tastes bad and/or smells funny, use a "taste and odor" water filter on the incoming water supply line.

▶ If you don't have an icemaker, you may want to add one.

People often don't realize that virtually all refrigerators are set up to accommodate an add-on icemaker. Many refrigerators have a tag in the back of the freezer with a kit number indicating exactly what kind of icemaker will fit in that model of refrigerator. Kits are available for virtually every refrigerator/freezer on the market.

Range, Stove, and Oven

▶ Most ovens have an interior light. If the bulb has been burned out for a long time, you may not even realize that you have one. The lightbulb is usually behind a small glass dome near the upper left or right side, inside of the oven. To replace the bulb, you must remove the glass dome, usually by sliding a wire off of it or rotating it counterclockwise. Be sure to use an appliance bulb.

▶ When cleaning your oven control panel, beware of "cream-type" cleansers, as they often contain tiny abrasive particles that can damage your stovetop or control panel. You can clean any porcelain stovetop or glass range/oven control panel with a non-abrasive cleanser or glass cleaner. If numbers are painted onto the face of a dial or panel, note that ammonia-based window cleaners might remove the paint.

▶ Drip pans and bowls serve multiple functions for a range. They catch food and spills, help radiate heat back at the pan for better efficiency, and protect you from accidentally touching internal components. It's important never to cover them with aluminum foil. Aluminum near the burner can cause many electric ranges to short-circuit, and you don't want to cover the oven vent, which is usually found at one of the burners. Try to clean the drip pans with a household nonabrasive cleanser. If they cannot be cleaned, replace them.

▶ Be sure to clean your over-the-stove vent hood periodically. The thin, silvery screen inside is the grease filter (there may be more than one). It traps airborne oils and grease to keep them out of the blower and exhaust vent. To clean the filter, remove it and

Quick Tip:
Drip Pan Duos

My friend Laura Dellutri, the Healthy Housekeeper, author and public speaker, comments: "I keep two sets of drips pans for my stove—one that gets dirty from everyday cooking use and one that is brand new and pristine for when my in-laws or guests are coming over. Then I just switch them out when necessary, one for cooking and the other for company."

Quick Tip:
Icky Rust

If your water has a high rust content or if your hot-water heater is showing signs of age by producing rust-colored water, the inside of your dishwasher will become rust-colored, too. To remove this coloring, fill the dishwasher cups with an orange-flavored breakfast drink such as Tang and run through the normal cycle. Voilà—it's like magic! The interior should go back to its natural color.

Quick Tip:
Devious Dishwashers

Are you finding puddles in front of your dishwasher? Don't worry: there is probably a simple solution. First, check the water fittings. To do this, simply remove the service panel that is on the front below the door. Look at the end of the drain hose that connects to the washer and the end that connects to the sink. If one is leaking, tighten the clamp with a screwdriver. Also, look for leaks around the water inlet valve. You can use a compression wrench to tighten the fitting that connects the water supply to the valve. If the fill hose is

soak it in a degreasing solution until the gunk is dissolved. Next, wash it with warm, soapy water to remove any traces of the degreaser. Then put it in the upper rack of the dishwasher and run it through a hot cycle.

▶ Some hoods circulate the air rather than venting it to the outside. You can sometimes determine this by looking in your attic to see if the fan exhaust pipe is visible. If so, your vent may have one or more activated charcoal filters. You cannot wash these. Just replace them when they lose their effectiveness and are not removing impurities from the air.

▶ Clean the smooth interior of the vent hood with a standard household degreaser/cleaner. Warning! Be sure the unit is turned off before you clean it. Also avoid spraying cleaner directly onto the lightbulb or lightbulb socket.

Microwave

▶ Clean the inside of your microwave frequently. Food particles and splatters absorb some of the microwave energy while the unit is operating and may cause burns and other damage to the unit. You can clean the interior with a microwave oven cleaner or other degreaser.

▶ Just like other electronic devices, microwave ovens are susceptible to damage from voltage spikes caused by lightning and other electrical surges. Plug your microwave into an appropriate surge suppressor to protect the circuitry.

Dishwasher

▶ You don't need to clean the interior of your dishwasher if you use it regularly. If it goes unused for a week or more and begins to mold or smell bad, run it with a deodorizing cleaner, such as baking soda or a few cups of vinegar.

▶ If your dishes aren't getting as clean as they used to, there's probably not enough water getting into the machine. This is usu-

→

ally caused by a broken or worn-out water inlet valve. These valves, located behind the lower service panel, need replacing every 3 to 7 years, depending on water conditions.

▶ Repair broken and rusted dishwasher racks when needed. If the plastic coating wears off the dish rack tines in your dishwasher, they will corrode and rust. The rust particles can then get into the pump and cause much more serious problems. Epoxy touch-up kits are available at most hardware stores. Prior to making the repair, be sure to clean up and smooth the rusted spots on the dishwasher rack with fine sandpaper to make the repair last much longer.

▶ Clean your dishwasher filter on a regular basis, at least every six months or so. Many dishwashers have a filter near the bottom or under the lower spray arm that needs cleaning. If you have this sort of filter, consult your owner's manual for how to remove and clean it. If the filter is damaged, replace it to protect the dishwasher's pump and motor seals.

▶ Check the dishwasher spray arms every six months as well. Over time, small holes in the spray arm(s) of your dishwasher may become clogged with bits of paper, toothpicks, glass, etc. Take a moment to clean out these holes with a small bristle brush to ensure you're getting the best cleaning ability from your dishwasher. If you find glass in the spray arm, there are probably glass pieces in the pump housing as well. You may want to disassemble the pump to check and clean it. Also, the glass may have damaged the motor spin seal, in which case you will often see a water leak at the main pump motor. Replace the motor spin seal if necessary. Visit www.repairclinic.com for diagrams of many common dishwashers and other small appliances.

Trash Compactor

▶ Thoroughly clean the interior of your trash compactor on a regular basis. Use a bacteria-fighting cleaner and/or degreaser to clean the ram (the platform that presses down on the garbage) and any other part of the compactor that comes into contact with the garbage.

leaking, you probably need to replace the spring clamp.

Your machine may simply be off level, causing water to drip out of the front. This is an easy fix, too. Under that same service panel, you can gain access to the adjustable feet. Unscrew the dishwasher from the countertop so it can move freely as you make any adjustment, then tighten it back in place.

Another possible culprit may be a leaky door. Check the door gasket, which may need to be replaced. Then test the door latch. If it's loose, a few turns of a screwdriver can usually fix the glitch.

If the puddle is filled with bubbles, you may be using the wrong detergent. Dishwashing soap for the sink is never okay in your dishwasher.

▶ Food waste can cause bacteria to grow on the inside of your trash compactor. For temporary odor control between cleanings, spray the interior with a germ-killing deodorant/disinfectant. Also replace the filter (if there is one) once or twice a year.

Water Filters

▶ Depending on how much you use a cartridge-type water filter, replace its cartridge one to two times a year. When you replace the cartridge, also thoroughly clean the canister that houses the cartridge. In addition, clean and lubricate the O-ring with food-grade silicone grease or a comparable lubricant.

▶ Dispose of a self-contained water filter (a filter without a removable cartridge) when it reaches the end of its useful life. This type of filter usually lasts from six months to one year.

Garbage Disposals

If appliances were movie stars, then the garbage disposal would be in the tabloids every week. It has been one of the more controversial appliances in recent history, and was actually banned in New York City until 1997. Dave Donovan, a former electrician, along with my buddies at www.doityourself.com, will help us grind through some common disposal issues.

Most garbage disposals take quite a beating on a daily basis. The function of the garbage disposal is to liquefy food and send it down the drain. Problems arise when we toss things in that can't be liquefied.

Here's an easy rule: if you can't shred an item apart with your fingers (e.g., chicken and turkey bones, onion skins, stringy celery, clam and oyster shells, corn husks, and other material with a high fiber content), toss it in the trash instead of the disposal. Under no circumstances should you put glass, plastic, metal, or other similar nonfood materials through a disposal. This includes bottle caps, tin covers, aluminum foil, and, of course, spoons.

So, how exactly does a disposal work? The disposal motor turns a rotating shredder plate with attached spinning lugs that grind food into mush that is flushed into your sewer system. The disposal is attached to the bottom of the sink with the use of a flange, a ring, and mounting bolts and then hardwired into an electrical outlet under the sink. Many dishwashers also send debris into the disposal. In this case, it's a good idea to run the disposal for about 15 seconds just before you turn on the dishwasher so that the ground-up food does not end up on your clean dishes. Yuck!

Always run cold water when grinding food in the disposal in order to move the waste all the way through the drain lines. Fats and grease congeal and harden in cold water and can then be flushed through the system. Don't use hot water, because it can dissolve fats and grease and cause them to accumulate in the drain line. Shredding eggshells and lemons actually helps clean the disposal by scraping away stubborn deposits in the process. Grinding ice cubes is another way to clean out deposits and get rid of odors.

Buying a New Disposal

If you're ready to buy a new model, or if you're getting one for the first time, check for regulations in your area, especially if you have recently moved to a new town. Some towns have strict rules about using one, especially if you have a septic tank. Also, have your plumbing system checked to see what kind of unit is compatible with your sewer and other plumbing hookups.

Next, choose the horsepower you need. Most disposals have a ½- to 1-horsepower motor. The average family will do well with a half horse-power motor, but if you tend to have heavier jobs, invest in the more powerful model.

If you have a dishwasher, make sure to select a unit with a dishwasher drain connection. Look for other special features like a manual reset, a corrosion protection shield, antisplash, and sound baffles. Installing a new unit is not difficult, but since each manufacturer's design varies, be sure to follow the instructions carefully.

PROJECT: GARBAGE DISPOSAL REPAIR

Level of difficulty: T T

Disposals are dependable appliances, but let's see if you've ever had this experience. You've just had a big dinner, and instead of throwing the debris left on the dishes into the garbage, you choose to stuff it all down the disposal. You hit the switch, the disposal screams to life, and then . . . nothing. You flip the switch a couple of times, only to be met with a humming sound and then a click. Now, when you hit the switch again, you don't even get the humming. Here's how to fix it.

You will need:
- ✓ Tongs
- ✓ Long screwdriver
- ✓ Allen wrench

1. HIT THE RESET BUTTON. Before attempting any fix, make sure the disposal switch is in the off position for a continuous feed disposal. For a batch feed disposal, be sure the stopper assembly is removed. When a disposal gets jammed, there is a reset button underneath it that trips out. It's best to wait about 15 minutes and then hit the reset button, which is located on the underside of most disposals and is usually red. If you push it in and you hear a click, then it has been reset. With the water running, try switching the disposal on again. If it's really jammed, it will probably trip again. If it does, leave the switch off for a few minutes and wait to hit the reset button.

2. CLEAR THE DEBRIS. Remove any large items from the disposal with a pair of tongs—never with your hands! Once you free the obstruction, hit the reset button, turn the water on, and hit the switch. It should be running smoothly now. Remember to throw the big debris in the garbage can next time!

3. TRY AN ALLEN WRENCH. If the disposal is still balking, locate the wrenchette that came with the disposal or use a ¼-inch Allen wrench. Insert it into the hex hole under the disposal and rotate it back and forth. Continue working the wrench until it turns freely in a complete revolution—both clockwise and counterclockwise. Be sure to remove the wrench!

Common Disposal Problems and Solutions

PROBLEM: The disposal isn't running at all.

SOLUTION: It could be an obstruction or it could be a power issue. Check the power to the circuit that feeds the disposal. If the circuit breaker is okay, then check the power at the switch. If you have power coming to, but not leaving, the switch, then the switch is bad. Turn the circuit off and replace the switch or call a service company.

PROBLEM: The disposal is draining poorly.

SOLUTION: Make sure that the water is running full blast when using the disposal. The more water, the better drainage. If it's still draining slowly, disconnect the J bend in the drainpipe under the sink and check for a clog. This is normally easy to do by unscrewing the pipe nut with a pipe wrench or channel locks. Be sure to place a bucket under it first to catch any water and debris. Sometimes grease and other nasty things will accumulate in your pipes over time. An old wire coat hanger can easily dislodge most clogs. Then just reattach the drain and tighten the pipe nut back into place.

PROBLEM: The disposal is leaking.

SOLUTION: If it's leaking around the mounting assembly, try tightening the screws on the sink-mounting ring. You will need an offset screwdriver to be able to reach the screws once the disposal is already assembled. Check to be sure that the disposal's lower mounting ring is fully engaged and locked to the mounting assembly. If the leak is coming from the drainpipe, tighten the screw that holds the drain gasket. If the leak persists, try replacing the drain gasket.

PROBLEM: The disposal is very noisy.

SOLUTION: While it's not the quietest appliance in normal situations, it can become really noisy if something gets in there to cause a ruckus. With the switch off, grab a flashlight and look down the drain for anything that might be causing the noise. Pay special attention to the area around the outer edge of the rotating shredder, where you will see V-shaped or window openings. Plastic or metal items are usually the culprits. Fish out the item with tongs. If there's nothing in the disposal, check the mounting screws. If they're loose, they may vibrate enough to cause a lot of noise when the disposal is turned on. The noise could also indicate that you have a damaged flywheel, in which case you're better off buying a new disposal than going through the motions of trying to repair it.

All in all, the garbage disposal's a pretty good fella'. He's dependable, he's there when you need him, and he doesn't complain about taking out the trash. If only your teenagers were so faithful! With these simple repairs, your relationship with him should last for years. ▪

Quick Kitchen Pick-me-ups

Forget the home equity loan. Cancel the appointment with the contractor. You don't need to spend a bundle and inconvenience your family for weeks to give the kitchen a face-lift. You will be amazed at what a few cans of paint or varnish or some new hardware can do for you. You can even leave the hammer in the toolbox this time. So set aside a weekend and let's get started!

Are your stained cabinets looking a bit dirty and sticky? Sometimes cooking grease can accumulate and settle on the surface, but underneath the finish still in good condition. Before starting a major refinishing project, try varnish-softening products such as Briwax or Howard's Restor-A-Finish. If the finish is not salvageable, you can often just lightly sand it and then apply stain and varnish. Be sure to use a good grease-cutting cleaner also. Colored varnishes, with the stain mixed in, work well as a topcoat to cover scratches and brighten the color of the original finish. Satin polyurethanes are often the best bet for going over an old finish. Be sure to read the manufacturer's directions for compatibility.

If you decide to paint over stained cabinets, be sure to degrease them first and then use a good primer, such as KILZ, to seal in the old finish. Lightly sand or steel-wool all surfaces, following the direction of the woodgrain, and then use a tack rag to remove dust before painting.

For painted cabinets and trim, if the color of the cabinets is satisfactory, leave it alone unless it is scuffed up. Enamel paint that is typically used on doors and trim is easy to sponge clean with mild detergent. If there is minor damage, try touching them up with leftover original paint, if you still have some. If you decide to totally repaint them, follow the directions in the previous paragraph.

Decorative wallpaper and other coverings can liven up any kitchen motif. Pick a paper that emphasizes or de-emphasizes your kitchen's strengths and weaknesses. For instance, a vertical stripe can make ceilings seem taller. A light-colored mini print can enlarge the space. And an embossed wallpaper installed as a backsplash, painted in a gloss silver, can imitate stamped metal panels.

If you have a higher budget, consider faux tin panels, installed as a backsplash, behind the stove, as the back or front of a bar, or in other accent areas in a kitchen. These beautiful designs are offered in a variety of vintage and contemporary patterns and finishes. They can be cut with scissors and installed in just minutes with ordinary construction adhesive. These are also great for cabinet fronts, ceilings, stairwells, and craft projects. Visit www.acpideas.com to see current styles and designs.

Another fun idea can be done in an afternoon, even if company is coming over that evening. IdeaStix makes tile appliqués that are self-adhesive, removable, reusable, washable, and heat-, water-, and steam-resistant—and they do not leave any residue if you remove them. They simply stick directly onto your tile backsplash and accessory items, such as canisters. They also make designs that apply instantly to light switchplates. This is a great kid project. (Visit www.ideastix.com.)

New hardware can also transform a kitchen in minutes. Think outside of the box. Try mixing and matching styles for a totally fun look. See chapter 5 for more tips on choosing cabinet hardware.

I was recently faced with a dilemma. My glossy white kitchen cabinets had gotten a bit long in the tooth. The paint was peeling off of some of the drawer fronts and needed to be completely stripped and repainted. Since I was a bit tired of the white look anyway, I decided to go radical and change the motif to aged farmhouse. With the help of my buddies the Painter Chicks, here's how I did it.

You will need:

- ✓ Blue painter's tape
- ✓ Drop cloths and plastic sheeting
- ✓ Screwdriver or cordless drill
- ✓ Dust masks
- ✓ Safety goggles or glasses
- ✓ Sanding blocks
- ✓ Belt sander and assorted belts
- ✓ Vacuum cleaner
- ✓ Tack rags
- ✓ Paintbrushes and rags
- ✓ Gel stain (in a color of your choice)
- ✓ Clear topcoat (polyurethane)

1. PREP THE AREA. Since you are going to be sanding, you should expect to make a mess. Spread drop cloths to protect floors and cover countertops and appliances with plastic sheeting. Tape off all adjoining areas, just as with any paint job. Remove all hardware, unless you want it to help "frame" the gel stain. We opted to remove the drawer handles but to leave the hinges in place. Just avoid sanding any delicate hardware that you decide to work around. Also, remove all glass from cabinet fronts or cover it with plastic and masking tape.

2. SAND THE CABINETS. Don safety goggles and a particulate mask. Sand the cabinet fronts with a combination of the electric belt sander and the handheld sanding block. The trick here is not to make things look pretty, but to create an aged, distressed appearance, so be aggressive and a bit crazy.

3. LIGHTLY WIPE THE SURFACES TO REMOVE MAJOR DUST DEBRIS AND THEN APPLY THE GEL STAIN WITH A RAG. Again, do not be neat, a messy hand will create a more authentic look. Gel stains are very forgiving, so you can try again and again to achieve the look that you want.

4. APPLY TOPCOAT. Allow the gel stain to dry overnight and then thoroughly vacuum the area. Use a tack rag to remove all dust, and then apply a thin coat of polyurethane varnish to the cabinets, if desired for added shine. Allow the varnish to dry overnight, and then reinstall hardware and remove all tape and debris. ■

Don't Take Clean Water for Granted

When you are refurbishing your kitchen, it's important to look beyond aesthetics. Do you know what could be one of the most significant threats to your family's health and comfort? Access to clean water. Daily doses of clean, pure H_2O are essential for hydrating ourselves and flushing toxins from our bodies. Children are especially susceptible to waterborne illness and parasites, as well as to lead and chemicals that may be in our water supplies. Chlorine, the very agent that is used to purify our water, has been linked to learning disabilities in children. Asthma and other illnesses have also been associated with waterborne chemicals and pollutants.

But don't go thinking that buying water off the grocer's shelf will solve your problems. Recent studies have actually found as many contaminants in bottled water as plain tap water. Moreover, bottled water usually does not contain fluoride, which helps maintain healthy teeth.

What's the solution? Home water filtration products and systems cost very little and yet are quite effective. If your refrigerator does not have built-in filtration, consider installing a filtering system on your kitchen water supply. At the very least, pick up a filtering water pitcher the next time you are at the store. It really works.

If your water supply comes from a private well, you may still be subject to toxins. During the rainy season, flooding can transport bacteria, pesticides, and other chemicals across many miles and contaminate the water supply, since the underground aquifers that supply wells are replenished by surface water.

One easy way to provide purified water for your family is to install a filtering kitchen faucet. Several manufacturers, such as Moen, are now offering built-in filters. You simply turn on the tap and the water is purified automatically. Some models offer bypass options for reverting to standard tap water. I have one of these faucets in my own kitchen and just love it. (Visit www.moen.com.)

If you suspect that your water supply may be contaminated, you can contact the Environmental Protection Agency (EPA), Centers for Disease Control and Prevention (CDC), and local health departments for assistance.

PROJECT: ORGANIZING THE PANTRY

Level of difficulty: ⊤

Unless you are one of "those people" whose pantries are immaculate with all of the cans and boxes facing forward (organized by category and alphabetically), you may often find it easier to order takeout than to locate particular food items behind all the clutter.

My chronically clean friend and TV personality Jennifer Humes, the Clutter Queen (www.clutterqueen.com), has partnered with me to provide you with seven easy steps to taking back the pantry.

You will need:
- ✓ Wastebasket
- ✓ Recycle bin
- ✓ Notebook and pencil
- ✓ Vacuum (handheld and push)
- ✓ Rag
- ✓ All-purpose cleaner
- ✓ Small stepladder
- ✓ Labeling machine or Sharpie

1. CLEAR THE WAY. Pull everything out of the pantry. This may sound like a real drag, but you may find items you stuck in there once when you were in a mad dash out the door. Time to return your neighbor's mixer that you borrowed (oops!).

2. GET SORTED. While clearing the pantry, sort like items together and group them on the floor, the countertop, or in boxes.

3. GET RID OF IT. When was the last time you checked the expiration or "best if used by" date? That hot chocolate from 1984 might not be so tasty today. Pull the wastebasket over and get busy. Go through every single item, including spices, food packets, oils, and cooking items, checking expiration dates. Be ruthless. Don't kid yourself into thinking that you will use that old package of gravy the next time the family gets together.

No expiration date? Find the code and check online or call the company for it. (You can find shelf life charts online at sites such as www.hormel.com, www.usda.gov, and www.mccormick.com.) If you find an item whose final date is soon approaching, plan a meal around it.

If you haven't needed the "Happy Birthday" paper plates and napkins in the past couple of years, it's time to donate them. How about that old toaster or coffeemaker? If the item is broken and beyond repair, it's time to trash it. If it is fixable, consider how much it will cost to repair. Is it worth your time? It may be time to donate it with a courtesy note indicating that the item needs some attention.

4. TAKE INVENTORY. Take a count of what is left and create a list of the items you use regularly. Referring to a standard grocery list prior to going to the store will minimize duplicate purchases and save you money.

5. DEEP CLEAN. Vacuum and thoroughly clean the shelves, walls, and underneath the shelves. Wipe all surfaces with a damp cloth—a vinegar and water solution is effective—to remove any sticky residue, which will help keep varmints away. Finally, towel dry and allow the area to air out so there isn't any moisture. Use a shelf liner if you want to dress things up a bit. You might even consider a topcoat of paint, if necessary.

6. CREATE A SYSTEM. Now, it is time to put the pantry in order. Place frequently used items at eye level. Larger items such as cereal boxes can be one shelf higher. A small stepladder for the kiddos will ensure they can easily reach their favorite foods. Less frequently used or bulky products, such as extra paper towels, can be stored either on the top shelf or near the bottom. If safety is an issue, put nonbreakables on the lower shelves, where children might get to them.

7. LOVE THOSE LABELS. Labeling shelves and containers will make it easier to locate food when you need it and will help everyone to put things back where they belong. If you remove food from the original packaging, label the container with the expiration date. Mark the tops of spice jar lids with a label maker or utilize a lazy Susan or wall-mounted rack for easy access and identification.

After admiring your work, it's time to head to the market with a grocery list to restock the pantry with items you may actually use! ■

Kitchen Cleaning Made Easy

Oven

Fortunately, ovens are easier to clean than ever. Oven cleaners have improved over the last few years as well. Be sure to follow the cleaning-product manufacturer's directions, as well as the manual that was supplied with your oven. In most cases, the following steps will make your oven look great and smell wonderful.

1. First remove oven racks and place them in soapy water to soak.

2. Preheat the oven to 200 degrees. Once it heats up, turn it off and spray the inside with oven cleaner.

3. Let the cleaner set for about 10 minutes and then wipe away with a damp sponge. Make sure you rinse several times and then simply dry with a soft cloth.

Sink and Drains

If you are fed up with a sink that keeps clogging up or has a foul smell, your pipes probably need a good cleaning.

▶ To reduce clogging and odors, run very hot tap water through the kitchen drain after each use. Avoid getting vegetable matter or excess grease in the drain. Instead, throw that goop into the trash.

▶ To eliminate odors, about once a week, pour a handful of baking soda into the kitchen drain, then run very hot tap water through it. Or pour a cup of vinegar or lemon juice in the drain and let stand for 30 minutes before running very hot water through it.

▶ To eliminate odors and to keep grease from building up, pour a strong salt brine down the kitchen sink drain regularly. Also consider buying a good drain cleaner, but read the label to make

Andrea's Choice:
A Biological Wonder for Your Drains

If your drains tend to clog often or if your disposal has an odor that just won't quit, pick up some Bio-Clean from your plumber or plumbing supplier. Bio-Clean is a blend of active bacteria and enzymes that act together to unclog and sanitize drains naturally. Safer than conventional drain cleaners, the little microbes work 24/7, eating all kinds of organic crud that can stop up your pipes. I think of it as yogurt for my drains. Bio-Clean is terrific for septic tanks, RV and boat holding tanks, as well as kitty litter pans. (Visit www.safedraincleaner.com.)

sure it's safe for your type of pipes, or choose a natural drain cleaner.

► When all else fails, you may have to call a plumber.

Crayon Marks

If you have little ones with crayons, chances are they have created a mural or two on your painted sheetrock walls. There is a simple solution—and little Sally or Scott can help!

1. Gently scrape away the wax with a plastic spatula or spoon.

2. Sprinkle baking soda on a damp cloth and let your little one scrub the marks right off the wall.

3. Then dampen a sponge and wipe away the residue. (If you have a really stubborn mark, Mom or Dad may have to step in with a little WD-40 or other lubricating oil.)

5. Finally, wipe the wall down with a clean, damp cloth. And next time you buy crayons, look for the kind that are washable or pick up pencils that can easily be erased.

3

beautiful bathroom boosts

Changes and Repairs That Will Make You
Want to Stay and Read the Paper

"What made the deepest impression upon you," inquired a friend one day of Abraham Lincoln, "when you stood in the presence of the Falls of Niagara, the greatest of natural wonders?"

"The thing that struck me most forcibly when I saw the Falls," Lincoln responded with characteristic deliberation, "was where in the world did all that water come from?"

This chapter is all about the bathroom, one of the most important rooms in the house. A bathroom update can smooth out the morning rush and greatly improve the quality of life for everyone in your household. The bathroom is also a key area to refurbish when you are considering the resale value of your home. Prospective buyers rate functional and attractive bathrooms near the top of the list when choosing a new home.

This H_2O haven provides not only cleanliness, but also an escape from the hustle and bustle of everyday life. If you are still showering in a tiny cramped cubicle or bathing in a rust-stained tub, now is a good time to modernize.

In this chapter, we'll explore some fun ideas for dressing up a boring bathroom, then a few updates that will make it the most popular room in the house. We'll also look at some options for choosing a new faucet and tackle refinishing a sink or bathtub.

▶ Add Some Zing to a Boring Bath

▶ Planning a Major Bathroom Remodel

▶ One-Hour Wonder: Add Some Fun with Wallpaper Cutouts

▶ Project: Organizing Bathroom Clutter

▶ Project: Choosing and Replacing Towel Bars and Accessories

▶ Choosing a New Faucet

▶ Project: Repairing a Leaky Toilet—Water Out of Balance

▶ Project: Replacing or Cleaning a Leaky Toilet Flapper Valve

▶ Project: Repairing the Lazy Toilet

▶ Grout-Cleaning Solutions

▶ Project: Regrouting a Tile Shower, Countertop, or Floor

▶ Project: Refinishing a Bathtub, Sink, or Tile with Epoxy

Add Some Zing to a Boring Bath

Many of us live in houses with sorely outdated bathrooms. Remodeling costs are high, and a lot of us don't have the time or the skills to do it ourselves. But you don't have to tear it up to improve it. Here are some easy and inexpensive ideas for updating your bathroom from DoItYourself.com and my own trial and error.

▶ Add some new towels. You don't have to buy a whole new set. Just buy a set of hand towels or washcloths in a new color that will complement your existing color scheme. You could get a mix of colors or just one shade. Sew some lace trim or rickrack on the hand towels to give them a custom look. Or have each of your children's names custom-embroidered on some colorful towels at a local T-shirt shop. Your kids will think you just won the lottery. Short on towel storage? Try rolling a few up and displaying them in a basket for an attractive decorative accent.

▶ Frame your mirror. Make a plain mirror more decorative by creating a custom frame. Cut your choice of molding to fit around the mirror and paint it, using neutral colors or a brushed gold or silver. The frame can be attached to the mirror with glue and a few small nails or brads to bind the corners.

▶ Cover the walls with your life. One of my friends used old road maps as the wallpaper in her guest bathroom. Instead of reading a magazine, her visitors can travel to exotic locals while they soak in the tub. She accented with souvenirs from each stop, such as keychains and seashells. Do you like horses? How about using discarded feed sacks to adorn your walls? In a kid's bathroom, choose some of their old school papers and photos. For the pool bath, how about brochures from some of your favorite beach resorts. Why not?

▶ A new paint color is always an easy way to update a bathroom. Have fun by choosing a color that complements your existing decor but is a bit unexpected. Choose colors and patterns that say, "Wow." Even a small bathroom in a cramped apartment can become a fun getaway for you and your guests when you let your imagination take over your decorating style. For instance, if you have 1950s green tiles, try pale yellow as a wall paint. Or if you have a black or white motif, highlight it by painting the walls sage green or pink. If you don't want to go too bold, update your color with tone-on-tone neutrals such as ecru, oyster, almond, or biscuit. Then you can add colorful touches with towels, soaps, and candles.

▶ Buy a new shower curtain. For around $20, you can find a distinctive shower curtain with decorative hooks that will make a big difference in your bathroom. Sew a few bangles or bows on it for a custom touch. Just be sure that they are washable. If the room is small, a clear shower curtain or one in the same color as your bathtub will create the illusion of a bigger bathroom.

Andrea's Choice:
Mirror Dressing

The edges of bathroom mirrors often blacken as moisture seeps in over years of use. In the past, the only solution was to replace the mirror. Now Mirr.Edge offers an ingenious edging system that solves this problem, making your mirrors look even better than new. Using simple tools such as a razor knife and tape measure, Mirr.Edge helps you change your bathroom from tacky to terrific in just minutes. It can even cover the metal clips on many mirrors. Choose a beveled glass design or a woodgrain finish—all under $50 for an average mirror. (Visit www.MirrEdge.com.)

▶ Get rid of an outdated medicine cabinet. You can make a dramatic difference in your bathroom by replacing an old cabinet with a simple wood-framed mirror. Once the mirror is in place, you may want to add a matching freestanding storage unit or small table.

▶ Lively wallpaper can infuse new life into a drab decor. The right design can fix flaws in just a snap. Choose a small print or stripe to enlarge a cramped space visually. A horizontal band can draw separate areas into one uniform zone. And an embossed paper installed as a backsplash painted in a gloss enamel can be used instead of tile to help waterproof walls and is perfect around a claw-foot tub or pedestal sink.

▶ Change your hardware. An easy way to alter the look of your room is to update details such as drawer pulls, towel bars, shower controls, robe hooks, and soap holders. You could even splurge on a new faucet.

▶ Don't have a good place to hang your toilet paper holder or towel bars? Many companies offer freestanding designs that work really well. I have a freestanding toilet paper holder in my own bathroom.

Planning a Major Bathroom Remodel

The bathroom gets a lot of use, and having an attractive and well-designed one can make your daily routine that much more pleasant. If small cosmetic fixes won't do the trick, it may be time to really rock and roll.

Among the many home improvement projects that can increase both the livability and value of your home, remodeling the bathroom is certainly one of them. If your bathroom is old and outdated, you may have considered a redesign or remodel but been held back by fears that the project would become too costly and complex.

While it is true that even a small bathroom project can quickly spiral into thousands of dollars, it does not have to be that way. With the right planning and knowledge, it is possible to create a painless bathroom makeover that will not break the budget. Just grab that hammer again and follow these tips from my friends at DoItYourself.com.

Outlining a Budget

It is important to start with a realistic budget before you begin. Map out the entire project, including any new decorations and fixtures, before you get started. After you know exactly what you will need to create your stunning new look, be sure to shop around carefully for the best price. The prices of exactly the same bathroom faucets, shower-heads, and other fixtures can vary quite a bit from one source to another, so be sure to shop around for the best value.

Selecting a Style

It is also vital to think carefully about the look you want your finished bathroom to have. Consider such things as the colors you favor, the types of faucets and fixtures you want, as well as the decorations you want to incorporate in your new bathroom. If a new tub, shower, sink, or toilet is in the works, shop according to your desired color and style schemes. As you redesign your bathroom, be sure to consider the decor of the rest of your home and how your new H_2O zone will fit in.

Assessing Home Improvement Skills

As you plan your budget and redesign project, be sure to also consider the costs of any plumbers, contractors, or other outside assistance you may need. Not everyone is comfortable doing basic plumbing and pipe installation. It is important to assess honestly your own home improvement skills and time and plan to get professional help where necessary. This, combined with shopping carefully for the right materials, will help you create the bathroom of your dreams at a price you can live with.

whirlpool jets are adjustable for pressure and direction. Buying a whirlpool tub is much like buying a car: you'll find many manufacturers who offer several models and options you never dreamed existed. (There are even whirlpools for your dogs! MTI Whirlpools has one available with a hand shower and rings mounted to help keep your puppy in place while you scrub him down.)

Once you've decided on the type of tub, determine where it will go and how much room you will need. If you are trying to save space, consider a corner unit, and then determine the right kind of material for it. Can your floor support cast iron, or do you need to go with plastic or fiberglass? Don't forget to test the water heater to make sure it will deliver enough warm water. Whirlpool tubs hold anywhere from 25 to 150 gallons.

Now it's time to take the tubs for a test drive. Visit local showrooms, and don't be afraid to climb in and see how they fit. Also look at self-cleaning systems if that's important to you. More important, look for units that have protected jets and sensors that will cut the motor when the water gets too low so the motor doesn't burn out.

ONE-HOUR WONDER: ADD SOME FUN WITH WALLPAPER CUTOUTS

Level of difficulty: T

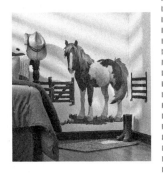

T *Andrea's Choice:*
Stick'n Stile Tile
Appliqués

"Too often people think they
are stuck with the tired old
tiles in their bathrooms," says
Todd Imholte, president of
Environmental Graphics, a
company that specializes in
decorative products for the
home. An easy fix is offered
by Stick'n Stile decorative
appliqués, which stick to plain
tile, giving it a new, updated,
designer look. You can create
your own effect to fit any
color scheme, and the
adhesive-backed appliqués
are easy to apply and remove.
(Visit www.designbiz.com.)

Self-stick wallpaper cutouts are just about the niftiest and simplest do-it-yourself products that I have come across in ages. They are incredibly easy to apply and can really transform a bathroom. They are great for other rooms in the house, too. Let your imagination run wild!

Some designs are made from a resin material that is self-adhesive, removable, reusable, washable, and heat-, water-, and steam-resistant—and they do not leave any residue if you remove them. Other patterns are more like conventional wallpaper but cut out to use as fun decor. Some even have coordinating murals. Three brands that I like are IdeaStix (www.ideastix.com), Wallies (www.wallies.com), and Stick'n Stile (see Andrea's Choice, this page).

All of these products allow you to decorate tiles and other nonporous surfaces—from canisters to switch plates, to lamps and appliances. Just be creative! They will instantly change the look of a room by adding color, design, and texture. Ranging from small artistic designs to life-sized plants, animals, people, and so on, they can even be used to create vibrant murals. For example, some of the whimsical images are perfect for designing unique rooms for kids.

It's so easy to do. Just clean and dry the surface first. If necessary, sand it lightly to prevent the texture from showing through the design. Carefully lift the design from the backing (save the backing for future storage) and place it on the application surface. Use a rag to burnish the design onto the surface, smoothing out bubbles and wrinkles carefully. Enjoy! ■

PROJECT: ORGANIZING BATHROOM CLUTTER

Level of difficulty: ⊤

Lotions, potions, salves, balms, oils, creams, toners . . . the next miracle is waiting for you at retail store counters. How do you contain everything and still find your favorite product when you need it—and still have space for the inevitable next great find? I seem to spend a large portion of my disposable income on cosmetics and toiletries, plus I like to test each new bathroom cleaner that hits the market. Over time, these miracle products tend to accumulate and create chaos. Once again, Jennifer Humes, the Clutter Queen (www.clutterqueen.com), provides easy steps to eliminate more than just fine lines and soap scum.

You will need:

- ✓ Recycle bin
- ✓ Wastebasket
- ✓ Label maker or Sharpie and labels

1. CLEAR OUT THE CHAOS. Pull everything out and clear the space. Turn drawers upside down. Pull out products from cabinets and under sinks. Spread it all out in front of you on the floor or on a table where you can see it.

2. SORT AND CATEGORIZE. Sort your beauty products according to type: cleansers, exfoliants, toners, creams, masks, and makeup, etc. Then sort your bathroom cleaners, sponges, brushes, etc., grouping like items together.

3. ELIMINATE EXCESS. Purge! Eliminate duplicate items and anything that you have not used in the past year.

4. LABEL, LABEL, LABEL. Use a permanent marker to label the purchase dates on products. The next time you clean out, it will be easier to say good-bye to the products not being used.

5. FIND A PLACE FOR EVERYTHING. Place frequently used products in front and less-used items behind or in back. If you can't see it, you might forget you have it. If you aren't going to use a product, don't waste it; instead, give it to a friend or donate it to a local charity if the product has not been used. Always recycle whenever possible.

6. KEEP YOUR TOOLS OF THE TRADE READY AT HAND. Applying makeup is easier when you have the right brushes, sponges, and sharpeners. Often, we have more gadgets than we really need or want. Choose your favorites and store nearby in a glass or decorative container for quick and easy application. The same goes for bathroom cleaning products.

Quick tips:

▶ If counter space is available, use decorative trays to display frequently used cosmetics.

▶ Store extras, such as soap or razors, in labeled containers. You might also store these near the shower or tub for those times when you run out.

▶ Label products with the purchase date. Some products lose their potency or dry out over time. An item purchased in the 1990s might not still have what it takes to banish that blemish or illuminate your locks.

▶ Makeup has a tendency to build up bacteria. Most makeup has a shelf life of only two years; mascara, only three to six months. If the product is clearly separating or you can see spots on your lipstick, it's time to throw it away.

▶ Dump any products that are caking, crackling, or crumbling. If it's your favorite product and you can't part with it, replace it with a new one.

▶ Pack a travel cosmetic bag for those times you are in a mad dash out the door. No need to pack the entire bathroom for a night or weekend away from home. Keep a clear plastic case with a small container of each essential item.

▶ Be sure to keep all toxic cleaners out of reach of children. Purchase some clear plastic shoeboxes so that you can store these items overhead and then pull them down on cleaning day.

▶ Avoid duplicates, and use multitasking products when available.

▶ Go through all products at least once a year, if not twice. Your favorite product may have been pushed to the back of the cabinet and finding it will be a pleasant surprise.

Your environment is a reflection of you. Be aware of what you create, because you create your reality. It takes only a minimal effort to create a stress-free haven in your bathroom. You'll feel the difference every time you're in there, and your nosy guests will envy your organization as they secretly peek into your drawers and bath cabinets! ■

PROJECT: CHOOSING AND REPLACING TOWEL BARS AND ACCESSORIES

Level of difficulty: ⊤ ⊤

Towel bars and bath accessories can be much more than functional. The trend these days is to match them to the faucets in the bathroom. Many faucet companies offer a line of bath accessories to complement their faucet styles. You may want to follow this trend or choose to mix and match. Whatever your choice, new bath accessories can definitely add new life and function to your bathroom.

You will need:

- ✓ New towel bars and accessories
- ✓ Screwdriver
- ✓ Drill
- ✓ Molly bolts or other fasteners

1. CHOOSE THE NEW FITTINGS. If you want to match your bathroom's decor, take a picture of it with you when you shop. It's also a good idea to remove the old fittings before you go shopping and take them with you. Most towel bars are offered in standard sizes, but measure your existing ones just in case they are metric or new versions may have to be cut to fit. Measure from the center of one post or base to the center of the opposite one. Make sure the new backplates will completely cover the old ones. Often, paint and wallpaper can fade behind the old ones.

2. CAREFULLY REMOVE ALL OLD FITTINGS. If you are trying to take off old towel bars and the screws are not exposed so you can easily see how to remove the towel bar posts, look for a setscrew at the bottom of the post or at the bottom of the baseplate. Some styles even have a notch with a tab holding them on. Just push in on the tab with a small slot head screwdriver to remove.

3. MOUNT THE NEW FITTINGS AND BARS. When replacing the bars, you can try to use the same mounting plates or hit the same holes. If you are successful, run out and buy a lottery ticket while your luck is on your side!

⊤ Andrea's Choice: Make it E-Z

For new towel bar installations, I often use a fastener called an E-Z Ancor. This gizmo drills its own hole, but I like to predrill a pilot hole into the drywall anyway. Then just screw the E-Z Ancor into the drywall like a corkscrew. It holds very well, but you must be sure the towel bar base will cover the holes. I use this type of fastener to attach many things to drywall, including shelves. But if the load is heavy, stay with wing toggles and make them as large as possible. Just take note of the size of hole that must be made into the drywall before you drill.

🔧 Quick Tip: Repainting

Don't try to paint a bathroom with all of the accessories still screwed to the wall. Just go ahead and remove them first, and then remount them after the paint has dried. It's worth the extra effort to facilitate a nice, clean paint job.

Often, when you remove the screws that hold the old mounting bracket to the wall, you'll find little space left for new screws. Sometimes, if you replace a horizontal screw pattern with a vertical pattern, you'll have enough fresh drywall for screws to be placed with the other orientation, which will allow for a stronger grip. If you have to remove Molly bolts, drill them out and push them into the wall. If your new backplates have holes that closely match, you can use wing-toggle bolts through the original holes. But the best bet is usually to start fresh with new holes. Just make sure the new towel bar base covers the old holes completely.

4. COMPLETE THE FINAL TOUCHES. Make sure that all fittings are attached securely. Then hang some new fluffy towels up to complete your new motif! ■

Choosing a New Faucet

Before shopping for a new faucet, it's important to determine exactly what size faucet you will need. Faucets are measured by the distance between the centers of the hot and cold water inlets, which is typically 8 inches for two-handle faucets. It may be necessary to remove the old faucet first to obtain accurate measurements. If you want to change from a two-handled faucet to just a single lever one, you can purchase a faucet with a cover plate to cover the existing holes.

For the easiest installation, replace the faucet you have with one that will fit the same openings. Otherwise, you might need to replace the sink or countertop, or drill additional holes. Also measure the supply line connections, as they are not all the same and this may be a good time to replace old rigid copper supply lines with steel flex lines. The flexible lines are less likely to leak and are easier to install.

If you haven't been plumbing shopping in a while, there are some technologies you should know about. First of all, most manufacturers don't use old-style rubber washers anymore. Ceramic disk cartridges last much longer and are easier to replace, as discussed earlier in this chapter. Tired of smashing your knuckles on a faucet that is hard to handle? Easy quarter-turn valves require only a small motion to turn the faucet on or off.

Never buy cheap faucets. You usually get what you pay for, and it is a real hassle to have to replace them in a year or two. Try to buy faucets with these options.

▶ A warranty of twenty-five years or more. Lifetime is the best.

▶ Choose your finish carefully. Although special colors such as bronze or pewter are beautiful, chrome will outlast all other finishes, regardless of warranty.

▶ Look for quarter-turn, ceramic disk valves for years of trouble-free service.

▶ Consider lever handles. When your hands are dirty or soapy, levers are easy to turn off and on. They are also terrific for kids and older folks or those with limited dexterity.

▶ When you go faucet shopping, take all of your measurements with you. Faucets come in a huge variety of sizes.

▶ Make sure that the spout of your new faucet will reach roughly to the center of the drain hole. (Don't you hate hitting your knuckles against the back of the sink when you're washing your hands?)

▶ Sinks can be found in almost any color and material, including wood and stone. These novelty products may look cool, but are they really practical when you are trying to brush your teeth? Save them for the powder bath, where they will be noticed by guests but not used as often.

Quick Tip:
Where to Buy New Faucets?

When you get ready to go shopping, you've got a handful of options.

▶ Home centers are generally inexpensive and good for more-common models, but your selection will be limited. Specialty items will usually take longer to get, if they are available at all.

▶ A decorative hardware store may charge a bit more, but the staff will usually be more knowledgeable, particularly if you want something unusual.

▶ Online sources are also an option; just be sure you can return the item if it does not fit or look good. Visit the resource section at the back of the book for some online suppliers.

Level of difficulty: T T

Quick Tip:
Know Your Limitations

Even though I have made many repairs to plumbing fittings, I limit myself to repairs outside the walls. To repair joints, valves, or drains inside the wall, I call a plumber to do the plumbing part and then make the wall repairs myself. Many good plumbers will make every effort to save your walls, but sometimes a little destruction is needed to access the problem. In such cases, drywall repair is preferable to tile repair, since removing tile can require a whole new shopping experience. Sometimes, it's best to access the problem from the other side of a tile wall, even if it destroys the wall in a bedroom or closet. You may even consider making the drywall opening into an access panel for later repairs, especially if it's in a closet, under the countertop, or inside a cabinet. In many homes, a tile wall backs up to an exterior brick wall, leaving no easy access. Some deck tub faucets and whirlpools don't have access panels because they were built before recent code changes required them.

Of all the plumbing repairs around the house, fixing the commode is the one that typically gets done most quickly. If you are like me, you'll agree that having a quiet, nonleaking commode is important enough to learn how to take care of problems when they first rear their ugly heads.

The toilet is the most common household water waster. A badly leaking toilet can waste nearly eighty thousand gallons of water a year. While repairing a leaky toilet is a major water conservation project, it is actually a very simple plumbing project. This diagram and the following instructions can help you understand the inner workings of your toilet and make adjustments as needed. For more troubleshooting with your toilet, visit Professor Flush at www.fluidmaster.com.

One of the most common toilet problems is excess overflow. This often happens because the water level in the tank is not balanced correctly. The water level should be a half inch or less below the overflow tube. When the water level in the tank rises above the overflow tube, the water will run into the toilet bowl constantly. When the level is too low, the toilet may not flush fully. Luckily, both problems are easily fixed with a screwdriver and a little know-how.

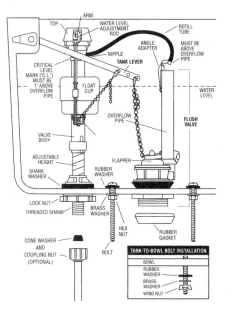

✓ Screwdriver

1. DETERMINE THE FLUSHING MECHANISM. Most toilets have one of three different types of flushing mechanisms: a float arm, a float cup, or a metered fill valve. A float arm looks like a balloon on the end of a metal rod, the rod part being the "arm." Usually, the float is made of black rubber, but it can be made of other materials as well. A float cup has the float part wrapped around the refill pipe rather than on the end of a metal arm. A metered fill valve is found on older commodes and does not use a float to control the water level in the tank.

2. ADJUST THE FLOAT ARM, THE FLOAT CUP, OR THE METERED FILL VALVE.

▶ *Float arm:* Adjust the level of the float. If the arm is metal, you can bend it either up or down to raise or lower the float. On plastic arms and some metal arms, there will be a knob at the ball cock, where the arm meets the vertical pipe that supplies water back into the tank. Be sure that the float rests halfway in the water. If it is covered by water, the float has a leak in it and needs to be replaced.

▶ *Float cup:* A float cup has its float situated on the intake pipe instead of on the end of a metal arm. To adjust the level of a float cup, find the metal clip that holds the cup in place along the refill pipe and squeeze it. Move the cup to the desired level and release the clip.

▶ *Metered fill valve:* If you have a metered fill valve, I recommend upgrading the flushing mechanism to a float cup or float arm to help minimize problems. If that is not an option right now, take a flathead screwdriver and turn the screw found on the fill valve clockwise to raise the water level, counterclockwise to lower it.

3. ADJUST THE WATER LEVEL. Check the level of water in the tank, which should be a half an inch or less below the overflow tube (see the diagram on page 68). Adjust the water level up or down accordingly, and flush to check that the level is balanced, and roughly one-half inch below the top of the overflow tube. Repeat until you get it right. ■

Andrea's Choice: An Instant Bidet

The Europeans have known it for years: bidets or cleansing toilets are a great way to stay as fresh as a daisy. If you would like a bidet but don't have the extra space or plumbing hookups, you can convert any normal toilet into hygienic luxury with the Purité Personal Cleansing Spa from Bemis. Simply touch a button and whoosh. The dual nozzles dispense warm water like a minishower for your underside. Each wash is followed with a warm-air jet dryer. The unit won't function unless the seat is occupied—so no water fights here, kids! It's particularly great for folks with disabilities and pregnant women, and for postsurgical care, too. (Visit www.bemismfg.com.)

Does a ghost seem to inhabit your toilet? Do you hear it running all night long? It may be leaking, which also means that you're wasting water. To determine if your potty is purging, put a few drops of food coloring into the tank. Wait a few minutes. If the water in the toilet bowl turns color, then you've got a leak coming from the tank into the bowl. If your toilet is leaking, one of the most common causes is a worn flapper valve. The flapper valve is a large rubber seal located in the middle of the bottom of the tank. It is usually attached by a chain to an arm that's connected to the toilet's handle.

You will need:

- ✓ Old towel
- ✓ Mineral-removing cleaner
- ✓ Screwdriver
- ✓ Pliers
- ✓ Replacement flapper

1. TURN OFF THE WATER SUPPLY. The best way to turn off the water for small repairs is to carefully turn off the supply valve to the faucet or toilet. (If plumbing repairs require that the water be shut off for the whole house, you may want to hire a plumber to do the repairs and provide a supply valve so you can do the next toilet or faucet repair yourself.) The supply valve is usually located under the lower-left part of the tank. Use caution when turning the handle, as these are notorious for breaking off. Have a towel handy to soak up any drips. Flush the toilet so that water drains out of the tank.

2. CLEAN OR REPLACE THE FLAPPER. Take off the lid of the tank and check the flapper valve. Make sure it's clean and smooth. If it's dirty or has a buildup of minerals or algae on it, it may not be able to seal properly. Also make sure that the tank drain is clean and smooth.

If either the flapper or the drain has any buildup on them, simply clean them with an old rag and, if necessary, a mineral-removing liquid such as Lime-A-Way, following the manufacturer's directions.

If the flapper is dried, warped, cracked, or pitted, replace it. Check for cracks in the flush valve (the piece the flapper seals against). Cracks seldom appear here, but if they do, you may need a whole new toilet if the part cannot be found or the toilet is too old. The silver lining in this case is that the newer 1.6 gallon toilets may save you enough water to pay for the replacement.

3. CHECK THE FLAPPER CHAIN. Before you replace the tank lid, check the chain that links the flapper to the arm. Make sure there is some slack in it. If it's too tight, it can hold the flapper open enough to allow the leak to persist. If there is too much slack, the chain can get caught between the flapper and the drain.

If you have taken all of these steps and the toilet is still leaking, it may be time to call a plumber or consider replacing the toilet completely. ■

Quick Tip:
Think Tank

When you are shopping for the latest technology in low-flush models, there are a couple of options to consider. First, make sure that the toilet flushes with enthusiasm. Nobody likes to flush twice. Ask the store staff about its flushability and check consumer Web sites such as www.consumerreports.com for ratings. Second, many brands are now offering an upgrade to a taller bowl, which is much more comfortable for grown-ups. Elongated bowls are more comfortable for men and keep the front part of the seat more sanitary. They take up only a few more inches of space and are required for some accessories, such as the bidet seat.

Andrea's Choice:
Bemis 1200 Slow-Close

This is a nifty toilet seat with snap-off hinges. Anyone who has raised children can appreciate a seat that can be removed for easy cleaning. Yes, it's best to have a good set of gloves, but once the seat is off, it's very easy to clean where the hinges meet the bowl: the dirtiest little spot in the whole house. The Bemis 1200SLOW seat and lid are also tempered to allow them to close slowly with little or no sound. The kids will be amazed when they drop the seat and see it drift down to the bowl.

If you have ever had a toilet that requires holding the handle down for the duration of the flush, you know how annoying those seconds can be. Fortunately, there is an easy solution. This project comes courtesy of my friend Ron Bevins, of Benjamin Franklin Plumbing in Dallas.

1. MAKE AN ADJUSTMENT. Remove the toilet tank cover carefully and observe the action of the internal parts as you flush the toilet without holding the tank handle down. Then flush the toilet again, but this time observe the action of the internal parts as you hold the tank handle down. You may find that the center rubber device known as the flapper may not be staying up long enough to allow all of the water to flush out before closing again. Most likely, the chain that connects the flapper to the tank handle is too long.

2. ADJUST THE CHAIN. Remove the upper portion of the chain from the handle and pull out some of the slack by reattaching the chain to the handle slightly above where the chain was previously attached. The problem should be solved. If not, you may be able to get a chain or a flapper with a small float attached. The float holds the flapper up until the water comes down, thus releasing water longer. ■

Grout-Cleaning Solutions

Whether you've got tile floors, backsplashes, or bathroom tile in your bathroom or kitchen, the grout between the tiles can get pretty grimy. Cleaning it is one of my least favorite chores, but with the right cleaning solution and a bit of elbow grease, you can get your grout looking fresh and brand-new.

Tile grout gets dirty in many different ways. In the bathroom, it's usually mold or mildew stains. In the kitchen, it could be a combination of food stains, general household traffic and grime, and mildew. No matter what the cause, start off with the simplest and least acidic cleaning solution first, then try harsher chemical cleaners as necessary.

For some grout stains, simple household items such as vinegar or baking soda can be effective cleaners. Make a solution of equal parts vinegar and water or a paste of baking soda with a bit of water. Spray or dab the cleaner onto a small length of grout and scrub with a stiff brush. Scrubbing in small circles rather than straight up and down will remove more debris. Rinse well with water and mop up any remaining moisture with a sponge or paper towels.

Generic household cleaners such as Mr. Clean, Lysol, or powder-based products can also work on tile grout. Lime-A-Way is effective on certain types of buildup, such as rust and lime deposits. Use these products as directed, wear rubber gloves, and make sure to rinse the grout well after cleaning. Alternatively, if you own or have access to a steam cleaner, try using it on your grout work. The pressure of the steam can loosen debris and stains that chemicals can't dissolve. Plus, there are no chemical odors or aftereffects.

If your grout hasn't come completely clean, the next step is to try a commercial tile-and-grout cleaner, which is available wherever home cleaning products are sold. Try to find a cleanser that is pH balanced so that the chemicals in the product won't erode the grout with continued use. To get the best result from a commercial cleaner, spray it on and let it sit for a few minutes before scrubbing, and always follow the directions on the label.

For heavy-duty stains, use even stronger products such as oxygen bleach powder, hydrogen peroxide, or chlorine bleach. These products should be well diluted before use. You can find heavy-duty cleaners at hardware stores or janitorial supply outlets. If you go this route, however, be sure to read labels carefully and follow directions to the letter. Also be careful about mixing different types of cleaners. Always rinse thoroughly between applications to avoid combination reactions.

A Few More Tips for Grout Cleaning

▶ Clean the grout first with water and allow it to dry. This will remove any loose surface debris.

▶ Never use bleach on colored grout, as it will discolor the grout.

▶ Use a stiff brush for scrubbing. Old toothbrushes will be too soft. Avoid using metal bristles, as they will wear away the grout.

▶ If you're using commercial cleaners, bleach, or other chemicals, make sure the room you're working in is well ventilated.

▶ Use gloves and protective eyewear when working with any chemical-based cleaners.

▶ Test your grout cleaner on a small, inconspicuous area first to make sure that it won't erode or damage your grout work. This is especially necessary if your tile grout is old or damaged.

▶ Never mix cleaners together! Chemical reactions can cause noxious fumes or burns if the mixture touches the skin.

▶ When your tile grout is completely clean, keep it looking fresh and new by applying a coat or two of grout sealer. There are various types of grout sealers available for different uses, such as floors or bathroom tile. Make sure you purchase the correct type. Reapply the grout sealer once a year or more often if necessary.

PROJECT: REGROUTING A TILE SHOWER, COUNTERTOP, OR FLOOR

Level of difficulty: T T T T T

Has your tile and grout seen better days? Have you tried every possible cleaning product, only to be left with stained grout that reminds you of a seedy motel? The good news is if your tile is still in good shape, you don't have to rip it out. You can simply replace the grout. It's a bit messy and time-consuming, but doesn't require special skills and costs almost nothing.

You will need:
- ✓ Plastic drop cloth
- ✓ Dust mask and goggles
- ✓ Masking tape
- ✓ Power drill with a Carborundum bit or Dremel tool and bits
- ✓ Handheld grout saw
- ✓ Paint scraper with a teardrop head
- ✓ Small grinding stone
- ✓ Grout
- ✓ Rubber grout trowel
- ✓ Grout sponge
- ✓ Shop vac
- ✓ Rags
- ✓ Grout sealer

1. PREP THE AREA. The grout-removal process is simple, but messy. Before you start, remove everything from the bathroom you don't want covered in grit and tape a sheet of plastic over the doorway to separate the work area from the rest of the house. Cover the tub with a drop cloth so that you don't grind the grit into the tub and damage the finish. Wear a dust mask and eye protection.

2. REMOVE THE OLD GROUT. Start on a horizontal grout line at a comfortable working height. (For me, that's about shoulder height.) Cover the tile on each side of the line with a 2-inch piece of masking tape to protect it if you slip.

With the drill or Dremel, cut down the middle of the grout line. The depth of the cut should be a little more than half the thickness of the tile. Avoid cutting into the drywall or backer board under the tile.

Use the handheld grout saw and the paint scraper to reach areas you can't get at with the power tools and to remove the grout along the edges of the tile. Repeat this process for the rest of the grout lines.

For the finishing touches, you'll have to use a handheld grout saw. These tools look like a straight razor blade attached to an offset handle. The blade is diamond studded and cuts through grout lickety-split.

Use the paint scraper and then the small grinding stone to remove the last of the old grout from the edges of the tile. Vacuum all surfaces with the shop vac and then wipe everything down with a damp rag.

3. REGROUT. When all the tile edges are clean, it's time to regrout. Complete a small area first to make sure you're happy with the result.

Mix a small amount of grout and apply it to the wall with the rubber grout trowel. Let it set up for a minute or two, then wipe off the residue with the grout sponge and clean water. After the water dries, polish the tile with a clean rag.

Once you're satisfied with the result, grout the rest of the tile. I strongly recommend sealing the grout once the regrouting is complete. Two coats of grout sealer, applied according to the manufacturer's instructions, will seal the tile and help resist the buildup of soap scum.
(Resource: www.doityourself.com) ◼

PROJECT: REFINISHING A BATHTUB, SINK, OR TILE WITH EPOXY

Level of difficulty: T T T T T

Is your bathtub stained with nasty rust? Or is your old tile an outdated color? This doesn't mean you have to buy a new tub or wait for those tiles to come back in fashion. With the types of refinishing kits on the market today, changing the color of your ceramics and putting a smooth new finish on them is truly a doable project for the do-it-yourselfer.

At your local hardware store or home center, look for a tub and tile refinishing product that provides a tough, hard, epoxy coating that acts like porcelain and ceramic. Make sure it is made for high-moisture areas. Products may have varying drying times, so be sure to read the label and follow directions. It is best to apply them when the temperature is between 65 and 90 degrees Fahrenheit and the humidity is below 80 percent to ensure that they dry properly.

You will need:

✓ Fan (if the room is windowless)
✓ Drop cloths
✓ Rubber gloves
✓ Wire brush or coarse sandpaper
✓ Patching compound such as Bondo or epoxy fillers (if there are chips or cracks to repair)
✓ Bleach
✓ Rags
✓ Abrasive scrub pads
✓ Abrasive cleaner
✓ Isopropyl alcohol
✓ 400- to 600-grit wet/dry sandpaper
✓ Vacuum
✓ Tack cloth
✓ Epoxy or tub and tile refinishing product/kit
✓ High-quality fine-bristle varnish brush or short 4-inch nap roller for kitchen/bath use
✓ Sprayer
✓ Lacquer thinner

Phase 1: Preparation

1. PREPARE THE AREA. Open window(s) for ventilation or, if there is no window, place a fan 5 feet outside the doorway to blow fresh air into the room. Cover nearby items with drop cloths. Be sure to wear rubber gloves and protect your clothing.

2. PREPARE THE SURFACE. This step is the key to a smooth, lasting finish. Remove metal drains and remove any loose paint with a wire brush or coarse sandpaper. Repair any chips and cracks with the patching compound or epoxy filler.

3. REMOVE MILDEW. Use a sponge or rag to treat the surface with a solution of equal parts bleach and water to remove any mildew. Repeat if necessary and rinse thoroughly with water.

4. SCRUB THE SURFACE CLEAN. Use an abrasive pad and cleaner to remove all dirt, grease, mold, oil, soap film, and hard-water deposits. Repeat several times to ensure that it is clean.

5. REMOVE ALL CAULK. Wipe those areas with a nonoily solvent such as isopropyl alcohol.

6. SAND THE SURFACE. Use 400- to 600-grit wet/dry sandpaper and water to wet sand the surface. Rinse completely to remove residue. Allow the surface to dry for at least 90 minutes, and make sure that it is dry before applying paint. Vacuum and wipe with a tack cloth immediately before painting to remove all dust and lint.

Phase 2: Application

1. PREPARE THE REFINISHING PRODUCT. If using a refinishing kit with an activator and base, be sure to stir each thoroughly before combining them. Pour the activator into the base can and mix. Mix only the amount necessary for two coats.

2. APPLY THE EPOXY OR REFINISHING PRODUCT WITH ONE OF THE FOLLOWING APPLICATION TECHNIQUES.

► *Application with a brush:* Using a high-quality fine-bristle varnish brush, brush on the product in one direction for a smooth surface. Feather the edges by smoothing with your brush as you paint to avoid a hard line between areas. Apply two coats, waiting at least 1 hour between coats. A third coat may be applied the next day, if necessary.

► *Application with a roller:* Using a high-quality short-nap roller made for kitchen and bath use (a 4-inch wide roller is recommended), apply two coats, waiting at least 1 hour between coats. A third coat may be applied the next day, if necessary.

► *Application by spraying:* Be especially sure to cover all surrounding areas with drop cloths, thick paper, and masking tape. Spray no more than 10 percent of the product (3 ounces per quart of alcohol) with 100 percent isopropyl alcohol (not rubbing alcohol). Refer to the epoxy manufacturer's directions for mixing suggestions. Hold the sprayer 8 to 12 inches from the surface and spray in a steady back-and-forth motion. Some hard-to-reach areas may require closer spraying. See sprayer instructions for proper adjustments. Apply a very-light mist coat, followed immediately by a light second coat. A third coat may be applied 1 to 2 hours after the first two coats, if necessary.

The coating should dry to the touch in less than an hour and to handle or move in 3 hours. It should be fully dry in 18 hours at about 70 degrees Fahrenheit with 50 percent relative humidity. Allow paint to cure for 3 days (72 hours) before exposing to water.

3. CLEAN UP. Clean painting tools and any paint spills with a lacquer thinner. ■

Quick Tip:
Grungy Showerhead Solution

To clean a clogged showerhead, remove it and soak it in white vinegar for about an hour. The vinegar will break up sediment and mineral deposits. But use caution on delicate finishes such as brass or pewter, as the vinegar might damage the finish.

4

paint and decorating ideas

How to Make Your Home Feel as Good as It Looks

Design is not just what it looks like and feels like. Design is how it works.
—STEVE JOBS

Do you ever feel overwhelmed by everything that you have to do to keep your home running properly? Sometimes it helps just to have a little fun. If you spend some time dressing up your house, you'll feel a bit more like keeping it in shape, too. When the idea of a major remodeling overwhelms you, think baby steps and work with what you have first. A quick coat of paint or some beads and baubles can work wonders for your home's self-esteem. You can brainstorm and beautify, adorn and accent, paint and plaster to liven up a drab decor. Let your imagination run wild!

▶ Get Started with "MTM": Money, Time, and Methods

▶ Project: Create a Design Inspiration File

▶ One-Hour Wonder: Quick Transformations

▶ Choosing a New Paint Color

▶ Project: Drywall Repair: The Bullet Patch

- ▶ Project: Let's Get Painting
- ▶ Decorative Painting Ideas: Color Blocking and Sheen Striping
- ▶ Project: Create a Faux Leather Wall
- ▶ Project: Painting Concrete Floors
- ▶ Project: Removing Wallpaper
- ▶ Tips for Measuring for New Wallpaper
- ▶ Project: Hanging Wallpaper
- ▶ Project: A Wallpapered Room Divider

Get Started with "MTM": Money, Time, and Methods

Before starting any decorating project, it is very important to evaluate your needs. Try thinking "MTM"—money, time, and methods. For most of us, money is the number one factor in how we decorate. Be as realistic as possible in evaluating how much you are able to outlay. How much value will you get in return for the time and money you are spending? Projects usually end up costing more and taking longer to complete than we anticipate, so allow for overages in both money and time. If you only have a limited amount to spend, you'll have to be selective in your choices.

Determine how long the project will take and how much time you can devote to it. Are you just trying to spruce things up for an impending event or are you headed for a major remodel? Are the in-laws coming to town in three days? Be practical—some projects cannot be done that quickly! You could throw on slipcovers and get new pillows for a spiffy update, but the average do it yourselfer cannot move a wall in three days!

It's important to determine if you know the methods and have the skills to complete a major project on your own. What are you trying to achieve? Do you want to give a room more pizzazz and make it more inviting? If you are a newcomer to home improvement, skills like painting are easy to master yet have a high rate of payback. Sometimes all a room needs is a new coat of color with clever painting techniques to liven it up. But if you want to move walls, install new cabinets, or raise a ceiling, you need to plan on a longer learning curve, or you may want to bring in professional help. Not only may a pro be able to handle a larger job, but you might actually save both time and money.

It's also important to follow a logical plan when remodeling. Do first things first. For instance, you may want to start a large redecorating job with painting, then carpeting or flooring the following month or year, then window treatments or new furniture, one piece at a time. Having a general plan will help you stay on track and allow you to watch for special sales on the items you may need in the future. If you are not in a hurry, ask store clerks when sales are coming up. If you can wait a month for that new carpet or couch, you might be able to save hundreds of dollars. You might also save money by buying leftovers from contractors. Check out "scratch-and-dent" stores, where manufacturers and retailers sell slightly damaged items, but keep in mind that you may have to pick up the items yourself, which may or may not save you cash in the end. For example, a tile supplier may have just enough tile left over from a big job for you to redo your bathroom, but if you have to rent a truck or take off a day of work to go to pick it up, it may not be worth it to you. But if your time is flexible and you can borrow your brother-in-law's pickup truck, there may be some good deals in your town just waiting for you.

Sometimes, it's better to pay a reasonable price at a store that includes delivery, allows returns, and includes product warranties. Certain types of materials tend to go on sale at specific times of the year. For instance, just as the best time for buying bed linens and towels is at the beginning of the year during the January "white sales," decorating and remodeling products (even items in special colors) tend to go on sale after the end of the summer and during cold weather. Watch for sales after holidays as well. I love to decorate with red, so I enjoy specials on red products after Christmas and Valentine's Day.

When is it a good idea to hire a professional decorator or designer? A reputable pro who knows the best places to purchase items

Quick Tip: The Degree Makes the Difference

What's the difference between a decorator and a designer? I asked my friend Ron Schaer, a top designer in Phoenix, Arizona. Ron's explanation was simple: A designer is a person who has earned a college degree in interior design. Most are members of the American Society of Interior Designers (ASID). A decorator is someone who has a love and talent for decorating, but does not have the degree. Both can be useful as advisers in your home improvement endeavors. In particular, I tend to bring in a designer when my projects involve major changes, such as moving walls or redesigning a space. I use my decorator to advise me about issues of color and style.

can save you money and time in the long run. He or she might also offer suggestions on how to rearrange the furniture and decorating items that you already have in a more pleasing or useful way. Let's face it, sometimes it's better to get an unbiased opinion. Your grandmother's antique lamp may have sentimental value to you, but it just doesn't go well with those chrome and glass tables! Also, some furniture stores and home centers offer design services for free when you buy their products.

PROJECT: CREATE A DESIGN INSPIRATION FILE

Level of Difficulty: T

Whether you are contemplating a new project or are already in the midst of one, organizing your thoughts and materials into one portable file folder, file box, or binder can help simplify the process, reduce stress, and save money. I prefer a big accordion file folder, because it's light enough to carry around with me but sturdy enough to hold a lot of information.

You will need:

✓ Decorating magazines and/or Internet access
✓ A floor plan of the designated room or graph paper
✓ Pencil or pen
✓ Tape measure
✓ Sticky notes and scissors (optional)
✓ File folder, file box, or binder
✓ File folders with labels
✓ Small three-ring binder
✓ Top-loading clear page protectors
✓ Notepad
✓ Digital camera

1. GATHER INSPIRATION. Having trouble thinking of ways to decorate? Just look through magazines, Web sites, and newspapers. Dream, explore, discover. Clip pictures and articles that catch your attention. Go crazy. You may find a picture of a room that could be a good starting point for your project—whether it's the spitting image of how you envision your new space or it just has the "feel" that you want to achieve. If you are working with a spouse, a partner, or a roommate, encourage her or him to do the same, so you can compare your inspiration folders to find common ground.

2. EVALUATE YOUR SPACE. Walk in the room (preferably without furniture or accessories) and start imagining the possibilities. Draw a floor plan if you don't have one. Make sure to note walk areas, doors, and windows measurements for a quick reference when shopping. A floor plan is a valuable tool for determining furniture arrangements and the "flow" of the room. If you plan to use existing furniture, draw and cut out general shapes on sticky notes that you can move around on the floor plan.

3. CREATE A FILE FOR EACH ROOM. Start a file for each room that you are working on. Not only will this help keep everything in one accessible place during the search and decorating process, but it may come in handy a few years from now when you want to retouch the paint, find a warranty, or recommend a product or subcontractor.

A room file should have enough space for everything, including your floor plan, photos of the room, fabric swatches, paint chips, flooring samples, brochures, business cards, receipts, contracts, warranties, etc. All of these items can help convey to a designer or salesclerk exactly what you're looking for. Ask clerks for their business cards or write down their names and numbers so you can call them by name and remind them about the item(s) you want.

Another important item to keep in the files is a running tally of expenses to help you avoid going over budget. Along the way, you may have to make some compromises to complete the room, such as waiting for that special sale to stay within budget or splurging on the more expensive item that will bring it all together for you. One easy way to keep track of costs is to save all of your receipts in one place. My favorite way to do this is to fill a three-ring binder with clear, top-loading page dividers. Slide one page of plain paper into each divider for stability. Then simply insert receipts into each page, dividing them into logical categories such as "Paint," "Tools," "Wallpaper," etc. Later, you can add warranty cards and other pertinent information. When your project is finished, the binder can be stored in the room for easy access at another time.

4. GO SHOPPING. When shopping for items for your decorating project, make sure to take your inspiration file, a tape measure (even a small pocket size one), a digital camera, a notepad, and a pencil. Take measurements of the things that you find to see if their dimensions will work in your room. Take pictures of the items you particularly like and might want to remember in the future. (How many times have you seen a sofa or an accessory that strikes your fancy, only to forget exactly what it looked like at a later date?)

Whenever you think of an idea or something that needs to be done, jot it down on your notepad. It will be a great reference when you're finalizing ideas or getting a to-do list off your mind. As you shop, write down the name of the person who helped you in each store (or staple his or her business card to your notepad) and the model number of the item that you are considering. Models and availability of furniture, carpet, tile, wallpaper, and even paint change from time to time. The very one that you have your heart set on may be gone by the time you're ready to buy, which is why it's best to have a second and third choice just in case. Ask the salesclerk if that item will be going out of stock in the near future or if you'll be able to order more if you run short. As you purchase wallpaper and flooring or other items, buy some extra for later repairs. A general rule of thumb is 10 percent to 20 percent overage just in case, especially when you are buying closeouts. ■

Andrea's Choice: The Decorating Assistant

If you would like to purchase a carry-along decorating file, the Decorating Assistant can hold everything! The carry bag is great for shopping. With the file holder and room files inside, throw it over your shoulder for hands-free shopping. The Decorating Assistant has space for your wallet, cell phone, and car keys, so you don't have to carry a purse. The bonus is that it's attractive so you can shop in style! Visit the Decorating Assistant Web site at www.decoratingassistant.com. You'll find directions on drawing your own floor plan, downloadable budget forms with automatic calculations if you have Microsoft Excel, room-by-room tips, and more!

If your budget is tight but you still want to make some changes around your home, sometimes you can do it without spending a dime. My friend Ron Schaer, a professional interior designer in Phoenix, offers this great tip: Take half of your decorative items, such as pictures, pillows, etc., and pack them away for six months. Then simply rotate items a few times a year and you'll feel like you just went shopping! Just replacing pillows, moving a few pieces of furniture, and removing clutter can make a difference and refresh a room.

Try using different bed linens in the fall and spring. Choose a warmer, heavier fabric during the cooler months and a lightweight one during the warmer months. Also consider the decorative effects of deep, warm colors versus pale, cool colors. Watch for bed linens to go on sale during the off-season.

One great idea is to make covers for your throw pillows with different patterns on each side that coordinate with your decor. Just flip the pillows now and then for a quick change. If your throw pillows are worn out, simply make some slipcovers from old sheets or clothes. My daughter loves to make accents from her old jeans and shirts. It gives her a way to remember a special event or time in her life. If you don't sew or simply don't have the time, cut a square piece of fabric about twice the size of your pillow, wrap the pillow neatly as you would a present, and tie it up with ribbon or decorative rope! ▪

Choosing a New Paint Color

Paint is probably the most cost effective home decorating tool. Paint protects, adds color, and extends the life of your home and furniture. But before you pull out the brush or roller, consider whether your walls or furniture need to be repaired first. If so, turn to the next section for tips on how to repair cracks and holes. If the wall is in good shape, then it's time to choose a color and a finish. Visit your local hardware store to look at paint chips and familiarize yourself with different types of paint. There are so many possibilities of color and texture! Some local stores offer free or low-cost classes on painting techniques. For your first visit, try to go when the store is not crowded (on a weekday) and a clerk can give you his or her undivided attention.

Choosing a color is a tough decision. Do not make it haphazardly. Some decorators say to start with a fabric, a piece of furniture that you like, artwork that you want to hang on the wall, or some other decorative item and coordinate your color scheme to it. My friend Carolyn Richardson, a professional color consultant and interior designer, says that the most important thing you can do when choosing a new color for a room is to think about exactly how you want to feel when you are in the room. Do you want this room to be energized, calm, neutral, warm, or cool? How do certain colors make you feel? Does red excite or irritate you? Does blue calm or depress you? Colors provoke emotional responses that vary among individuals as well as cultures. Colors and color combinations also go in and out of fashion. However, Carolyn offers some basic color guidelines, both positive and negative connotations that generally apply.

▶ Yellow is sunny, cheerful, radiant, and happy. Pale, soft yellows are good for kitchens. But yellow is also associated with caution and can be glaring and intense.

▶ Orange, a mixture of yellow and red, can be warm, invigorating, friendly, fun, and lively, but it can also be overpowering, flamboyant, conspicuous, and offensive.

▶ Red is exciting and stimulating, indicates warmth, and can stimulate the appetite, making it great for kitchens and dining rooms. Red is also the first color an infant will respond to. On the negative side, red can be aggressive and make a room feel too warm.

▶ Purple strikes a balance between stimulating red and calming blue. It is commonly associated with royalty, spirituality, and creativity. On the downside, purple can be overpowering and heavy.

▶ Blue, the favorite color of the Western world, represents sky, water, and tranquility. Blue has actually been known to lower blood pressure, but it can also be depressing and cold. Since many of us love blue, it can also be overused, so try to balance it with other colors.

Quick Tip:
Color Chips

Most paint companies offer their colors on paint strips or chips that showcase a few color choices together, like a little family. These groupings are carefully selected to complement each other and to harmonize well in a room. So when you are choosing colors, it can be a good idea to stay within the same color card. Ask your paint professional to help you if you are unsure if your choices will blend with each other.

▶ Green is the calming color of nature, a balance of uplifting yellow and calming blue. It represents harmony, balance, hope, sincerity, stability, growth, and spring. On a negative note, green can be associated with jealousy, detachment, and disappointment.

▶ Brown is associated with comfort, warmth, protection, dependability, and the earth. However, brown can be dull or boring, so spice it up with some brighter accents.

▶ Black is elegant, strong, creative, powerful, and sexy. Too much black can be difficult to live with, as it can also connote superiority, evil, sorrow, and emptiness.

▶ White symbolizes purity, brilliance, truthfulness, cleanliness, and simplicity. It can be hygienic and uncluttered, but also cold, stark, and clinical. White can be hard to keep clean for those of us with children or pets.

Once you have selected your color, you'll need a sample packet or a quart. It is best to paint your sample (at least two coats) on a piece of mat board that you can place in different positions around the room. Light has the most effect on your color choice. Since sunlight is constantly changing, your paint color will also change throughout the day. What appears as one color in the morning light will transform a little in the afternoon. Take several days to study and carefully consider your paint choice. If you have doubts, try another color. You may want a warmer or cooler version. Remember that colors tend to darken as they dry, so go with a lighter hue if you are not sure of the intensity.

In addition to color, you need to choose the proper type of paint for the job. Latex (water-based) is the most common choice because it's easy to clean up. For a surface that will be exposed to water often, oil-based is best. Paints come in a variety of sheen or gloss levels, ranging from "high gloss" (the shiniest) to "flat" (virtually no shine). Those with higher gloss reflect more light, so they can make a room look brighter and may be easier to wash, but they also are harder to apply and may accentuate imperfections or previous repairs. Be sure that you're completely satisfied with your choice before you begin to paint.

Level of difficulty: T T T T

Before you begin painting, it's important to repair cracks and holes in your drywall. Sometimes, just a bit of spackling compound or a smear of caulk is enough to do the trick. But occasionally, a larger repair is necessary.

Here's something that frequently happens in remodeling projects. The electrician installs a light fixture or receptacle in the wrong location. It's easy enough to get him to move it, but asking an electrician to repair drywall is like asking a demolition laborer to cut dovetail joints—ain't gonna happen.

A great patch technique is called the bullet patch, so-called because you can do it pretty darn fast. It is the kind of site-born invention that clever carpenters, drywallers, and painters probably devised individually until the word spread and it became part of the tradesman's bag of tricks. Mark Clement, a remodeler and the author of *The Carpenter's Notebook,* recommends it highly. The bullet patch is a smart and easy solution because it minimizes the size of a patch and doesn't require cutting drywall back to existing studs for fastening purposes. It works great for holes around the size of a two-gang light switch, but can be used for bigger or smaller repairs, too.

You will need:

- ✓ Drywall saw
- ✓ Blue painter's tape or masking tape
- ✓ Tape measure
- ✓ Drywall pieces (ask at your hardware store for a small piece)
- ✓ 6-inch utility knife
- ✓ 10-inch utility knife (optional)
- ✓ Skim coat ("mud compound")
- ✓ Screwdriver

1. MAKE A CLEAN CUT. The first step in the bullet patch process is to clean out and square the hole. This is pretty much done for you in the case shown here, where the repair is being made because of an errantly

Quick Tip:
Drywall Repair 101

It is much easier to use a piece of drywall that is not from the factory edge of a piece of wallboard because the paper folds over at that location and the ends are usually banged-up, cracked, or have labels you have to remove. For better results, use a piece cut from somewhere inside the factory edge of the wallboard. Ask the folks at your local hardware store if they have small pieces that you can use for repairs.

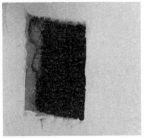

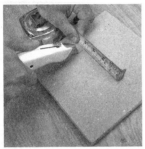

placed switch box. But if the hole is made by a fist, a hammer, or some other blunt force, then use a drywall saw both to remove broken or damaged drywall (it will also work on plaster and lath) to make it square or rectangular in shape for ease of fitting a new piece. Next, if there are any obstructions or finishes near the patch location (such as a light switch cover), remove what you can. If the finish can't be removed (such as wallpaper or molding), protect it as necessary with blue painter's tape.

2. MEASURE AND CUT THE NEW PIECE OF DRYWALL ("THE BLANK"). Once the hole is squared out, measure it. Now, cut a piece out of the new drywall that is 2 inches bigger in width and height than the hole. For example: if the hole turns out to be 4 by 4 inches, cut a new piece of drywall 6 by 6 inches.

3. MAKE THE PLUG. Now, flip the blank over so that the front is facedown and the back (the brown side) is faceup. Use a tape measure to locate the center of the blank. Mark it. Keep the blank lying facedown. From the center point of the blank, measure the plug. This plug will help to hold the new bullet patch in place, so it should fit into the hole in your wall. Make the plug about ½-inch smaller in width and height than the hole. For example, if the hole is 4 by 4 inches, make the plug 3½ by 3½ inches. Measure the size that you will need and mark the back of the drywall.

Using a utility knife, cut through the back of the drywall from one edge of the blank to the other, but do not cut through the front paper of the drywall. You should now have a grid that looks like a tic-tac-toe game on the back of your blank.

Now, grasp the drywall firmly in both hands and break it forward along one line. Then—and this is the cool part of this process—carefully peel the gypsum (the white chalky material) away from the paper.

Discard the gypsum and leave the paper flange. Do this all the way around the piece until you have exposed the center plug.

4. APPLY THE MUD COMPOUND. With any finished surfaces, masked as necessary with blue painter's tape from step 1, apply a thin coat of mud (skim coat) to the wall before installing the bullet patch. Don't wipe it down tight. Allow a little extra mud to remain on the surface. You need enough mud on there so you can embed the back of the paper flanges into it.

5. ATTACH THE PATCH TO THE WALL. Put the patch on the wall and lightly press the paper into the wet mud compound with your fingertips (don't press on the plug) to hold it in place.

Now, put a little compound on the edge of your knife (a 6-inch knife works well for this job) to "lubricate" it and enable it to ride across the paper. Pass the knife across the patch, pressing hard enough on it to squeeze the mud out from behind the paper—but be careful not to press too hard or you risk rippling the paper. A couple of passes will ensure a tight bond. Now, with the paper adhered from the back, wipe a light coat of the mud on the front of the paper. Smooth down all rough spots, but don't expect perfection. The key here is to create a thin light coat that will bond that paper to the wallboard.

6. APPLY A SECOND COAT OF THE MUD COMPOUND. Once the first coat has dried, after an hour or so, you can apply a second coat. Some muds dry faster than others, so you may be able to proceed in less time. You may want to use a 10-inch knife on the second coat for an easier wide application. First, use the knife without any mud compound on it to lightly scrape down the area, knocking off any rough, raised spots. Then, apply the second thin coat of mud compound. Again, the goal is not perfection, but to fill in more imperfections.

7. APPLY A THIRD COAT. These repairs usually take three coats. After the second coat has dried, smooth the surface lightly with a 100-grit sanding block. Add a third thin coat of compound, filling in any final imperfections and feathering out the edges.

8. SAND THE SURFACE. Sand as necessary to flatten and feather the edges of the patch. It's easier to add a fourth coat than to sand off three thick ones. Less is more here. Once sanded, you're ready to prime and paint.

Thanks to my buddy, Mark Clement, for teaching me this technique. For more information on drywall patching and other projects, visit Mark Clement's Web site, www.thecarpentersnotebook.com. ■

Now that you've picked your color, it's time to get painting, but first you need to gather your painting tools. As with any DIY project, the key to success is preparation. Professional painters offer these "must-haves":

▶ *All-purpose caulk:* Reinforce joints to prevent cracking by using a water-based, paintable, mildew-resistant, all-purpose caulk.

▶ *Five-in-one tool:* This is a multipurpose tool that allows you to open paint cans, clean rollers, scrape peeling paint, remove old caulk, open cracks, and apply putty. I have also seen seven-in-one and even twelve-in-one tools. They are all very handy.

▶ *Patching products:* To repair holes, chipped paint, or other wall defects, use a paintable, fast-drying, shrink-free patching compound—also called mud or spackle.

▶ *Sandpaper or sanding blocks:* Sanding is important to create a smooth surface to which paint can adhere. A durable aluminum oxide, A-weight paper with 100- to 150-grit is suitable for most general-purpose sanding applications. Finer grits will be needed for varnished wood projects.

▶ *Blue painter's tape or masking tape:* To keep paint only on the surfaces you want to paint, use blue painter's tape or masking tape to cover woodwork or hardware. The blue tape does not leave a residue like old-style masking tape can. Look for low-tack adhesives for use on delicate surfaces such as wallpaper and drywall for easy removal without damaging the surface.

▶ *Drop cloths:* Protect your floors from grit, sawdust, caulk, and paint spills. Plastic drop cloths are inexpensive enough that you can throw them away when you're done and not feel too guilty about it. Cloth drops are more expensive, but they also work the best, especially over carpets. There are also drop cloths that feature a pretaped edge, making it easier to adhere them around baseboards and other flat surfaces.

▶ *Paintbrushes and rollers:* A quality brush makes it easier to apply paint evenly and accurately. I recommend selecting a 1- to 2-inch,

---

T Andrea's Choice:
Erase That Hole!

For filling nail holes and other small repairs on textured walls, try Erase-A-Hole. It's really a thick spackle that's packed into a stick form, like a deodorant dispenser. It's easy to use by simply smearing it into the hole—and kinda' fun. You just smooth it off with a damp finger and you're done. It's available at most hardware stores and home centers.

Quick Tip:
Taping Techniques

Applying masking tape before painting a room seems simple enough. But anyone who has painted before knows that working with masking tape can be tricky. Here are a few tips.

▶ Select blue or green painter's tape rather than standard masking tape. It allows you more time to finish the project without leaving a sticky residue.

▶ Press the tape firmly to the surface, using your fingernail to adhere it to

→

high-quality, nylon/polyester angled brush because it can be used with all coatings, holds paint well, and provides better brush control where detail is necessary. I also keep a few disposable foam or poly brushes on hand for quick touch-ups. Choose rollers based on the type of paint you are applying and the desired texture. The roller label should indicate what it's meant for. The shorter the nap, the less stipple will appear in the finished paint job.

▶ *Rags or disposable cloths:* There will be spills, drips, and "oops, didn't mean to paint there" moments when you'll want to wipe up the paint immediately. Baby wipes work great for small accidents.

▶ *Primer (or sealer):* This is a specially formulated paint designed for use on bare metal, wood, and other surfaces. Using a primer can smooth uneven surfaces and make the finish coat beautiful and long lasting. Primers are often recommended to ensure the true paint color is achieved; increase paint adhesion; get better paint coverage and penetration, particularly on wood surfaces; increase corrosion resistance on metal surfaces; hide stains and surface imperfections; seal porous surfaces; and make the finish coat smooth and uniform. Consider having your primer tinted to match your finish coat. Most paint suppliers can do this for you. (Resource: Krylon)

▶ *Good-quality paint:* It pays to spend a little more for quality paint. The Rohm and Haas Paint Quality Institute recommends buying top-quality paints that glide on easier, provide superior adhesion and coverage, offer better stain resistance, and resist yellowing for a professional, longer-lasting finish.

Now it's time to paint. Get ready to divide and conquer. Take it one step at a time for great results.

1. CLEAR THE ROOM. Move your furniture out of the room if possible. If you can't move it, make sure it is completely covered.

2. PREP THE ROOM. Remove all pictures, switch plates, nails, etc. and do any necessary patching. Caulk all corners and cracks. Cover or tape off any areas you don't want painted: window frames, baseboards, etc. Spread drop cloths and overlap them. You may want to tape down the edges to prevent accidental tripping.

edges and corners. Watch out for folds and bubbles.

▶ Paint as though the tape is not there. Even the best masking job cannot stop every dribble of paint. So do your best not to get any paint on the tape and you will be ensured of a clean edge.

Now comes the tricky part— removing the tape. It's tricky because sometimes the paint grabs the edge of the tape and peels off right along with it. My friends the Painter Chicks, a professional outfit in Dallas, recommend cutting the joint between the tape and the painted surface with a utility knife before peeling. I have had some success with this technique also. In any case, wait until the paint is dry to remove the tape, but not more than 24 hours, if you can help it. Then you may still need to touch up any "holidays," or areas where the paint has bled through the tape.

3. PROTECT YOUR CLOTHES. Wear old clothes or inexpensive painting coveralls, gloves, and a kerchief or hat for your hair. Shoe protectors that easily slip on and off are also a good idea. Be sure to remove the shoe protectors when you leave the painting area so that you don't track paint throughout the house.

4. WORK IN SECTIONS. If priming is needed, now's the time to do it. If not, just use your normal paint as a primer. Once everything is primed, apply either one or two coats, depending on the paint manufacturer's recommendations. You may also find that some colors simply require two coats, especially darker tints.

Many professionals paint the trim first and then the walls, but this is a common area for debate. You can do whatever makes you comfortable. I prefer to paint my walls first and then trim them in afterward. In any case, when working on the walls, paint all the corners and the areas around windows and doors with a brush, then come back with a roller to fill in the large areas.

When painting, work in 3-foot squares, roughly the area of one paint-loaded roller. Make the first roller stroke away from you. On walls, roll an M pattern, and on ceilings, roll a W pattern, distributing the thickest part of the paint evenly over the 3-foot square. Roll with smooth back-and-forth strokes in the M or W pattern and fill in the unpainted areas. To avoid roller marks, don't lift the roller off the surface.

5. FINISH UP. Remove all tape as soon as you are done painting, using caution not to damage the painted edge. Allow the room to dry naturally, without drafts, which can cause dust to enter the room. ■

Decorative Painting Ideas: Color Blocking and Sheen Striping

Out of ideas, budget, or both? Decorative painting goes high style with these two exciting interior painting techniques: color blocking and sheen striping. And all you need are a few gallons of paint. Here's what you need to know about these cutting-edge techniques, courtesy of my friends at the Rohm and Haas Paint Quality Institute. Another great resource for fun painting techniques is www.prismaticpainting.com.

Color Blocking

Color blocking involves painting several colors (usually at least three) in various-sized "blocks" on the wall. Because of its visual interest, this technique is usually done on one wall in a room, and often takes the place of artwork—behind a sofa, for example.

The key is to draw the blocks in different dimensions, varied sizes of squares and rectangles, and map them out in a geometric, visually balanced arrangement on the wall. Begin by sketching the blocks on paper, transferring them to the wall, outlining them lightly in pencil, and then filling them in with paint. Make several copies of the final design on paper for practice. Use these to play with the arrangement of colors in the design, then pick your favorite and start painting.

Choosing colors for this technique can be fun, but there are some things to keep in mind to help achieve the look you're after.

▶ Colors from the same color card, but in varying intensities, will give your room a sophisticated, monochromatic appeal. If you're looking for subtlety, choose colors that are next to each other on the card.

▶ Two or three harmonious colors and a third accent hue of either black or white creates a dramatic look.

▶ For a fun, playful look, choose complementary colors (those that are opposite each other on the color wheel), such as yellow and violet.

▶ It is helpful to use colors of the same value, or intensity, by choosing ones that are in the same position on several color cards: the second up from the bottom, for example. This helps achieve a feeling of balance.

▶ If you decide to use colors of varying intensities, you may want to experiment with several practice designs. Using more of the brighter hue will give you a bold look, while using more of the lighter one will be more soothing. Remember that the practice design is much smaller than the final product, and any color you use will intensify once it's on a wall.

Sheen Striping

Sheen striping is a technique that involves painting vertical stripes of the same color but of differing sheens, for a subtle, sophisticated look. It is often used in dining rooms, above the chair rail, or in low-ceiling areas that could use some visual "height."

First, choose the sheen levels you want to work with. In ascending levels of gloss, the sheen levels are: flat, eggshell, satin, semigloss, and gloss (or high gloss). For this technique, you might choose an eggshell and a semigloss product, which will create visual interest without being overwhelming. The sheen difference should be somewhat subtle, so a flat and a high gloss may not be the best combination.

Then, choose a color according to your personal preference and the effect you want to create in the room. (See page 88 for more information on color.) In any case, choose a durable, top-quality, interior latex paint. These paints go on smoothly and evenly, cover well, resist stains and damage from cleaning, and hold their color for many years.

PROJECT: **CREATE A FAUX LEATHER WALL**

Level of difficulty: T T T

Think you can't faux finish? My friend Cheri Van Bynen, host of the DIY Network's *Tool School,* says anyone can learn this easy technique for faux leather finishing. This is a great project for a den or an office. First of all, choose colors for your project that have the look of real leather. Look in books and magazines, paint some samples, even look at real leather to get ideas. Dark over light green is a fun combo that can look like the cover of an old book. Deep brown or black over red or tan works well, too. Lighter colors can create a rawhide effect. Then have fun—and remember, it's only paint!

You will need:

- ✓ Blue painter's tape
- ✓ Drop cloths
- ✓ Spackle
- ✓ Primer
- ✓ Semigloss base coat (in a light color of your choice)
- ✓ Gloss topcoat (in a darker color of your choice)
- ✓ Paint roller and ½-inch nap cover
- ✓ Paintbrushes
- ✓ Floetrol (or any other thinner that does not change the pigment-to-binder ratio)
- ✓ Plastic drop cloths

1. **PREP AND PRIME.** Fill in any holes and scratches with spackle. Let dry, then sand the spackled spots and any other rough areas (like paint globs from previous paint jobs). Prime your wall if necessary to create a flawless finish. Primer is especially recommended when you need to seal in a former painted area or finish, such as when covering a dark paint color or previous faux effect.

2. **PROTECT SURROUNDING SURFACES.** Trim the ceiling with blue painters tape. Protect the floor and furniture with drop cloths.

3. **APPLY THE FIRST COAT.** Using a good roller cover and brush, apply a light base coat of semigloss. Let dry overnight.

4. PREPARE THE SECOND COAT. Mix approximately one part Floetrol or other thinner with two parts topcoat (no need to be exact as long as you mix a little bit more than you'll need). This will make the paint flow easier. Save the extra paint mixture in a sealed jar for future touch-ups.

5. APPLY THE TOPCOAT AND GO WILD WITH THE PLASTIC DROP CLOTHS! Before rolling on this topcoat, make sure you have a friend handy, especially if you're painting a big wall. Keep your plastic drop cloths nearby. Roll on a few feet of the top coat, getting close to the edges, then start draping the plastic all over the wall. Mush it around with your hands to make wrinkles. Roll a few more feet and keep spreading the plastic. Continue until the whole wall is done, then come back and peel all the plastic off. It may be messy, but it's fun—and the result looks so cool! If you don't achieve the look that you want on the first try, just apply the plastic and peel it off again. It may take some practice to perfect your technique.

6. TOUCH UP. When you're all done, go back with a small brush and lightly touch up the edges that the roller couldn't reach. If you don't like the glossy finish of the topcoat, you can always go over it with a matte clear when it's dry. This will also protect the finish. Enjoy your new faux leather wall! ■

PROJECT: PAINTING CONCRETE FLOORS

Level of difficulty: T T T T T

Looking for a durable and fun treatment for concrete floors? Why not paint them? It's inexpensive and will hold up well to kids, pets, and high traffic.

You will need:
- ✓ Filler for holes in concrete
- ✓ Trisodium phosphate (TSP) or other cleaning product
- ✓ Adhesive remover (if necessary)
- ✓ Heavy rubber gloves
- ✓ Heavy rubber boots
- ✓ Goggles
- ✓ Old rags and mop
- ✓ Broom and dustpan
- ✓ Bucket for mixing the acid solution
- ✓ Muriatic acid
- ✓ Stiff fiber bristle brush
- ✓ Vacuum cleaner
- ✓ Latex floor paint or oil-based floor coating

1. CLEAN THE AREA. Remove all old carpeting and floor tile. Use an appropriate adhesive remover or TSP, if necessary. Fill any gaps or holes with a filler that is made for concrete. Remove all loose paint, cement particles, or any other foreign matter and eliminate any sources of moisture before painting.

2. BEGIN ACID ETCHING. Allow new concrete floors to cure for 90 to 180 days before painting. Once they have been cured, raw concrete floors should be acid etched before painting. Previously painted concrete floors do not need to be acid etched where paint is sound, but etching should be done where bare spots occur or are revealed by scraping loose or peeling paint. Just remember to wear full protective gear—rubber gloves, boots, and goggles—whenever working with muriatic acid. Carefully prepare a solution of 1 part full-strength muriatic acid with 3 parts water.

Use 1 gallon (3.785 liters) of this solution per 100 square feet (9.3 square meters) of floor and scrub with a stiff fiber bristle brush while apply-

Always add the acid to the water to prevent splashing the hot acid. Never pour water into acid.

Caution: Don't Get Burned

Muriatic acid is an aqueous solution of approximately 35 percent hydrochloric acid. It is capable of producing severe chemical burns as a result of contact with skin or eyes. Muriatic acid is also capable of producing marked irritation of the nose and throat resulting from the inhalation of vapors. In some cases, contact with the eye will cause blindness. All persons handling this material should be aware of this danger and avoid these hazards. Any eye contact with muriatic acid solution should be followed immediately by irrigating the eyes with plenty of water. Areas of the body contaminated with etching materials should be washed immediately with plenty of water. Burns should be treated according to medical advice. Always wear rubber boots, rubber gloves, and work goggles when using muriatic acid. Always follow all label instructions.

ing. Allow the solution to remain on the floor until it stops bubbling. Flush the solution off thoroughly with clean water. If you can use a garden hose and allow the water to drain off, that is preferred. If not, mop up the acidic water carefully and rerinse the area several times. If the total surface is not dry within a few hours, flush it with water again. You may have some residual acid remaining. The surface must dry evenly. If puddles develop, the solution will become more concentrated and this will affect the performance of the coating applied over it.

After the surface has dried, use a vacuum cleaner to remove the powder that is created by etching. Failure to remove this powder will result in poor adhesion. Painting can begin when the surface is chemically neutral and dry. When a proper etch has been attained, the concrete will have a surface texture like sandpaper.

3. APPLY THE MASONRY PAINT. It's important to choose the correct paint for your project. If your floor already has a plastic moisture barrier under it, you can use either an oil or latex product. If not, you must use a latex paint, which allows moisture to pass through once it's dry. Oil base coatings will hold in the moisture and eventually peel off.

Paint the edges of the room first with a good-quality bristle brush or disposable poly brushes. Then complete the main floor with a short-nap roller, following the manufacturer's recommendations. Allow the room to dry completely before adding any embellishments.

4. GET CREATIVE. Now it is time to have some fun! For a fun look in children's rooms, let them step in a contrasting color of paint and walk around the floor barefoot, leaving footprints everywhere. They will love that they get to help decorate their room, and walking in paint is one of those fun things we rarely get to do without getting in trouble. Stencils work well, too, and are easy to use. If you love bowling, paint bowling lanes on the floor; all you'll need to add are the bowling pins and a bowling ball. If bowling is not your game, try your hand at shuffleboard. Can't play miniature golf because it's raining? You'll be the envy of the neighborhood with your own indoor golf course. Paint the team logo of your favorite sports team on the floor, the walls, anywhere you like. Or try painting the whole baseball, basketball, or even football field on the floor.
[Resource: www.doityourself.com] ■

PROJECT: REMOVING WALLPAPER

Level of difficulty: ↑ ↑ ↑

In every room, the time comes when your wallpaper has seen better days. It's damaged, or you're just ready for a change. But before you can redecorate the walls, the old wallpaper needs to come down. The following tips, provided by my friends at DoItYourself.com, should help. It's a good weekend project—one that will probably take most of the day for an average-sized room.

You'll need:

- ✓ Old towels and drop cloths
- ✓ Blue painter's tape
- ✓ Wallpaper scorer
- ✓ Wallpaper removal agent or home steam stripper
- ✓ Rubber or latex gloves
- ✓ Wide brush or sprayer
- ✓ Putty knife and/or scraper

1. PREP THE ROOM. Remove everything from the walls and as many items and furniture from the room as possible. Cover the baseboards and floors with drop cloths and painter's tape to avoid getting wet scraps on the floor.

2. USE A SCORING TOOL. Use a scoring tool to create holes in the surface of the old wallpaper to allow water to penetrate it and loosen the glue.

3. SOAK THE WALLPAPER WITH A WALLPAPER REMOVER SOLUTION OR A STEAM STRIPPER. A chemical wallpaper remover attacks the glue behind old wallpaper and helps to make it easier to scrape off. For many years, this has been the favorite method of most DIYers, because it is quick and requires less effort than steam. Mix it with water according to the manufacturer's directions. Wearing rubber gloves, apply the solution to the wall in sections, using a brush or a sprayer. Work from top to bottom. Let it soak in for about 10 minutes. Using the putty knife, carefully pry an edge/seam of the wallpaper and see if you can pull it away. If it is still resisting, soak the section again and try pulling it away with the scraper.

A steam stripper can require a bit more elbow grease, but it does not leave a chemical residue on your walls. Follow the specific manufacturer's instructions, but, generally, you need only fill it with water. No brushes, chemicals, or sprayers are necessary. It takes approximately 20 minutes to warm up the tank of water each time it is refilled. An average-sized room will require about two tanks. (While waiting for it to heat, it is a good time to score the wallpaper.) Once ready, hold the steam plate over a section of wallpaper for about 15 seconds. When the wallpaper is damp, scrape it off with one hand while soaking the next section of wallpaper with the steam plate.

4. REMOVE ALL OF THE WALLPAPER. Sometimes there are multiple layers of wallpaper or stubborn patches where the paper won't come away easily. Using the wallpaper remover or the steamstripper, keep soaking and scraping until you've removed all bits of paper.

5. WASH THE WALLS. Once your walls are completely bare, wash them completely with warm water. Be sure to remove all traces of glue residue, as this can cause new paint to crack and peel and leave bumps beneath new wallpaper. ■

Tips for Measuring for New Wallpaper

If you're going to repaper, you need to determine how much wallpaper you'll need for your project. Many stores special-order paper for each job, so make sure you can order more if you need it and that you can return any unused rolls. Ask how long the store will allow returns from the original purchase date. My friends at the National Retail Hardware Association have shared some tips to make measuring easier.

To determine the amount of paper you'll need, first, measure the height of the wall from the top of the baseboard to the ceiling or molding. Next, measure the length of each wall. Add the lengths of the walls together. Find the total number of square feet by multiplying the wall height by the length.

American-manufactured single rolls of wallpaper usually have about 36 square feet. Double rolls have about 72 square feet. Triple rolls have about 108 square feet. However, American rolls are being phased out and may be hard to find. Metric or Euro rolls have about 29 square feet per roll. Double rolls have about 58 square feet.

Use the metric single roll chart. If your pattern does not repeat or if it repeats every 0 to 6 inches, each roll yields approximately 25 square feet. If your pattern repeats every 7 to 12 inches, each roll yields approximately 22 square feet; and so on. Divide the total number of square feet to be covered by the number that is appropriate for your pattern. This is the total number of single rolls of paper you will need for your wallpaper job.

Wallpaper is usually packaged in single or double rolls. To find the number of double rolls you need, divide the number of single rolls by two. To find the number of triple rolls you need, divide by three.

For example, suppose the ceiling is 8 feet high and the room is 10 feet by 12 feet with two 3-foot by 7-foot doors and two 3-foot by 4-foot windows. This means the total wall length is 10 feet + 10 feet + 12 feet + 12 feet, or 44 feet. Find the total number of square feet: 44 feet × 8 feet, or 352 square feet. Find the number of square feet per door: 3 feet × 7 feet, or 21 square feet. Remember, there are two doors and two windows. Find the total number of square feet not to be covered: 12 feet + 12 feet + 21 feet + 21 feet, or 66 square feet. Then find the total number of square feet to be covered: 352 − 66, or 286 square feet. Phew! Aren't you glad you paid attention in math class?

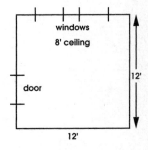

PROJECT: **HANGING WALLPAPER**

Level of difficulty: T T T

Now that the old wallpaper has been removed, it's time to hang the new. Be sure to follow the manufacturer's directions for preparing your walls before getting started. Thanks again to my friends at DoItYourself.com for help with instructions for this project.

You'll need:

✓ Wallpaper sizing
✓ Prepasted wallpaper (If your paper requires paste, follow the manufacturer's directions for applying it to the paper)
✓ Flat work surface (overlaid with cardboard or plywood, if necessary, to protect it from cuts)
✓ Straightedge and utility knife
✓ Scissors
✓ Soaking tray
✓ Tape measure and yardstick
✓ Broad knife or plastic smoother
✓ Smoothing brush
✓ Large sponges or lint-free rags
✓ An old table or other waterproof work surface
✓ Pencil
✓ Drop cloths
✓ 4-foot level or laser lever or wallpaper level (a straightedge with a level bubble)
✓ Ladder
✓ Bucket
✓ Extra lighting, if necessary
✓ Blue painter's tape (3 foot wide is recommended)
✓ Soft-bristle smoothing brush
✓ Seam roller
✓ Vinyl-over-vinyl adhesive for corners

1. PREPARE THE AREA. If you haven't already done so, remove as many items and furniture from the room as possible. Cover the floors with drop cloths to avoid getting wet scraps and adhesive on the floor.

2. APPLY SIZING TO THE WALLS. Apply a coat of wallpaper sizing to the wall, if necessary. Sizing makes the wallpaper hanging easier if there is flat-finish paint on the walls you are papering. It helps you slide the paper into place when hanging it. The sizing gives your walls a light gloss, which allows paper to slide into place. Apply the sizing to your walls using a paint roller, just like you would apply paint. It is inexpensive and makes a better surface to hang wallpaper on. If your walls have just been primed, you can skip applying sizing to the walls. If you are not sure whether your walls need sizing, it is best to do it because it is quick and makes hanging wall-paper easier.

3. CUT THE WALLPAPER. If you have patterned wallpaper, make sure the pattern will break at the ceiling line wherever you believe is most attractive. Hold each piece up against the wall before you cut it and mark where it will meet the ceiling and baseboard lines.

Place the wallpaper on a broad, flat surface. Using a straightedge and a utility knife or scissors, cut the paper 2 inches outside the ceiling and baseboard lines so that there will be a 2-inch overlap along the ceiling and the floor. This excess will later be trimmed away. Check each piece as you cut it. Start with just a few strips to make sure that you are not making errors. It's hard to fix once it's all cut up. If you make an error, save the cut pieces. You may be able to use them later for patching or small areas. Change the blade in your utility knife often, as it becomes dull from paste and debris. This will help you to make clean cuts and avoid ripping the paper.

4. SOAK THE WALLPAPER. Roll up the paper with the pattern side in and the adhesive side out, then place it in a soaking tray filled with lukewarm water, which should be next to the wall directly below the area to be hung.

Unlike the older types of wallpaper that needed paste spread on the back, most wallpaper today is prepasted with adhesive already applied. You simply soak the wallpaper in water and hang it. However, be sure to follow the manufacturer's instructions closely, because there is a set period of time that you need to let the paper sit in the soaking tray.

5. BOOK THE WALLPAPER. After the paper is removed from the tray, there is also set period during which it must be allowed to dry before being applied to the wall. Upon removing the wallpaper from the tray, fold it, pasted side to pasted side, loosely and without creasing the folds, so that it comes out flat. This is called "booking." Place it on a water-proof surface for a period of "curing" (I use an old card table for this pur-pose). Allow it to cure according to the paper manufacturer's directions before applying. Be sure that no dust or debris settles on the paper while it is curing.

6. MARK A LEVEL LINE. Starting at an inconspicuous corner, measure along the long edge of the wallpaper to a point that is a distance of 1 inch less than the width of the wallpaper roll from the corner. Make a mark at this point. For example, if your wallpaper rolls are 20 inches wide, make a mark 19 inches from the corner.

At this mark, you will need to make an exactly plumb (vertical) line, which requires the use of a level, because there is a good chance that the corner is not plumb. A common and drastic mistake in hanging wallpaper is to hang it out of plumb by following a wall that is not vertical and true plumb.

Use a 4-foot level, a laser lever, or a wallpaper level (a straightedge with a level bubble) to mark this line on the wall. Also, a chalk line can be used. Be sure that the level bubble is reading true level, and then mark the line from the ceiling to the floor.

7. HANG THE FIRST SHEET. You are now ready to hang your first piece. Keep a damp rag or sponge handy to mop up any dripping glue. Apply the paper so that one edge is exactly vertical and aligned with your plumb mark. Leave the bottom fold folded and begin work only with the upper part of the sheet. Be sure the mark for the ceiling is aligned so that there is a clean pattern break along the ceiling line. If you are working at an inside corner, which is often the case, wrap the 1-inch overlap into the corner (see page 110 for more tips on wallpapering inside corners).

Use a wallpaper brush to work out any bubbles, stroking from the middle of the sheet of wallpaper toward the edges to push the air out. Start at the top and work your way down the paper. Keep working with the brush until all the bubbles are out and the paper is perfectly smooth on the wall. Be sure the paper stays aligned with your plumb mark as you work with the brush. Be sure there is no debris on the wall that you now see poking through. When necessary, gently lift the bottom edge of the strip to free the sheet of any wrinkles. After the upper part is smooth, release the bottom fold and position it carefully against the wall, using the palms of your hands. Then use the smoothing brush, as you did above. Leave the wallpaper untrimmed to allow it to "set" for a few minutes; you will trim it after the next sheet is hung.

8. HANG THE SECOND SHEET. Before cutting the second sheet, be sure to mark it so that the pattern will match at the seam line alongside the first sheet. This second sheet should butt snugly against the first; do not overlap the seams. Apply this sheet as you did the first and maneuver it against the edge of the first with your hands.

After the second sheet is in place, go back and trim the first. Use your straightedge or broad knife to assure a good trim job, changing the razor blade for each strip of wallpaper applied. Trim the second piece after the third piece is hung, and so on. Smooth out all of the remaining small bubbles and wipe up excess paste.

After the first two sheets are in place, go over them with a large damp sponge or lint-free rags or towels to smooth out all the small bubbles. Be sure to wipe up any excess paste at the seams and ends with the sponge before they dry.

9. HANG THE REMAINING SHEETS, FOLLOWING ALL THE SAME STEPS.

10. USE A SEAM ROLLER. (Note: omit this step if you have raised or flocked wallpaper.)

After 20 to 30 minutes, use a seam roller on all seams to be sure they are well secured. Press the roller lightly to avoid a producing a glossy area on the paper. Wipe up any excess paste with the damp sponge and dry carefully with a soft towel.

Tips for Applying Wallpaper to Corners

Applying wallpaper properly to corners can be demanding. In and of themselves, corners are not that difficult. The problem is that they are seldom true plumb or vertical. You need to be able to hang your wallpaper plumb, even if the corners are not, which can take some time and care. Go slowly here, since this is where your new skills will be challenged the most.

For inside corners:

▶ At both the top and bottom of the wall, measure the distances from the sheet of wallpaper next to the corner to the actual corner itself. Add 1 inch to the greater of the two measurements and cut a sheet lengthwise to this width measurement. However, if this measurement is within 6 inches of the width of your full sheet, use a full sheet. If there is a sheet next to the corner, its edge can be used as a plumb line—if you have managed to hang it plumb!

▶ If there is no sheet at the corner, simply measure out from the corner a distance equal to the dimensions of a wallpaper roll less 1 inch (for corner overlap) and draw a plumb line. This will be your guideline when hanging your first sheet. Since many times your first sheet is installed in an inconspicuous corner, this is the process you will use to hang your first sheet.

▶ Now simply hang the sheet and wrap the excess into the corner. Since few corners are perfectly plumb, you will need to strike a plumb line on the adjacent wall, again at a distance from the corner of 1 inch less than the dimension of the roll. Then apply another sheet and wrap the excess so it overlaps the first sheet. Now, simply use your broad knife and your razor knife to cut the overlapping sheets in the corner and peel away the two excess pieces.

For outside corners:

▶ In the rare occasion that an outside corner is exactly plumb, you can simply wrap the paper around the corner and begin from its edge on the other side of the corner. If it is not plumb, a little more attention is needed.

▶ As with inside corners, measure at the top and bottom of the wall the distance from the last sheet to the corner. Add 1 inch to the longer measurement and cut a sheet to that width. If the measurement is within 6 inches of a full sheet, use a full sheet. After cutting a diagonal slit at the corner at the top so it will bend around the corner, hang the sheet so that it's smooth and fold it smoothly around the corner. Now, create another plumb line on the intersecting wall with your wallpaper level. The plumb line should be the width of the wallpaper roll from the corner. Now, simply hang your intersecting piece to that plumb line. After both pieces are in place, make a new plumb line ¼ to ½ inch from the corner. At this line, cut through both pieces of overlapping paper and peel away the excess strips. Finish up as normal with a seam roller, and then clean up.

The Wallcoverings Association offers many other tips on its Web site for both novice and professional wallpaper hangers. Check them out at www.wallcoverings.org. ■

Quick Tip:
A Wee Bit of Wallpaper

Just want to add a touch of wallpaper and create some visual interest? Think about covering a ceiling or a wainscot instead of a whole wall. A wallpapered ceiling can create a fantastic effect as well. For a quick and easy project with some leftover paper, use it inside the back of shelf units or cabinets and paint the shelves to coordinate. Just make sure to do any painting first.

PROJECT: A WALLPAPERED ROOM DIVIDER

Level of Difficulty: T T T

A room divider or a folding screen can be used to divide a large room, create privacy, or simply add a nice decorative accent. Save money and make your own room divider using simple doors and your favorite wallpaper. You can use almost any kind of doors. Be creative! Purchase three doors, either solid or French, and hinge them to each other. You can even mix and match antique doors or builder's salvage. If they have hardware on them, that's okay—it just makes them more interesting.

You will need:
- ✓ Three hollow-core interior doors (18 by 80 by 1⅜ inches); solid doors can be used, but will be heavier to move around
- ✓ Paintbrush
- ✓ Primer suitable for paint and wallpaper
- ✓ Paint to coordinate with the wallpaper
- ✓ Wallpaper of your choice
- ✓ Six double-action hinges (1⅛ by 2 inches) with screws
- ✓ Drill and drill bit (size depends on size of screws for hinges)
- ✓ Six 1-inch glides

Phase 1: Decorate the Doors

1. PREP THE DOORS. Apply the primer to the doors, then paint the side edges of the doors, extending the paint about half an inch around the edges to the front and the back. If you are only going to be applying the wallpaper to the front of the door, paint the back. Apply a second coat of paint if necessary.

2. PREP THE WALLPAPER. Cut the wallpaper to the dimensions of the door. Use a framing square to ensure 90-degree corners.

3. APPLY THE WALLPAPER. Adhere the wallpaper to the door and smooth it in place with a damp sponge.

4. FINISH UP. Trim the wallpaper about ⅛ inch from the edges of the door to prevent peeling or fraying. Embellish and decorate as desired. For a bit of visual interest, use cutouts or a wallpaper border to add some finishing touches.

Phase 2: Build the Screen

1. INSTALL THE HINGES. Position the middle door on one outer door, aligning all edges. Place an open hinge centered on the edge of the doors, with the center of the hinge between the doors. Mark the placement of the screws. Mark the placement for the top and bottom hinges about 10 inches from the upper and lower edges of the door. Predrill the holes and attach the hinges.

2. CONNECT THE DOORS. Position the remaining outer door on the middle door. Attach the three remaining hinges to the edges of these doors on the opposite side of the previously attached hinges.

3. FINISH UP. Tap the glides into the bottom of the doors near each end. Enjoy your new screen!
(Resource: Wallcoverings Association) ■

5

doorknobs
and whatchamacallits

Fun Modifications to Your Home's Hardware

"I'm not a locksmith, I'm a magician!"
—FROM THE MOVIE *HOUDINI* (1953), STARRING TONY CURTIS

Well, maybe you're not a locksmith, but that doesn't mean you can't be a hardware hound. Updating your knobs and knockers can be one of the easiest projects to do around the house, plus one of the best ways to improve the everyday comfort level of your home and raise its resale value.

In this chapter, I have included some ideas gleaned from over twenty-five years in the hardware business. I am joined by Keith Lowery, my good friend and fellow hardware specialist from Renaissance Restoration in Dallas, who loves to share his wealth of information.

If you haven't been hardware shopping lately, you'll be amazed at the vast array of products in store for you. The selection of doorknobs alone has increased tenfold over the last few years. Whether you want cabinet knobs that reflect your love of trout fishing or door hardware that makes your house look like a vintage Victorian, you can find and install it, usually in one afternoon. Get a grip with these fun projects.

If you are tired of your old doorknobs, now might be a good time for an update. In the last few years, prices of doorknobs have come down quite a bit, while quality and selection have increased. Just ten years ago, mushroom-shaped knobs were all the rage. Now, anything goes. You can find many beautiful sets priced from $20 and up. Whatever you choose, be sure that they will fit your doors before you buy them.

You will need:
- ✓ Notepad and pencil
- ✓ .Tape measure
- ✓ Screwdriver

1. MEASURE YOUR EXISTING HARDWARE. Before you go shopping for new hardware, you must remove the doorknob set and measure the hole diameter and backset.

If your house was built after 1950, chances are the doorknobs fit through the doors via a standard, predrilled hole. In most parts of the country, that hole is 2⅛ inches in diameter and is "backset" 2⅜ inches from the edge of the door, on center. In other words, on a standard door, the center for the hole for the doorknob is 2⅜ inches from the edge of the door. In some regions, a 2¾-inch backset is more common, even though this is normally a commercial backset. Also measure the thickness of your doors, as some hardware will only fit on certain thicknesses.

If your house does not have predrilled doors, it may have mortise locks (you will see a long rectangle on the edge of the door) or even rim locks (a box-shaped lock mounted on the surface of the door). To learn about the installation process of older lock styles, visit my buddies at Nostalgic Warehouse (www.nostalgicwarehouse.com).

2. CHOOSE THE TYPE OF HARDWARE YOU WANT. Do you want standard doorknobs, antique or decorative knobs, or perhaps levers? Doorknobs are the mainstay in most homes and come in the widest range of styles and prices, but levers are worth considering because they are convenient, add visual interest to your doors, and can boost your home's resale value. They're also easier on aging or arthritic hands that may have trouble gripping a slippery doorknob. Now that levers are gaining in popularity, prices are coming down, but watch out for cheap versions. Lesser brands will use an inferior latch that can tend to sag after a few years. Choose sets that have an extra backup spring in the lever itself, as well as in the latch, and make sure the manufacturer or the dealer will stand behind the product's quality.

If you decide to install levers, note that some styles come in both left-handed and right-handed configurations, so ask your hardware dealer to make sure handing is not and issue.

3. CHOOSE THE MATERIAL. Most quality hardware is made from solid brass, even if the finish is made from something else, such as chrome. "Forged" brass is generally considered better than "cast" brass because it resists breaking and tarnishing. Forged and cast irons are popular for hardware as well, especially if you are looking for a style that was originally made from iron, such as Colonial Williamsburg, also known as just Williamsburg. Bronze is gaining in popularity for its strength and rustic charm. Glass and porcelain doorknobs are also making a comeback, but watch out for inferior quality ones that can break under heavy use. If breakage is a concern, check out acrylic options.

4. CHOOSE THE FINISH. Polished brass is the most popular finish for door hardware. Since it is so common, brass is usually relatively inexpensive and matching accessories, such as a brass kickplate or door knocker, are easy to find. Look for brass that has a "lifetime" finish or "PVD" coating, which is made to resist tarnish.

Alternative finishes such as chrome or oil-rubbed bronze express your individuality and may actually outlast brass finishes, but you may have more difficulty locating accessories that are a perfect match. These types of finishes may be trendy and can "date" your remodeling project.

5. COUNT THE NUMBER OF DOOR SETS THAT YOU WILL NEED FOR EACH OF THE FOLLOWING FUNCTIONS.

▶ Passage sets that do not lock and are normally used on most doors in a home.

▶ Privacy sets that utilize a lock for bedrooms and bathrooms but also feature an emergency release on the outside of the door.

▶ Dummy knobs that are like large cabinet knobs and are often used for closet doors that do not need to latch via the doorknob.

▶ Keyed locking sets that open with a key and are normally used for exterior doors. (Ask your hardware dealer to match all of the locking sets to function with one key, if that meets your needs.)

6. GO SHOPPING! Head to your local hardware store or home center. If you are looking for something a little different—for instance, lion's head doorknobs—you may want to visit decorative hardware showrooms. These stores specialize in unusual products that are not normally available, but be aware that they may have stricter return and exchange policies than you are used to. Wherever you buy your hardware, be sure to understand the store's policies before you special-order products. What is the manufacturer's warranty? Choose a company that has a solid reputation and will stand behind its products for at least 10 years. ■

Quick Tip:
Salvage Solutions

If you have a house that was built prior to 1970, use caution when replacing old hardware. Incorrect replacements can severely damage the value of a vintage home, making it difficult to resell. Original hardware can often be matched from salvage, especially since most builders tend to use the same hardware in a particular region. Old locks can be refurbished and the knobs and faceplates can be polished up. And if you run short, there are quality reproductions available that are so similar to the old ones that it's hard to tell the difference.

PROJECT: **INSTALL A DEAD-BOLT LOCK**

Level of difficulty: $T T T$

It's amazing how many people depend on undependable security. The biggest culprit in the security business is the one who recommends that you install a chain on your door. No matter how well it's installed, if you open the door with a chain engaged, you'd better stand back, because it only takes a good kick or shove into the door to break out the screws, rip up the jamb, and let the intruder in your home. Chains can also scratch the door and the doorjamb.

A well-installed, high-security dead bolt is your best chance of slowing or preventing a break-in. Police call it "hardening the target," which simply means that you make it so difficult for a burglar to enter that he chooses an easier target. Even more amazing than the use of undependable security is how many dead bolts are installed incorrectly. Most intrusions are accomplished by breaking the doorjamb.

If you have just purchased an expensive new door and it is not drilled for hardware, you may want to hire a locksmith to do the installation for you—not because it's difficult, but because a poor job can permanently damage the door, making it hard to correct misaligned hardware. This can be an expensive mistake. But if you have someone else do the installation for you, make sure they do it right! Some installers will throw away the strike-reinforcing plate and long screws that come with the better locks and try to save time by installing just a thin brass strike plate. One kick and the jamb is gone. Ask your installer to use the most secure strike plate available—and pay a little extra, if necessary.

If you have decided to install your own lock, read the manufacturer's instructions first. I know this is not the usual practice, but you never know when a lock maker will come up with a new idea. Here are some basic steps and hints that may help.

You will need:

✓ Dead bolt with a steel plate and long screws or a steel plate that installs under the decorative strike

✓ Latch

✓ Paper template (usually supplied with the dead bolt)

- ✓ Awl
- ✓ Power drill
- ✓ Hammer
- ✓ Boring kit made just for doorknobs and dead bolts that includes a 1-inch edge bore spade drill bit and a 2⅛-inch hole saw
- ✓ Pencil
- ✓ Sharp chisel
- ✓ Carpenter's rule with a sliding depth gauge or a sewing hem ruler
- ✓ Bar of soap

1. PLACE THE DEAD BOLT. The placement of a doorknob and the dead bolt is often up to you. In most cases, the lock is centered 5 inches above the doorknob center. You almost never install a dead bolt without a latch to hold the door in place while you engage the bolt. Most sets come with a paper template that will help you mark the holes with an awl. Both backsets are shown on many templates, and often the latch can be modified to fit either a 2⅜ inch or 2¾ backset, so measure the doorknob backset so the dead bolt will match. Visit www.schlage.com to download a free template and some more great tips on lock installation and security hardware options.

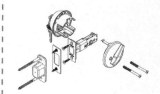

2. DRILL THE EDGE BORE. (Your hardware store may rent a boring kit that can help you.)

Make sure the drill bit point is centered on the width of the door and just get the bit started. If you are not an experienced installer, you may want to have someone watch from your side to help you keep the vertical alignment by telling you to move up or down. Then drill approximately 3 inches into the door.

For the horizontal alignment, try to eye the door itself as if you are looking far ahead when driving. Don't count on the edge of the door being straight. Most doors have a beveled edge, so lining up to this surface will have you drilling toward the inside of the house and give you an angled latch bore. Make sure that you are drilling straight and true before you ever turn on your drill. You will only get one chance to do it right.

3. DRILL THE CROSS BORE. Make sure your hole saw is tight in the drill. Drill slowly into one side of the door. As you work into the door with the hole saw, wiggle it slightly by moving the drill in a slightly circular motion. This will help prevent the blade from binding. As you drill into the face of the door, you will feel it become easier as it hits the cross bore. Continue drilling until the pilot bit breaks through to the other side. Move the drill to the other side and slowly drill out the 2⅛-inch plug. Slow down and use caution, because you are close to breaking through the door. The drill can slip from your grip as the hole saw completes the hole—and may cause injury to you or damage to the door.

4. INSERT THE LATCH. Slide the latch into the edge bore hole, keeping it straight with the edge of the door. Using your awl, trace around the edge of the faceplate. Remove the latch. Use a hammer to sink the chisel edge into the traced line. Keep your edges straight and make just the right-sized cut into the wood for the faceplate to fit into. This is called a mortise. Chisel the top and bottom of the rectangle to give the mortise a stopping place. Then chisel the vertical lines gently and toward the center of the hole, taking care not to split the wood. When you go with the grain (vertically), the wood is easy to split, especially if it has crooked grain lines. Once you have framed your faceplate mortise well, you can put the chisel into the edge bore about 3/16-inch deep and split the pieces out from the top and bottom. Only a little cleanup should be necessary to make room for the latch face. Insert the latch; it should be flush with the door edge. If not, use the chisel to clean it up a bit more until you are satisfied. Insert screws.

5. INSTALL THE STRIKE. Close the door until it latches. To measure the distance from the edge, use a carpenter's rule with a sliding depth gauge (or a sewing hem ruler that is thin enough to go between door and jamb). While pushing the dead bolt toward the jamb, use the depth gauge to measure from the edge of the jamb to the side of the deadbolt latch. Open the door and transfer that distance to a line on the doorjamb. Use a pencil to measure the height of the latch by engaging the dead bolt about ¼ inch as you ease it against the jamb. Mark the top and bottom. Transfer these lines to the jamb face. Now you can use the strike itself to line up the cutout area with the depth mark and the height marks. (It should look like a big U turned on its side.) Hold the strike in place and scribe the edges. Draw the entire inside of the screw hole with a pencil. Drill pilot holes for

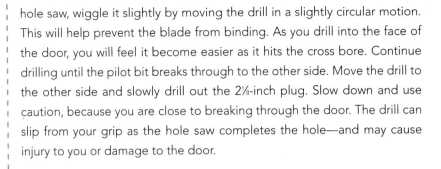

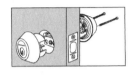
Quick Tip:
What a Drag!

If the bolt does not engage or drags and you have to push on the door to lock it, you may be able to fix it by adjusting the knob strike. Move the knob strike toward the outside by mortising the outside edge and tapping wood into the old screw holes. Then when you close the door, it will be tighter and won't need to be pushed to engage the lock. Sometimes, it is okay to file the decorative plate to free up the bolt.
(Resource: Keith Lowery, Renaissance Restoration)

the screws and install the strike. Test the doorknob to make sure it all aligns before moving on to the dead-bolt installation.

6. SET THE DEAD BOLT AND THUMB TURN. To drill the hole for the dead bolt, it is actually better to drill two ⅞-inch holes that overlap. Since you have drilled the screw pilot holes, you can see where not to drill. Clean up the two overlapping holes with a chisel to make a nice oval. Now when the doorjamb settles or shifts, the bolt won't stick or drag against the wood as it would if a single hole were drilled.

Chisel the mortised area just as you did the latch faceplate, only deeper so you can put in the strike-reinforcing plate. Insert the steel strike plate and drill very deep pilot holes, all the way into the wall stud behind the jamb. Rub some hard bath soap on the long screws and use a bit that fits securely. Drive the screws home. Install the decorative strike and test the lock. ∎

Quick Tip:
Perfect Professional Polishing

If your existing front-door hardware is especially good quality and just needs polishing, you may want to have it professionally refinished. Properly recoating brass hardware yourself is difficult and does not usually result in a durable finish that can withstand the elements. The question is, how do you lock the door while the hardware is at the refinishing shop? Check with plating and polishing companies in your area. Some offer same-day service on front door hardware so that you can remove the door set early in the morning and reinstall it that evening. If this service is not available, buy a cheap dead bolt to use while your entry set is being refinished or plated. Also, when you're having the set redone, consider changing it to an alternative finish such as pewter, chrome, or satin nickel. These may hold up better than polished brass in highly used areas.

ONE-HOUR WONDER: **UNSTICK A STICKY LOCK**

Do your keys get stuck when you try to unlock a door? Before you spend money on new hardware, try this locksmith's trick, compliments of my friend and lock expert Keith Lowery: At your local hardware store, buy a small tube of powdered graphite. Puncture the end of the tube and squeeze some of the graphite in through the keyhole. Then slide the key in and out several times. Problem solved!

Graphite is also available in a squeeze can, suspended in a molybdenum disulfide base—a fancy term that just means that the liquid base carries the graphite into the lock parts and lubricates them. The liquid base soon evaporates away. Either option, powdered or liquid graphite, should solve the problem. If it doesn't, you may need to take the lock to a locksmith for adjustment or replacement. ■

PROJECT: FIX A SAGGING DOOR

Level of difficulty: ⊤ ⊤ ⊤ ⊤

If a dead-bolt lock is dragging or the doorknob latch is not catching the strike, moving the strike is not always the best idea. Often, the door has shifted in its space or the frame has tilted due to settling of the home's foundation. Examine the gap at the top of the door when it is closed. If the gap is uneven, either the jamb has moved or the hinges are weak. The cure for this problem is often at the hinges. Many prehung doors have inexpensive, lightweight hinges that start to sag after a few years. If you have a sagging door, the problem may be more than aesthetic; you may be spending extra energy dollars due to the draft around the door. If you don't want to replace the hinges or the door set, try this easy fix first.

You will need:

- ✓ A power drill, screwdriver tips, and assorted bits
- ✓ 3 to 3½-inch wood screws
- ✓ Bar of soap
- ✓ Heavy corrugated cardboard or ⅛-inch plywood door shims (if necessary)

1. REMOVE AND REPLACE ONE SCREW. Open the door and use your drill and a screwdriver tip to remove the top hinge screw that is closest to the exterior.

2. DRILL A PILOT HOLE. Using a bit that is slightly smaller than the new screw diameter, drill a pilot hole through the old screw hole, but angled toward the home's exterior so you can catch the stud behind the doorjamb.

3. INSERT THE NEW SCREW. Lubricate the screw with a bar of soap to prevent splitting the doorjamb. Press your shoulder against the opposite side of the jamb and push hard as you drive the screw home. The door should be lifted off the threshold away from the lock side and up at the top.

So you've tightened that wood screw too many times and now it just spins? Grab the wood glue and some toothpicks, matches, or ideally a ⅛-inch hardwood dowel. If you are handy, you may be able to use wood golf tees or whittle your own plugs. To remove the screw, edge the corner of your chisel under the head while you turn it with a screwdriver. If the screw head is stripped, use a high-speed rotary tool with a metal cutting disk, but be sure to wear eye protection as you grind a slot into the head of the screw. Then you can use a flat-edge screwdriver and back the screw out.
(Resource: Keith Lowery, Renaissance Restoration)

4. SHIMMY, SHIMMY, BABY! If the door still sags, add enough heavy cardboard or thin plywood shims under the bottom hinge until you have an even gap around the door. You may have to try this several times until the fit is correct. It is a good idea to consider replacing the screws on all hinges with slightly longer screws, especially if they seem loose.

5. IF NECESSARY, TRY THIS LAST RESORT. Replace the old, cheap hinges with better-quality versions. Just take one of your old hinges to the hardware store with you to match it up for size and thickness. Also consider using longer screws for more stability. ■

ONE-HOUR WONDER: AN EASY FIX FOR WOBBLY DOORKNOBS

How many times have you tightened screws on a doorknob, only to have it wiggle loose again? Many things can become wobbly under normal operation and, if they are not repaired, lead to costly replacements. One of the most useful tools in this battle is liquid thread lock, which is available at any hardware store.

First, determine how your doorknobs attach. On older doorknob sets, the doorknob is held onto a square spindle by setscrews that tend to loosen over time. Look for the setscrews on the side of each knob and remove them, if possible. Look into the setscrew holes. The spindle should fit at a perpendicular angle to the setscrew holes. Apply a dot or two of thread lock onto the threads of the setscrews. When you screw them back in, they shouldn't wiggle loose. When you add thread lock, be sure that the setscrews are tightened against the flat side of the spindle, or matters will worsen. You may want to test the sets to make sure they are properly aligned before you apply the thread lock and accidentally bind them in the wrong position.

A doorknob that does not have exposed setscrews is usually held in place by a tab. This is common on doorknobs made after 1960. Look on the bottom of the doorknob shaft for a slot with the tab in it. (If you cannot find the slot or tab, try visiting the hardware manufacturer's Web site for instructions before proceeding). Once you have located the tab, try pushing it inward to release the knob so you can pull it off the shaft. After that, there is often a stamped brass cover over the round backplate. Look for an opening around the top where you can insert a slot head screwdriver to pry off the cover. After you have exposed the screws, remove them, coat them with thread lock, and reinsert them tightly. Then snap the cover back on and slide the doorknob back on the shaft. ■

Quick Tips: A Few Ideas to Make Drilling Easier

▶ Always use a screwdriver bit that fits tightly in the head of the screw.

▶ Drill pilot holes for all screws when installing hardware. Predrilling is even important for a hollow-core door because the screw can act as a wedge and split the door vertically.

▶ Using a flip-around drill bit holder along with slide-in hex head drill bits and screwdriver bits make it very easy to change from a predrilling bit to the screwdriver bit.

For greater security, it's a good idea to install door viewers on the front and back doors of your home. How many times have you opened your front door without being sure of who is on the other side? For just a few dollars and less than 10 minutes, you can install a door viewer that lets you see outside without letting someone see in.

Installing Security Hardware

Before you go to the trouble of installing security hardware, make sure it really works and does not compromise your safety in case of fire. Some security devices, such as double-cylinder dead bolts, are more secure, but if you do not practice fire drills with the assurance of the spare key under a rug near the door, you have a safety hazard.

The opposite of this problem can also be a hazard. If you have a lever on the inside of the front door or a thumb turn on the deadbolt, your toddler might escape from the house before you knew he or she could open the door! Many people add double-cylinder dead bolts to exterior doors for this reason alone, only to ruin the front of their home by drilling an unnecessary extra hole in the door. The only reason to use a double-cylinder dead bolt is if you have a door with a glass window that could be broken by an intruder, allowing him to unlock the door.

A very easy way to keep the kids in is to add an inexpensive flip lock. This device looks like a doorknob strike, except the curved lip can be lifted, rotated in front of the door, and dropped into position to keep the door from being opened. It screws to the doorjamb, not the door itself, so it will not harm your beautiful door. To exit, just lift and pivot the front part out of the way.

Door chains will not protect your loved ones because they can easily be kicked in. There is one device that is okay if you want the capacity to open the door just enough to talk with visitors, but it should be placed high on the door so it is not an option for children who do not know who to trust. The device is called a door guard or swing lock. You may have seen them at a hotel on the inside of the door. A curved, hooklike piece screws to the door and a triangular-shaped hinged piece attaches to the jamb. When you want to open the door but still have some resistance, just swing the triangular-shaped portion over until the door piece is in the center. The bulbous end of the hook will catch once the door has opened about 3 to 4 inches. If you decide a swing lock is right for you, be sure you use long screws that will tighten into the stud behind the jamb. You may want to replace the manufacturer's screws with some longer ones from the hardware store.

PROJECT: SELECT AND INSTALL NEW CABINET HARDWARE

Level of difficulty: T T

It is said that nothing does more for raising one's spirits than a new haircut. The same can be said for updating cabinet hardware. Shiny new knobs and pulls can make all the difference in the world. The best part is that your guests will think you've made major renovations—and it's an easy fix that almost anyone can do.

You will need:

- ✓ Tape measure
- ✓ New cabinet pulls
- ✓ Awl or large nail
- ✓ Blue painter's tape
- ✓ Safety goggles
- ✓ Electric drill
- ✓ ¹⁄₁₆-inch drill bit for drilling pilot hole
- ✓ Drill bit, sized according to hardware screw diameter (³⁄₁₆- to ¼-inch usually work fine)
- ✓ Drill guide, available at most hardware stores (optional)
- ✓ Screwdriver

1. MEASURE YOUR EXISTING CABINET PULLS BEFORE SELECTING NEW ONES. Cabinet pulls come in lots of sizes, so be sure to measure your existing hardware before buying new pulls. The standard size is 3 inches (or 96 millimeters), but there are many other sizes. To measure, hold one of your old pulls and determine the distance from the center of one screw hole to the center of the next screw hole. For single-hole knobs, make sure to measure the backplate to ensure coverage.

You may want to begin your cabinet hardware search on the Internet so that you can select from the widest variety of styles, but I recommend that you go to a local source for the actual purchase. Most decorative hardware dealers can order almost anything that you see on the Web, and they will usually match or beat the price. Take a door or a drawer to the hardware store, if possible, so you can see the new pulls against your cabinet's finish.

Quick Tip:
Hassle-Free Holes

If the spacing for your new pulls does not line up with your old holes, or if you want to install oversized hardware, you can use wood filler or a backplate to cover exposed holes.

Andrea's Choice: Oversized Pulls

For a unique look in ultramodern kitchens, select cabinet pulls that are much longer than traditional styles and enhance their decorative effect with accents that match their finish. For instance, use brushed chrome pulls in an extra-long design with stainless steel film accents on cabinet fronts and fixtures.
(Resource: MNG Designer Hardware/
www.mnghardware.com)

Quick Tip: Soapy Screws

If you feel too much resistance while hand-tightening the screws into the new hardware, back the screw out and try again. You may have cross-threaded the screws. If the little misfits still won't tighten, rub a little bit of soap or oil lubricant onto the threads and try again. Also, to prevent the pulls from loosening over time, dab a little clear fingernail polish or thread lock onto each screw before tightening them.

Once you've made your choice, purchase a couple of extra pulls, knobs, and hinges and keep them in a drawer for future use. If you ever snap off a knob or want to add a drawer, it may be impossible to find a match at a later date.

2. MARK THE DRILLING POINTS ON YOUR CABINETS FOR THE MOUNTING HOLES. If your cabinets have not previously had pulls on them, tape a 4- to 5-inch piece of blue masking tape on the outside surface where you want to mount new hardware. There are no specific rules about where to position the hardware, as long as it's practical for opening the cabinet. Just be careful to not drill closer than 1 inch from the edge, as the wood might splinter.

Using your tape measure and awl (or a large nail), measure and mark the locations for the mounting holes on the blue painter's tape, spaced according to the fastening points for your hardware. Also take care to measure evenly from the vertical and horizontal edge of each cabinet door or drawer so the hardware appears straight and symmetrical. If necessary, make a cardboard drilling template to help speed up the marking process. Simply cut a piece of cardboard and line it up against the side or top of the door or drawer. Mark the proper hole placement into the cardboard and pierce a small hole on each mark. Then mark a centerline on the template to help place it in the correct position on your door or drawer. If you are replacing a large quantity of cabinet hardware, consider ordering a hard plastic drilling template from my friends at www.hardwareandtools.com.

3. INSTALL THE NEW HARDWARE. Sporting safety goggles, drill a $\frac{1}{16}$-inch pilot hole through the tape wherever you've marked it and then follow up with a $\frac{3}{16}$- to $\frac{1}{4}$-inch bit. Keeping the drill aligned, not angled, drill straight through the cabinet, front to the back, to avoid wood splintering. (If necessary, use a drill guide.) After drilling holes for the first pull, remove the tape from the cabinet surface and test the fit. Install the screws into the pull or the knobs and tighten them as much as possible by hand. Then tighten the screws further (but do not overtighten) with a screwdriver. If all is well, continue mounting the rest of the hardware. If necessary, make any measurement or positioning adjustments first. ■

Functional and Decorative Hardware

From floor vent covers to a weather vane on the roof and everything in between, decorative and functional hardware comes in a wide variety of options. These are the details that sparkle and enhance the mood of your home. They have a practical side, too. A weather vane can help guests find your house for their first visit. A decorative kickplate can protect the wood on your front door. Don't be afraid to play with themes and let your hardware reflect your sense of style. Here are a few fun options.

▶ **SWITCH PLATES:** Changing light switch plates is easy and can make a big difference in a room's decor. You'll find a huge selection of switch plates with dozens of styles and hole configurations on the market. Many are oversized to cover previous damage. Others are wallpapered to blend into a room. Some designs even glow in the dark with dinosaurs or ballerinas. Wooden plates can be stained to match the furniture. Since many switch plates are made to order, be sure you purchase ones with the right configurations.

▶ **AIR-REGISTER COVERS OR VENTS:** Whether they are mounted on the wall or in the floor, air registers are an oft-neglected accent. Most register covers are plain, painted steel. Replacing them can transform a room from blah to beautiful. Options abound on the Internet, from Victorian brass styles to wood models that can be stained to match your floors. You can even use a pretty register cover to hide an unsightly doorbell ringer inside the wall.

▶ **DOORBELLS AND KNOCKERS:** When guests want to get your attention, let them ring for you on a doorbell that expresses your individuality. Or perhaps you prefer an old-fashioned door knocker or even a nostalgic twist doorbell. Whatever your preference, a quick search on the Internet will likely uncover a model that reflects your favorite hobby or interest—from fishing to Scottie dogs or even the logo of your college football team.

▶ **KICKPLATES, PUSH PLATES, AND DOORSTOPS:** Protect your door and add shine at the same time with a kickplate that matches

Quick Tip: Hinge Headaches

If you need to replace your hinges, be sure to take one to the hardware store when you go shopping. Hinges come in a huge variety of shapes and sizes, and it will be important to compare your originals with the samples in the store. If your home is very old, you may have difficulty finding new hinges that fit. Sometimes, it is easier to have your old hinges refinished or replated and then just use them again. If so, consider using new, slightly larger screws when you replace them so they will grab better in the original holes. You might also try squirting a dab of carpenter's glue into each hole before inserting the screws, to give them better holding power. If your home is historic, avoid Phillips-head screws, as they were not commonly used in homes until the 1960s and 1970s.
(Resource: MNG Designer Hardware)

your door hardware. Designed to help protect a wooden door from weather and abrasion, a kickplate is just that—a place to kick a door or, more likely, to place your foot against it to open or close it. A push plate serves a similar function, except it is smaller and designed to protect a door from handprints and key scratches. As well as protecting walls from doorknob punctures, doorstops and holders can help prevent hands from being pinched or crushed in doors and door hinges

▶ **HOUSE NUMBERS:** Do you know how common it is for emergency vehicles to have trouble finding homes because the house numbers are not visible? Seconds can mean the difference between life and death, so be sure that your home is clearly marked, both in the front and back. Drive down your own street and make sure that your house number is legible during the day and illuminated or reflective at night. Don't sacrifice beauty, though. House numbers are available in many gorgeous designs.

Level of difficulty: T T

If your old electric doorbell has been dead forever but you haven't a clue how to fix it, it's easier than you think. First, turn off the power to the doorbell at the breaker or fuse box. Most doorbells are wired at 12 volts, which is minimal electrical flow. You probably wouldn't feel it even if you did touch the live wires. However, in very rare cases, the bell may be wired with a higher voltage than you expect, and it could hurt you. The best saying for electrical work is "better safe than dead." Always turn the power off.

Then unscrew the doorbell cover plate and remove it. You should then be able to pop out the unit with your hand, but avoid the metal parts as you do this—they can be sharp. Unscrew the two electrical wires from the back of the doorbell button and take the whole unit with you to the hardware store to make sure you get the right replacement.

Attach the wires on the new doorbell to the screws on the back of the doorbell button. Remount the doorbell to the wall and replace the cover plate. Turn the power back on and wait for your next visitor to be announced with a nice clear ring!

Another option is to replace your old doorbell with a wireless unit. These battery-operated units are available at most hardware stores and home centers and can be installed in just a few minutes. These are great for an area, such as rear entrance, that did not have a doorbell to begin with. ■

6

attractive antiques, charming chairs, and fabulous floors

Waxing Your Way Through Furniture and Wood Care

I spend hours in junk shops buying furniture. I do all the upholstery work myself and it's like therapy.

—PAMELA ANDERSON

Do you have a piece of furniture that needs a makeover? Don't toss it out. Restoring it is usually much less expensive than replacing it. Replacing a chair's worn-out fabric is a snap. And if you're feeling more adventurous, you can save hundreds or perhaps thousands of dollars by refinishing your own wood furniture and floors. In this chapter, we will begin by turning trash into treasures. Then we'll move on to a crash course in finishes, followed by some projects that you can accomplish over a weekend. Along the way, you'll find some quick tips and quips from the wonderful world of wood care.

▶ Trash to Treasures

▶ Project: Reglue a Wobbly Chair Frame

▶ Project: Re-cover a Chair Seat with Fabric

Trash to Treasures

If you are in the market for a new dresser, bed, or seating for your home, or if you are furnishing your son or daughter's first apartment or dorm, consider picking up some older pieces at the local thrift store or antique shop. A little bit of elbow grease can go a long way and potentially save you some bucks, too. Vintage items are often better quality than what you can find in today's furniture stores. Here are some ways to turn boring into beautiful.

Whether you are shopping for a nifty collectible or deciding whether to refurbish a hand-me-down, ask these questions before spending time and money on repairs.

Is the piece made from softwood or hardwood? Hardwood is generally better quality, has higher resale value, and will last longer. An easy way to tell if a wood is "hard" is to scrape it with the sharp edge of your fingernail in a hidden spot under the seat. Hardwoods such as oak or walnut will not scratch easily. Pine, fir, and gumwood will indent without much pressure.

Are replacement parts available? If parts are not available at your local hardware store, many catalogers specialize in replacement pulls, knobs, casters, and even wood parts for restoring vintage pieces to their former glory. (See page 271 for a listing of resources.) Just be sure that you're not spending more on parts than you would on a whole piece of furniture that has already been restored—unless, of course, the item has sentimental value.

Once you've decided to refurbish an item, there are many options for bringing new life to it. Here are a few . . .

▶ **DECORATE IT:** Use stencils and sponges to create eye-catching designs on surfaces. Stencil flowers and butterflies on a drab storage chest for garden tools or create depth and texture on an old hutch with some paint and a sponge. Hand-painted designs lend a personal touch to any object, while also adding style and elegance to the decor.

▶ **DECAL IT:** Many companies offer fun decal designs to dress up furniture, cabinetry, and bookcases. Choose from themes such as southwestern, floral, whimsical, and classical to blend with the balance of your room.

▶ **PAINT IT:** Paint can often be used to make an inexpensive piece sport a unique, new appeal. Try nontraditional colors, such as gloss black or red, for a dramatic effect. Experiment with an interchange of color; for instance, blue drawers on a green dresser. Another idea is to paint the inside of shelves or cabinets a contrasting hue. White or black can be used in this way to create a shadowbox effect. Try leaving a portion of the piece unpainted with natural wood as an accent.

▶ **DISTRESS IT:** Give items such as dressers and bookcases a hint of sophistication and age by distressing the surface. Kits are available at most craft and hobby shops to achieve a vintage appearance, or you can improvise with leftover paint. Start with a base coat on the object and then age it with a second color. Using a rag, wipe a bit of the second color on the corners and edges. You may want to create a grained or "aged" appearance as you wipe some of the paint off. Then, using a paintbrush, fling tiny speckles of paint everywhere to give your furniture a stylish yet aged look.

▶ **PERSONALIZE IT:** Add a unique touch to any room with personalized furnishings. Stencil an old rocking chair with your baby's name or birth date to create a special place to rock the bundle of joy to sleep. Or paint a child's desk with letters of the alphabet or numbers to create a cozy place to study or color while encouraging learning. Decals are also available to help personalize a special keepsake.

▶ **RESTORE IT:** If you have a piece of furniture that is starting to look dull, re-stain the piece to restore it to its original beauty. This will bring a fresh new look to the piece while preserving its original charm.

▶ **TILE IT:** Add beauty and color to boring tables and chairs with mosaic-tiled artwork. Create a design of your choice with broken pieces of tile and stained glass, adhering each piece with super-glue. Next, fill in the spaces between tiles with grout. Whether you want to give old furniture a new look or make a unique housewarming gift for someone special, this is a great way to add style and elegance to any decor.

PROJECT: REGLUE A WOBBLY CHAIR FRAME

Level of difficulty: T

Regluing a wobbly chair is usually an easy project, even for a novice. Yellow wood glue is best for most jobs of this type. It's important to clamp all of the glued parts together for several hours to allow the glue to adhere and dry thoroughly. You don't even need wood clamps. You can improvise with a rope or an inner tube.

You will need:

- ✓ Yellow wood glue
- ✓ Thin rope (approximately ¼ inch thick, 3 to 4 feet long) or deflated tire inner tube
- ✓ Thick wooden dowel or heavy wooden spoon
- ✓ Medium-sized spring clamp (or extra piece of rope)
- ✓ Damp rag
- ✓ Heavy books (or cinder blocks or other ballast)

1. MAKE SURE THE CHAIR IS SITTING ON A FLAT SURFACE. Squirt a moderate amount of glue into any loose joints. (Don't worry yet about any excess glue; you'll wipe it away in a minute.)

2. WRAP A ROPE (OR INNER TUBE) AROUND ALL FOUR LEGS OF THE CHAIR, SECURING THE FRONT WITH A STRONG KNOT. Using a wooden dowel (or the handle of a wooden spoon), twist the rope (or inner tube) around it several times until the rope is tight on all four legs. Lock the dowel into place with a spring clamp (or extra piece of rope).

3. USE A DAMP RAG TO WIPE AWAY ANY EXCESS GLUE WHILE IT'S STILL WET.

4. WEIGHT THE CHAIR SEAT WITH A FEW HEAVY BOOKS OR OTHER BALLAST. Allow the chair to sit overnight before removing the clamps (or rope or inner tube). ■

T Andrea's Choice: Alternatives to Conventional Glue

Sometimes, older chairs become loose from lack of humidity. Often, these can be repaired without conventional glue. The advantage to avoiding glue on chair frames is that as chairs flex when one sits on them, the glue will eventually break down, requiring the repair to be done over and over. Two products that work well in such cases are Wonderlok and Chair-Loc. Wonderlok is considered a glue of sorts, because it quickly forms a tight wood bond. Chair-Loc actually swells the wood fibers, creating a tighter joint. Both products are available at most hardware stores.

Chairs with an upholstered seat that fits into a frame are easy and inexpensive to recover, using just a small amount of cloth. Often, you can use old drapes or even discarded clothes as new seating fabric. Try mixing and matching patterns. This is a great job for a beginner or a teenager. Supplies are available at most fabric stores.

You will need:

✓ Staple remover and pliers
✓ Tape measure
✓ 1- to 2-inch thick foam upholstery rubber
✓ Thick cotton upholstery batting
✓ Fabric—usually nonstretchy, closely woven varieties
✓ Staple gun
✓ Scissors and/or utility knife
✓ Wood screws

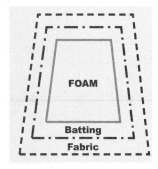

1. CUT THE MATERIALS. First, remove the old seat from the chair frame, watching out for sharp nails or staples. If the old batting or foam is brittle or hardened, it should be replaced with a new piece of foam rubber, cut to the same size as the chair seat. Also, cut a piece of cotton batting approximately 4 inches larger than the chair seat. Finally, cut a piece of new fabric approximately 4 inches larger than the chair seat in each direction, making sure the fabric design is straight and centered on the chair seat.

2. INSTALL FOAM AND BATTING. Center the new foam on top of the piece of batting, then place the top of the chair seat (facedown) on top of the foam. Pull the batting up and over the edge of the side of the chair seat and staple it into place on the underside of the seat. Repeat on the other side, then the back, and finally the front, pulling tightly and stapling all edges into place. Keep the corners as neat and flat as possible. Trim any excess batting with scissors or a utility knife.

3. INSTALL FABRIC. Lay the fabric facedown and center the newly padded seat on top of it. Look at the design in the fabric and make sure it is straight and centered. Repeat the stapling process with the fabric, starting at the sides first, then the back, and finally the front of the seat. Trim off any excess fabric with a scissors or a utility knife. Drop the seat into place, and secure with wood screws, if necessary. Enjoy! ■

PROJECT: REPLACE A PREWOVEN CANE CHAIR SEAT OR BACK

Level of difficulty: T T T

There are two major types of cane panels in chairs: hand cane and prewoven cane. A hand-caned chair has holes that go through the wood into which strands of cane are woven. Hand caning is a fairly involved process, requiring both skill and patience. But prewoven cane is as easy to replace as installing a screen in a screen door, and the process is very similar. Prewoven cane panels can be easily identified by the woody spline (a wedge-shaped piece of wood that holds the cane in place, along with glue). Again, this compares to the rubber gasket that holds a screen in place in a door. Most prewoven seats and backs are not difficult to replace, but some skill is required. The hardest part is usually getting the old cane out. Allow approximately 2 to 4 hours per chair to get the job done.

If you cannot locate caning products in your area, mail-order supplies are available. Check the resources section for listings.

You will need:

✓ Utility knife, preferably with breakaway blades
✓ Spline chisel or sharpened screwdriver (must be narrower than the width of the spline)
✓ Vinegar and small bulb syringe (if necessary)
✓ Needle-nose pliers (if necessary)
✓ Small hammer or mallet
✓ Tape measure
✓ Hand router (optional)—this is a power tool that can be used to cut grooves
✓ File or coarse sandpaper (if necessary)
✓ New cane
✓ New spline
✓ Bathtub or large pan
✓ Damp rag or sponge
✓ Rag (approximately 12 by 12 inches)
✓ Small bucket of water
✓ Small spray bottle of water

- ✓ Two large clamps
- ✓ Thin, sharpened hardwood wedge
- ✓ Yellow wood glue
- ✓ Scissors

1. CUT OUT THE OLD CANE PANEL. Use a utility knife to cut around the periphery of the spline next to the wood, holding the blade in a vertical position. Push down firmly but gently around the chair frame until the blade starts to dig into the space between the spline and the wood to separate them. This eliminates damage to the outside edge of the wood while making the old spline easier to remove. Cut the old cane out as close to the spline as possible. Save the old piece of cane to match stain color later. Caution: Always point sharp tools away from your body to avoid injury.

2. CHISEL INTO THE OLD SPLINE. Carefully, use a spline chisel or a sharpened screwdriver to remove the old spline. Starting at a joint in the spline, hold the chisel upright and hammer it into the spline until it bottoms out, usually about 5/16 inch deep. Make a series of indents into the spline approximately 2 inches apart all around the edge of the cane panel.

3. POP THE SPLINE OUT AND CLEAN THE GROOVE. Sometimes old spline and cane will pop out easily with the use of a spline chisel or a screwdriver. More often, the glue that held the cane in place will remain intact and need some persuasion to come out. My father, Phil McEwan, installs cane seats as a hobby. His special technique for softening and removing old glue is warmed vinegar. Heat ¼ cup of vinegar in the microwave for about 30 seconds and, using the bulb syringe, thoroughly fill indents (as mentioned in step 2) around the spline with the vinegar. Let sit for approximately an hour.

Hammer the chisel into the indents and pry up the spline. The spline should pop out of the groove. Don't be concerned if it doesn't all come out cleanly. It may have been well glued or have small nails or staples, which must be removed. If it has nails or staples, pry them out with great care, as they may have rusted. If they snap off and you can't get them out with needle-nose pliers, hammer them down below the surface of the chair groove bottom.

Thoroughly clean and scrape the groove with the edge of a screw-

Quick Tip:
Extend the Life of Your Cane Panel Chair

If a cane panel in a chair is just loose, you may be able to tighten it up and prolong its life. Turn the chair upside down and place a damp paper towel on the underside of the cane seat to moisten it. After the cane is sufficiently dampened, for 30 minutes or so, allow it to dry normally. If the cane does not shrink back to its original shape, dampen it again and then set it in the sun. Never use a hair dryer to dry cane. When it's all tightened up, apply tung oil, linseed oil, or an oil-based varnish to the topside of the cane. Never coat the underside with anything. Your seat should look as good as new.

driver, then check the depth of the groove. It must be $\frac{5}{16}$ to $\frac{3}{8}$ inches deep. If it's not deep enough, the new spline might not insert properly. If necessary, deepen the groove carefully with a router or a spline chisel. Allow the vinegar in the groove to dry thoroughly before proceeding.

4. ROUND OFF EDGES TO PREVENT CUTTING THE NEW CANE. Examine the inside edge of the chair frame, against which the new cane will be placed. If it has a sharp edge, round it off with a knife, a file, or coarse sandpaper. A sharp edge is often what causes cane to break out in the first place. Also round off the inside edge (not the outside edge) of the narrow groove to prevent cutting the new cane during installation.

5. CUT AND SOAK THE NEW CANE AND SPLINE. Measure the groove from side to side of the chair and add 2 inches. Then measure the groove from front to back of the chair and add 2 inches. Be sure to measure from the widest points. Cane comes in standard sizes, so you may have to buy a bit more than you need. For example, if the chair measures 15 inches, you may have to buy 18-inch cane. If possible, take pieces of your old cane and spline to the store with you or measure them very accurately.

Spline is sold in about a dozen sizes, in $\frac{1}{64}$-inch increments. It is imperative to use the correct size. If it's too small, it will pop out. If it's too big, it will not fit into the groove. If in doubt, take the chair to the store and try a piece of spline. It should fit into the groove snugly but not too tightly (like a pair of shoes). If you are ordering your spline through a mail-order supplier, buy a couple of sizes just to be sure that you get the right fit. It is usually fairly inexpensive.

Using a sharp utility knife or scissors, cut the length of cane and spline needed for the chair seat. If it has sharp corners, cut each section of spline individually. Cut the ends straight and do not miter the ends, as it is difficult to do it properly and very few chairs have perfect 90-degree corners. If the chair seat is round, oblong, triangular, or curvy, and the original spline was in one piece, cut a single piece of new spline that will be long enough to reach all the way around.

Soak the cane and the spline for at least 1 hour in warm water in the bathtub or a large pan so the cane is lying flat under water, but do not soak it longer than 4 hours or you will have to discard it and start over. Keep the spline in the water until needed. If any of the materials turn gray, it has soaked too long. Cut a fresh piece.

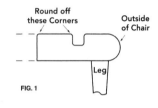

Round off
these Corners

Outside
of Chair

Leg

FIG. 1

6. INSERT THE NEW CANE. Set aside at least an hour to install the new cane panel. Minimize distractions so you can complete the job without stopping. Unless you are very sure of yourself, do only one chair at a time. Have a rag and a bucket of water handy, as well as a hammer, hardwood wedge and misting bottle. You must keep the cane wet during the installation so it doesn't shrink prematurely. Mist it with the spray bottle of water every few minutes.

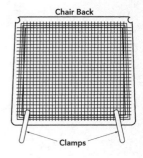

Chair Back

Clamps

Lay the new cane over the surface of the chair, centering it over the opening. Make sure the front of the cane is straight or symmetrical with the groove at the front. The front is the most critical, because that's what people see first. Using clamps, secure the cane in place at the two corners.

Using the wood wedge and starting at the back center, push the cane down into the groove, going from side to side and around the corners, working your way forward to the front middle. Keep checking to be sure the front edge is still straight. Do not force the cane all the way into the corners of the groove; the spline will do that later.

When you reach the front corners, remove the clamps and then resume pushing the cane down into the center of the groove, using the wood wedge. If necessary, tap the cane in with the hammer from side to side. If the pattern has become crooked, carefully pull the cane out and straighten it.

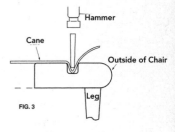

Hammer

Cane

Outside of Chair

Leg

FIG. 3

Remember to keep the cane damp at all times during the installation process by misting it or wiping it with a wet rag or sponge.

7. INSERT THE NEW SPLINE. Squirt a bead of glue into the groove, but don't overflow it. Push the spline in (narrow edge down) and gradually tap it down into the groove, with the hammer, but not all the way in, working your way around the chair. It's important not to hammer the spline in all the way, as we'll see in the next step. Keep a damp rag handy for glue cleanup. When you reach a joint (or corner), cut the ends off square, or cut them at a 45-degree angle, or "miter," as you prefer. It is merely a matter of personal preference. If the joint is at the back, such as in a round seat, repeat this step by cutting the spline so that the two ends meet in the middle of the back of the seat. You should have a tight fit. Wipe off the excess glue with a damp rag.

8. TRIM THE SPLINE. Now you will see why you didn't hammer the spline all the way in. Hold your knife at a 45-degree angle away from you and cut off the excess cane very carefully. Don't accidentally cut into the new seat.

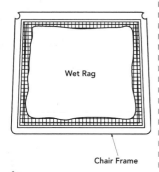

Wet Rag

Chair Frame

Quick Tip: To Finish or Not to Finish

It is usually recommended to leave cane natural (unfinished) so that it can be moistened later to keep it supple, if necessary. If you wish to stain the cane to match other chairs, test the stain on the scrap pieces that you cut off earlier. Gel stains work well on cane; they're less messy and adhere to cane better than thinner-bodied stains. Brush the stain on the underside of the cane first, and then brush the top surface. Once the stain is dry, it may need another coat or two of stain, as cane does not stain easily. You may want to topcoat it with lacquer or varnish to add shine, but only use a final finish on the shiny side of the cane. Leave the rough side unfinished so that it can "breathe" and be moistened periodically. Follow manufacturers' directions for drying time on both the stain and the finish.

Use the spline sticking up as a backdrop for the knife, but cut gently and with caution so it doesn't slip. You do not want to cut your newly installed cane or nip your other hand!

9. LEVEL THE SPLINE. After you have removed all the little bits of cane sticking out, invert the wood wedge on the spline and tap it with a hammer to knock the spline down to the bottom of the groove. This will tuck away all the little hairy pieces of cane around the edges. Wipe off any excess glue with a damp rag.

10. KEEP IT DAMP. Lay a damp rag (approximately 12 by 12 inches) on the cane so that its edges are about 1 inch inside the wood of the chair. Keep the cane damp by moistening it every hour or so, for at least 24 hours. This allows the glue under the spline to dry into the wood of the chair.

11. CHECK FOR FLAWS. Remove the rag and examine the cane for any minor flaws or "flags," which you can carefully cut away with a tiny fingernail or sewing scissors. Wait another 48 hours before using your chair. ■

Furniture Care Tips

It's important to care properly for your wood furniture, cabinets, and moldings. Here are a few tips of my own, plus some from DoItYourself.com, to help wood last longer.

▶ Excessive dampness, dryness, heat, or cold can damage wood furniture. Make sure that your furniture is kept in an appropriate place.

▶ You can give most pieces a rubdown with lemon oil or any other fine wood-feeding product. Products will often say "wood-feeding" or "moisturizing" on the label. First, coat the wood completely and allow the product to penetrate for about 30 minutes. Then, wipe the entire surface with a soft cotton rag (an old T-shirt works well), turning the rag frequently. The oil or other feeder will help protect your wood from fluctuating temperatures and humidity and prevent cracking and chipping, just as hand lotion does for our hands.

▶ Do not mix different types of polish; for instance, oil-based furniture polish can cause a wax finish to become gummy. Clean the furniture surface thoroughly before changing furniture care products.

▶ Treat your wood no more than 3 or 4 times a year unless it sustains heavy use. More than that can cause a buildup of polish. Always use a polish recommended for its particular kind of finish. Too much polish may create a cloudy film, so wipe off the polish before it dries completely.

▶ Wipe up water-based spills immediately to prevent spots that require refinishing.

▶ Vacuum wood surfaces with a dusting brush attachment to gently remove dust and prevent buildup. If you don't have a vacuum cleaner, use a clean soft cloth or soft paper towels to pick up dust. If the finish is water resistant, a barely dampened towel or cloth will do the trick. Use a soft-bristled paintbrush to remove dust from grooves. Dust furniture before vacuuming floors.

▶ Occasionally, vacuum upholstered furniture and window treatments. Dust can be a contributor to fabric erosion, as well as allergies and odors.

▶ Keeps a coaster handy to place under drinks. Use pads or mats under vases and potted plants to protect them from spills, stains, and heated objects. Do not use plastic or rubber on natural wood surfaces, because they may stick and damage finish. Use felt under objects to prevent scratches on furniture.

▶ Avoid placing wood items in sunny windows. Sunlight can damage fine wood finishes as well as fade your upholstery.

Quick Tip: Vintage Odors

Does your antique furniture smell musty? Mold spores are the culprits. Try this antique dealer's trick. Wear rubber gloves and old clothes and work in the garage or other safe area to avoid damaging surroundings. Mix a weak bleach solution of 1 teaspoon of bleach per gallon of water. Using an old paintbrush or poly brush, coat all of the unfinished wood surfaces (inside drawers and the underside and the back) with the solution, avoiding varnished areas. Let the piece dry out completely. Then coat all unfinished surfaces with thinned-down varnish or lacquer to seal in any remaining odor. If you're sensitive to bleach, try using 1 part lemon juice to 1 part water.

PROJECT: STRIP WOOD FURNITURE USING SAWDUST

Level of difficulty: T T T

Quick Tip:
Choosing the Right Stripper

Although most stripping chemicals can be used on a variety of surfaces, here are a few tips for selecting one over another. Of course, follow all manufacturers' recommendations and instructions.

▶ *Liquid and paste strippers:* Great for small projects in cool weather. Liquid stripper will evaporate quickly in warm weather, so you may end up wasting some of it. Paste strippers are ideal when vertical cling is needed or when covering a large surface area. Paste strippers will usually stay wet longer than liquids. The downside is that the paste is actually a wax (paraffin) that can sometimes leave a residue of its own.

▶ *Spray-on stripper:* If the furniture is painted or if total finish removal is necessary, spray-on strippers actually work very well and are similar to the formulas used by professional refinishing companies. They apply just like foaming bathtub cleaner.

→

Sometimes, the finish on wood furnishings must be stripped down to bare wood and new stain and finish applied. The project can be messy and time-consuming, but it can also save hundreds of dollars over having it professionally done. Over my many years of refinishing wood, I have found a technique that makes the job much easier—using something that's normally thrown away.

If you or someone you know enjoys woodworking, be sure to save the sawdust. It's quite handy when you're stripping the paint or varnish off old furniture or cabinets. Sprinkling sawdust on top of the stripping chemical keeps it wet longer, allowing it to work better. Then you can use the sawdust for sanding. Here's how to do it.

You will need:
- ✓ Drop cloth and/or newspapers
- ✓ Work apron or old clothes
- ✓ Rubber gloves
- ✓ Eye protection
- ✓ Stripping chemical
- ✓ Old paintbrush for applying stripper
- ✓ Lots of sawdust
- ✓ Chemical-resistant plastic scraper or metal scraper
- ✓ Small brass or plastic brush
- ✓ Paint thinner or denatured alcohol
- ✓ Fine steel wool
- ✓ Rags or paper towels

1. PREPARE THE AREA. Work in a well-ventilated area, away from open flame. Prepare the work area with a drop cloth and old newspapers to absorb the mess. Wear old clothes, rubber gloves, and eye protection to shield yourself from splatters.

2. APPLY THE STRIPPER AND SAWDUST. Using an old paintbrush, coat the furniture with paint stripper and then cover it with about a ½-inch-thick layer of sawdust while the stripper is still wet. You may need to work on horizontal surfaces so that the sawdust will stick, then turn the piece to work on other surfaces, as needed.

3. WAIT AND CHECK. Let it sit for 15 to 30 minutes, and then test a small area with a scraper. If the paint comes off easily, move to the next step. If not, wait a bit longer, dabbing dried areas with more stripper, if necessary.

4. SAND WITH SAWDUST. Grab a handful of sawdust and gradually sand the entire piece of furniture with sawdust until all the paint is removed. You may need to repeat the process several times. If necessary, use a scraper to help remove paint or varnish from stubborn areas.

5. FINE-TUNE. If paint or stain is imbedded in the grain, the carvings, or the moldings, use a brass or plastic brush and firm pressure to help remove it. Always work in the direction of the woodgrain. Never use a brush across the grain, as it will leave fine scratches that will be hard to remove.

6. RINSE. Wipe down the entire surface using fine steel wool soaked with paint thinner or denatured alcohol. If you still have stubborn residue in the grain, try soaking the brass brush with your rinse medium to aid removal. If the area has dried, simply apply more stripper and start the process over.

7. DRY. Dry the wood with more sawdust, paper towels, or old rags. When you are done, dispose of these materials properly, following the stripping-chemical manufacturer's directions. They can sometimes self-combust if disposed of improperly. ■

Just watch out for overspray, so you don't strip something unintentionally or burn your skin.

▶ *Refinisher:* If the piece is not painted, products such as Formby's Conditioning Furniture Refinisher are often easier to use than strippers and more gentle on the patina of antiques, but they do not always work. Purchase a small can first to see if the old finish responds to a refinisher. If it does, you might also buy a can of denatured alcohol and try it on the old finish. Often, the alcohol is enough to clean off old dirt and grime so that a new finish can be applied. Denatured alcohol also works well as a rinse after the refinisher or stripper is used.

Quick Tip:
No Water on Wood

I do not recommend using water as a rinse on wood furniture, even when the stripping-chemical manufacturer recommends it. Water tends to raise the woodgrain and can actually cause veneers and glued-on moldings and trim to separate. Always use paint thinner, denatured alcohol, or lacquer thinner. These products evaporate quickly and will not raise the grain.

Quick Tip:
Removing Stains from Wood

To remove discoloration from stripped wood furniture, such as a water ring or other defect, check to see if your drugstore carries oxylic acid. It is usually sold in a powder form that you mix with water. First, work in the garage or other safe area to avoid damaging surroundings. Wear rubber gloves and old clothes. Soak the entire furniture panel (not just the stain) with a weak solution to begin with (1 teaspoon of crystals/powder per 1 cup of warm water). It may take a couple of applications. Rinse the area with water and let it dry overnight. Since sanding will release the acidic dust, wear a particulate mask while you sand the entire top surface with fine sandpaper, working in the direction of the grain. Then proceed with stain and final finish. You can achieve similar results with a weak bleach solution, but bleach tends to raise the woodgrain and may damage your wood.

If you have a piece of wood furniture that has a dirty, scratched, or worn finish, don't immediately assume that it will need complete stripping and refinishing. Older pieces can often be refurbished using special wood-cleaning products that have been formulated to remove residue and blend in old varnish or lacquer. This is especially important when restoring antiques, because stripping and refinishing will damage their value.

Products such as Briwax or Howard's Restor-A-Finish can usually revitalize worn or cracked surfaces with minimal work. Briwax is a thick paste that has good cling, so you can use it on vertical surfaces. It contains beeswax and carnauba wax, along with a strong solvent that dissolves old, cracked wood finishes, moisturizes dry woodgrain, and leaves a thin wax coating for protection. It comes in several colors to help blend in scratches and worn areas.

Briwax is also a lifesaver for removing paint splatter, crayon, permanent marker, stickers, and other residues from wood. As with all products, you should test Briwax on an inconspicuous area to be sure it is color safe and does not remove more of the finish than you desire. Other good formulas for removing splatter and sticky residue are Un-Du, Goo Gone, and Goof Off.

Howard's Restor-A-Finish is a thin liquid, so it works well to refurbish large areas. It is also offered in a variety of tints to help blend in surface imperfections. A word of warning about Restor-A-Finish: Apply it to a rag or other applicator first. Do not apply it directly to the furniture, because it can discolor a finish if it is not applied evenly. Follow the manufacturer's directions and heed any warnings carefully. ◼

PROJECT: **APPLY WOOD STAIN AND VARNISHES**

Level of difficulty: T T T

When coating a new or stripped piece of wood furniture, it's important to choose the correct stain and finish and then apply them properly. The most popular finishes for home use are traditional oil-based stains and varnishes, but there are many other options on the market. Most people still opt for a traditional two-step stain and finish process, which allows you to control each step independently; for instance, adding additional coats of stain to darken a finish or extra coats of varnish to deepen the gloss. Many products combine both the stain and the final finish, which makes the whole process easier, although you lose some control over the final results, because these products are usually only offered in limited color choices, plus you build up color with each coat.

Remember, the same stain will react differently on different varieties of wood. Softwoods, such as pine and poplar, will soak up stain like a sponge, while harder varieties, such as oak or maple, will absorb much less color. If you have a scrap of your wood, take it to the store with you. Most paint and hardware stores and even home centers allow you to try a color before you buy it.

Also, it is easier to create a professional-looking finish with satin rather than glossy finishes. Satin helps to hide flaws and imperfections, and it is especially nice to use on antiques for a more authentic look and feel. Gloss is harder to work with and can leave a "plastic" appearance—a dead give-away that it was a do-it-yourself project.

Here are some popular options for stains and finishes.

Stains

▶ *Gel stains:* These are heavy-bodied stains that have the advantage of being able to cling to vertical surfaces. They are also recommended for blending in blotchy or discolored wood. Sometimes, gels can create a bit of a "painted" look that may obscure the natural beauty of fine woodgrain. Most gel stains are water based, which makes cleanup easy. Typical drying time: 2 to 4 hours.

▶ *Oil stains:* These are the most popular option for fine furniture and cabinetry. They are designed to highlight wood's natural grain and character. Typical drying time: about 24 hours.

▶ *Water-based stains:* Many new water-based stains apply like traditional oil-based products. They are great for beginners because they dry quickly and offer easier clean up; however, they do not produce results that appear as professional as oil-based products. Typical drying time: about 2 hours.

▶ *Aniline dye stains:* These are often used by professional wood finishers and are supplied in a powder form that can be mixed with water, alcohol, or finishing oil to create exceptionally vivid tints on fine woods. Aniline dyes can also be blended with wax for a hand-rubbed shine. Note: Ask for aniline dye at your local hardware or paint supply store. Typical drying time: 24 hours or less.

▶ *Combo stains and finishes:* These are easy-to-use combination products that are a mixture of stain and some type of finish, usually either a varnish or an oil finish. Typical drying time: 24 hours or less.

Finishes

▶ *Varnishes:* These are a popular choice for most projects. Watch for the term polyurethane varnish when water resistance is needed, such as on floors and dining tables. Conventional varnishes have always been petroleum based; however, some polyurethane finishes are also offered in water-based versions that dry very quickly. All come in your choice of satin or gloss. Typical drying time: 4 to 24 hours.

▶ *Oil finishes:* These are usually made of tung oil or linseed oil in a hand-rubbed and easy-to-use base. Some brands also contain tints and are a great option for beginners because they can be applied in one step and are hard to mess up. Typical drying time: 12 to 24 hours.

▶ *Lacquer:* This is the professional choice for most cabinetry and furniture because it dries quickly and can be applied in multiple coats for a "mile-deep" appearance. Exercise caution when using lacquer on refinished furniture, because it can react badly to trace residues left from the stripping process—so make sure to rinse off any stripping chemicals thoroughly. Lacquer is available in gloss and satin. Typical drying time: 2 to 4 hours.

► **Wax:** Wax has been popular for centuries because it is easy to apply, dries quickly, and is almost foolproof. Many wax products are available in assorted tints so that you can stain and finish in one step. The disadvantage is that no other finish can be applied once wax is on the surface. You will have to completely strip and refinish the piece if you ever want to change its appearance. Typical drying time: less than 1 hour.

Once you've chosen your finish, it's time to apply it. Here we go!

You will need:
- ✓ Work apron or old clothes
- ✓ Disposable or rubber gloves
- ✓ Newspaper or drop cloth
- ✓ Sandpaper (medium, fine, and superfine)
- ✓ Sanding block and/or electric sander
- ✓ Tack cloth
- ✓ Vacuum cleaner
- ✓ Stain of your choice
- ✓ Poly brushes for stain
- ✓ Cotton rags or paper towels
- ✓ Final finish of your choice
- ✓ Good bristle brushes (for varnish)
- ✓ Steel wool
- ✓ Wood filler (if necessary)

1. PREP THE SURFACE. Before you begin, don't forget to spread drop cloths to protect the surrounding area and to change into old clothes that can get messy. Then using a sanding block and/or an electric sander, sand the raw wood with medium sandpaper and then follow up with fine and superfine sandpaper until all sanding lines are smoothed away and no longer visible. Always work in the direction of the grain. If you have applied wood filler, sand it until all excess is removed.

2. REMOVE ALL DUST. Vacuum the wood, the work area, and even your clothes, then use a tack cloth to pick up all remaining dust. Dust is an enemy to a good final finish.

Caution:
Flammable

Most finishing products are highly flammable, so take all necessary precautions. Keep all finishing processes away from open flame or heat sources. Also, allow rags to dry out completely after use and do not store them in a bag. Hang them or lay them flat. Rags soaked in flammable substances can self-combust, even after they are dry.

If you have a chip or a ding in a piece of furniture, the problem may be that the wood finish or the varnish has been damaged, rather than the actual wood itself. Clear fingernail polish can sometimes be used to hide tiny defects. If the damage is larger and you don't want to refinish the entire piece, wood filler can often do the trick. Famowood and similar products come in several colors to match existing finishes. Famowood stays soft so that it molds to fit a chipped area. Wax fillers, another option, are melted with heat so they fill an area and form a permanent bond. After you are finished, choose a good-quality, tinted furniture polish to help even out the repaired areas.

3. STIR IT UP! Make sure to stir the stain thoroughly before you apply it. It is important to mix all pigments and solids into the stain base to achieve an even coat. Do not shake stain unless the manufacturer recommends it.

4. APPLY STAIN. Brush on the stain in the direction of the woodgrain and use a cotton rag to wipe off any excess. If a second coat of stain is desired, follow manufacturer's directions. Many stains must completely dry between coats, which usually takes 24 hours. Allow the final coat of stain to dry overnight before applying the finish.

5. GET READY TO VARNISH. Use a tack rag again to rub down all surfaces before varnishing.

6. STIR AGAIN. Stir your varnish completely. Do not shake it, because this can create bubbles in the finish.

7. APPLY FINISH. Using good bristle brushes, brush the finish on across the grain and then quickly rebrush it in the direction of the grain. This assures that all grain is filled with the coating.

8. BE PATIENT. Follow the varnish manufacturer's directions, but generally allow each coat to dry overnight. Do not try to rush the drying process with fans, because this can stir up dust that will necessitate sanding and finishing again.

9. APPLY A SECOND COAT. If more than one coat is needed, lightly buff the previous coat with superfine steel wool, then rub down all surfaces again with a tack rag, and then apply the next coat. ■

Wood Floor Care Tips

You and your hardwood floor will shine when you use the right care to keep it looking like new. Here are some sensible do's and don'ts from the experts at BonaKemi.

▶ Do remember that cleaning your wood floors with vinegar and water, oil soap, furniture polish, or window cleaner may ruin your costly investment. While these cleaners may work well on some surfaces, hardwood floors are not one of them.

▶ Don't wet-mop your wood floors with water-based products, which can cause wood to expand, possibly permanently damaging the floor in addition to dulling the finish. Other cleaners that have silicone, wax, or oil soaps can leave a residue on the finish that will adversely affect the adhesion of a new coat of finish, requiring a complete sanding and finishing of your floors to remove it.

▶ Do use cleaners that won't leave any residue, especially if you have polyurethane-finished hardwood floors. These will allow you to periodically "pad and recoat" your floors, which means to add a new coat of finish; this dramatically conserves time and money and keeps your floors looking like new.

▶ Do take preventive care of your hardwood floors to keep them looking like new. Simple activities such as regular vacuuming and sweeping, promptly removing spills, placing mats at exterior doors to keep out sand and grit, and using protective pads or caps on furniture feet can all help to keep your hardwood floors fresh. Also, avoid walking on your floors with high-heeled shoes and keep your pets' nails trimmed.

Andrea's Choice: Better Floor Care

Hardwood floor refinishing has traditionally been a dusty and inconvenient process. However, newer products and services, such as BonaKemi's Environmental Choice System, include Swedish waterborne finishes without the toxic fumes and sanding systems that eliminate dust. The BonaKemi system is certified by the GREENGUARD Environmental Institute for indoor air quality. To learn more about caring for your floor, visit www.bonakemi. com.

7

our utility bill
is how much?!

Easy Energy-Saving Ideas

It's money. I remember it from when I was single.
—BILLY CRYSTAL

Whether we're fighting the dog days of summer or winter's frosty grip, many of us break into a sweat when we see how much it costs to heat, cool, and light up our homes each month. This chapter is packed with ways to make your home more energy efficient and avoid skyrocketing utility bills.

According to the U.S. Department of Energy (DOE), the average American family living in a single-family home spends close to $2,000 a year on utility bills. If you live in the Sunbelt or a cold zone, your bills are probably even higher. Now is the time to plug into these great energy-saving ideas and projects for increasing the comfort of your home while saving some cold cash and the environment, too.

▶ Project: Eliminating Energy Wasters

▶ Caulking Techniques

▶ Weather-stripping Basics and Tips

▶ Appliance Energy Solutions

- Water: A Precious Commodity
- Project: Tip-top Tips
- Project: Installing Window-Tinting Film
- Project: Choosing and Installing a Ceiling Fan

It's a long weekend, and you're wondering what you can do to fill the time. Why not have a little home energy audit and then make some changes around your castle to make it more energy wise? Many of the following ideas are free or very inexpensive and can begin paying you back immediately. This is a great project to do with the whole family. Even young children can help!

You will need:
- ✓ Notepad and pencil
- ✓ Partner
- ✓ Candle and/or matches
- ✓ Flashlight
- ✓ Vacuum or cleaning brush (for outdoor air-conditioning units)
- ✓ Other supplies may be needed, such as caulk or weather stripping, if leaks are found

1. BECOME A LEAK DETECTIVE. The exterior of your house, a combination of walls, windows, insulation, doors, ceilings, and floors, creates a seal or "envelope" that regulates airflow into and out of a house. A good seal keeps drafts to a minimum. Once you discover the places where air is moving into and out of the house, you can begin the sealing process.

▶ Start by examining the outside walls to identify cracks or holes where air might escape and make notes of all spots that will need caulk, siding repair, or other attention. You may need to trim back shrubs or other obstacles to get a good view of hidden areas.

▶ Pay close attention to where brick or siding fits against another material, such as wood.

▶ Check outlets and switches on exterior walls or house-to-garage walls for drafts and repair. Consider installing special foam inserts into them to provide added insulation. Just be sure to shut off the power while working around any electrical outlets.

▶ Note any holes where plumbing, ductwork, or electrical wiring enter your exterior walls, floors, or ceilings that need to be sealed with caulk or expanding foam.

▶ Make note of any drafty windows and exterior doors. Also look for cracks and holes around attic fans and window unit air conditioners. Air ducts, attics, and basements are areas where air commonly comes into the house. While these drafts seem small individually, they can add up to the same energy loss that results from an open window.

Here are two easy ways to determine if there's a leak with the help of a friend or family member.

1. *Candle method:* Hold a lit candle near the edges of each door or window and run a hair dryer on the other side toward the flame. If the flame flickers or goes out, you have a leak.

2. *Flashlight method:* Have one person shine a flashlight along the edges of doors and windows, looking for potential gaps. If the second person can see the light, it's time to get caulking.

2. LOSE THOSE LEAKS. Once you've discovered as many leaks as possible, now it's time to seal them up. Many of the following suggestions are covered in more depth later in this chapter.

▶ Caulk or use an expanding foam sealant on any exterior leaks. Make sure to caulk around windows and doors. You may even need to remove door and window casings to adequately seal all leaks. Pay a few extra dollars to buy the best caulk that you can find. Make sure that it is labeled for your use—for example, "Exterior" or "Brick and Siding." See more tips on caulk later in the chapter.

▶ Weather-strip doors and, if necessary, add a door sweep to help keep air infiltration to a minimum. Also, don't forget to weather-strip around attic doorways as well, using stick-on foam if they are inside the heated and cooled part of your house. If a door opens into the garage, you don't need to worry about sealing it. You can check your local yellow pages for professional weather-strip installers. They are usually fairly inexpensive. However, this is a project you can definitely tackle yourself. I will cover weather stripping in more detail later in this chapter.

▶ Cover exterior vents on your home during winter months. Covers are available at most hardware stores and home centers. Just be sure to remove them in warmer months.

▶ If you have window air-conditioning units, cover them in the cooler months to prevent cold air from entering the house and warm air from escaping.

▶ Make sure the fireplace damper is closed when not in use and consider an inflatable fireplace plug to help control heat loss.

3. BE WINDOW WISE. Old-style single-pane windows can account for major heating and cooling costs. If you can afford to replace them, you can often pay for new windows fairly quickly in energy dollars saved. The energy lost through windows can account for as much as 10 to 25 percent of a home's cooling bill. During the summer, sunlight streaming through windows can make your air conditioner work two to three times harder, which also costs money. According to the U.S. Department of Energy, new windows that meet the ENERGY STAR rating are twice as energy efficient as the average windows produced just 10 years ago. ENERGY STAR–labeled windows can be 35 percent more energy efficient than common double-pane windows.

Choose windows with dual panes and low-emissivity (Low-E) coatings to reduce heat loss and argon blend-filled glass for maximum energy efficiency. Also, spectrally selective coatings can reduce heat gain. Look for the NFRC (National Fenestration Rating Council) label on windows. This label provides easy-to-understand numbers that represent a window's energy efficiency in terms of its U-Value factor (insulating ability) and solar heat gain coefficient (SHGC). For both, look for the lowest number possible.

Vinyl-coated wood windows are particularly efficient and have the added bonus of requiring little or no maintenance. A typical home can save hundreds of dollars per year in heating and cooling costs by simply switching to energy-efficient wood windows in place of single-pane aluminum windows. To calculate your home's energy efficiency and potential savings, go to the Efficient Windows Collaborative Web site at www.efficientwindows.org.

If you cannot afford new windows, you can help keep your old ones from leaking by making sure that they are well caulked and weather-stripped. If your windows are historic and you do not want to replace them, it's especially important to caulk them completely. Check your local hardware store for removable caulk, which allows you to virtually seal your windows closed, yet permit you to peel the caulk off when you want to open the windows, such as in the spring or the fall. Self-adhesive weather stripping can also be used to create a seal if you are going to be opening and closing the windows often.

Also consider easy-to-install, clear-plastic window covers. For outside weatherproofing, simply nail or tack the cover over the window. For indoor weatherproofing, simply tape down the edges. Then blow a hair dryer over the plastic to shrink it and seal it tightly over the window. Check your local hardware store for supplies.

One last idea, for newer or older windows, is to install window-tinting film. This easy project is covered later in this chapter.

4. PLANT A TREE AND SAVE THE WORLD. Trees, vines, and other shrubs around a house can provide shade that will keep the home cooler and reduce your overall utility bills. A well-placed tree can offer shade and act as a windbreak for your home; plus, they add to your property value and help to clean the air for all of us. Plant trees close enough to offer some shade to your home, but not so close that root growth can damage the foundation. An easy rule is to place the tree the same distance from the house as it will be in height when it is mature. If your lot is too small for that, plant the tree at least 10 feet from the home and then water the roots regularly on the far side of the tree, which will encourage them to grow away from the house.

5. SHED SOME LIGHT ON IT—OR MAYBE NOT. During the summer, keep blinds and drapes closed to prevent sunlight from warming the house, especially on south- and west-facing windows, where you might also consider awnings. During the winter, keep those same blinds and drapes open during the day to allow sunlight to enter and heat the home. Just be mindful of furniture and carpets that might be damaged by frequent sun exposure.

Solar window screens can also stop an amazing amount of radiant heat from entering your home. Some products claim up to 90 percent efficiency.

6. HAVE ANOTHER BRIGHT IDEA OR TWO. Energy for lighting accounts for about 10 percent of your electric bill. Take stock of your home's lighting needs and replace short-lived incandescent lightbulbs throughout the home with lower-wattage and fluorescent bulbs, high-pressure sodium fixtures, or new LED lights that are even more efficient. In fact, by replacing 25 percent of lights in high-use areas with energy-efficient bulbs, you can save about 50 percent or more on lighting-related energy expenses. These newer bulbs also last six to ten times longer than regular lamps, so they don't need to be changed nearly as often.

Did you know that dimmers also save energy? When you dim a light, it reduces the amount of electricity that the bulb requires. Also consider motion sensors and timers that operate lights only when needed, inside and out. Another idea is to determine if there are areas where natural light can be utilized in place of extra light fixtures. And one last tip on lighting . . . Instead of running costly wires to outbuildings or less frequently used areas such as gates and barns, install solar-powered lights. Not only do they save energy, but since solar lights do not need to connect to your home's electrical system, you can also eliminate wiring hassle and expense.

7. COOL TO BE KIND. Heating and cooling your home can account for more than 40 percent of the average home's utility bill and is typically the largest energy expense. To keep your home's heating, ventilating, and air-conditioning (HVAC) system running at peak efficiency, have it checked out by a certified heating and air-conditioning technician at least every couple of years. If you have an oil-burning system, have it done yearly. Just like a car's engine, an HVAC system that is out of tune can waste energy.

One of the main jobs for your HVAC pro is to clean the indoor and outdoor coils of your air conditioner. The indoor coil is the part of your air conditioner that removes heat from your house, and the outdoor coil is the part that ejects the heat outside. Just $\frac{1}{100}$ inch of dirt on the coil can reduce your system's efficiency by 5 percent. If you have not had your coils cleaned in a while, it would be a good idea to do so. You should have the indoor blower fan checked as well.

If your HVAC system is more than 10 years old, it may actually be less expensive to replace it with higher-efficiency equipment than to nurse along an old system. To cut down on climate control costs, consider replacing older, less-efficient furnaces or air conditioners with new, state-of-the-art equipment that surpasses minimum government standards for energy efficiency. If you think you may need a new heating and cooling

Quick Tip:
A Job for the Pros

Your heating and cooling technician can also examine for leaks in ductwork and make sure that the airflow is balanced properly throughout the house. He or she can also check for drafts by using special diagnostic tools that pressurize the house and detect leaks. The air pressure will be higher outside than inside the house, causing air to rush in through unsealed cracks and openings. A smoke pencil or an incense stick will often be used to help detect the source of air leaks.

system, set up an appointment with a reputable, licensed heating and air-conditioning company to inspect your home's unit.

If the equipment needs to be replaced, choose an ENERGY STAR–labeled system, which will be more efficient and can save hundreds of dollars in utility costs per year. In particular, be sure to look for a SEER (Seasonal Energy Efficiency Ratio) rating as high as you can afford on air-conditioning units and an AFUE (annual fuel utilization efficiency) rating of at least 90 on furnaces. Although the government minimum is 13 SEER, you can save up to hundreds of dollars per season on utility costs with higher-efficiency units. Some companies offer SEER ratings over 20 that can be nearly twice as efficient as systems that were available just a few years ago. Check out the Air Conditioning Contractors of America Web site at www.acca.org/consumer for more tips on choosing a new HVAC system.

8. CHECK VENTILATION. Between professional HVAC tune-ups, spend some of your own time making sure that your HVAC system is running at peak efficiency. What does changing your filter have to do with air-conditioning? Everything! Proper air movement is critical for your system to operate at optimum efficiency. A dirty air filter drastically reduces the air moving through your conditioning system, so check your filter monthly and change it regularly, especially if you have pets.

Also, your home's HVAC system was designed for a certain amount of airflow. Make sure that indoor registers and return air vents are not blocked by furnishings and rugs. And be aware that blowing air can also damage some items by either drying them out from heated air or adding moisture from air-conditioned air.

Outdoors, remove any foliage that is within 3 feet of the outdoor air-conditioning unit to allow the system to take in adequate outside air and operate efficiently. Use a Shop-Vac and an old paintbrush to remove pet hair, leaves, and other blockages. Make sure to turn off the unit before cleaning it to avoid static electricity. Rub your paintbrush with a dryer sheet to reduce static as well.

9. CHANGE YOUR THERMOSTAT. Your thermostat is used to control most central heating and cooling systems. If your home has an outdated, conventional model that you must regulate manually, consider installing a programmable thermostat that allows the climate control system to run only at certain times of the day, saving energy when you and your family are away or sleeping. It's one of the best investments that you can make to increase your home's energy efficiency—and a great Saturday afternoon project. See complete details later in this chapter.

10. LOOK TOWARD THE FUTURE. If you follow all of the advice in this chapter but your energy bills still seem unusually high, you might want to invest in some major home improvements. When deciding whether to spend money to save money, you should consider the value of potential government incentives, the actual amount of energy savings that will be reflected on your utility bill, and the improved home comfort and increased resale value of your home.

One nice thing is that energy-saving products, particularly in the solar (photovoltaic) and wind-driven (windmill) arenas, are becoming more affordable as well as more efficient every day. If you are remodeling or if you are considering building a new home, research all of the new technologies on the market as much as possible. With the rising costs of fuel, many products can pay for themselves in just a short time. ■

Caulking Techniques

Caulk is a puttylike substance, most often made from silicone or latex. Caulks are available for a variety of needs, ranging from concrete repair to simple weatherproofing. Caulk is used to fill and seal all kinds of small gaps or cracks in brick, wood, drywall, and other construction materials. These gaps can allow heated or cooled air to escape (thus raising utility bills), moisture or insects to enter a home, or more serious damage to occur if not corrected. Caulking can be messy, so wear old clothes and spread a drop cloth if necessary.

Choosing the Right Caulk

Have you ever used caulk in an area where it just doesn't seem to last? You might be using the wrong product for that particular application. In other words, only use interior caulk inside the home and exterior

Quick Tip: Your Tax Dollars at Work

While there are many ways to make your home more energy efficient, the U.S. government periodically offers tax incentives for select energy-saving home improvements. Incentives are normally around 10 percent of the total cost of the improvement, with a maximum per home. ENERGY STAR–rated exterior doors, windows, metal roofing, water heaters, insulation, heating, air-conditioning, and even new cars have qualified for tax credits during recent years. Tax credits have also been available for qualified solar water heating and photovoltaic systems. Check out www.energystar.gov to see if your home might qualify.

caulk outdoors. Buy the best grade available to help the seal last longer. Choose waterproof products with fungicides in bathrooms and basements. Read those manufacturers' labels. They know their products better than anyone. Here are some other basics guidelines to help you choose the right caulk.

▶ Use exterior caulk for filling in the line between a window and the molding around it, as well as gaps where different outdoor surfaces meet, such as where the foundation meets siding or a sidewalk.

▶ Use interior caulk for preventing moisture from getting into cracks between walls, bathtubs, countertops, and sinks, as well as filling in joints where different surfaces meet, such as ceramic tile and baseboard.

▶ Silicone-based caulk will stick to almost anything, but it cannot be painted. It must be cleaned up with a solvent that can be messy.

▶ Any hole 1 inch or smaller can be sealed with a high-quality acrylic latex caulk, which can be painted. Latex-based caulk is easy to apply and cleans up with soap and water.

▶ Like standard caulks, foam sealants can be used in a variety of locations, including the attic and the basement. It is great for filling larger gaps around doors, windows, and siding, but it is not recommended for use around heat sources, such as chimneys and wood-burning stoves. Foam is available in polyurethane-based or latex-based formulas. Latex has the advantage of cleaning up with soap and water.

▶ Concrete or masonry caulk is ideal for concrete and masonry surfaces. These sandy formulas simulate the look of mortar or mixed concrete. They can help to repair air leaks as well as fix minor cosmetic cracks.

▶ Caulk is normally sold in two types of containers: cylinders and squeeze tubes. Cylinders require the use of a caulk gun, while squeeze tubes can be applied directly to a project surface. Some new caulks come in handy dispenser packs with built-in triggers.

▶ Many types of caulk come in colors to match the surface color. Some can even be matched to your paint color.

▶ Caulk can only fill in spaces about ½-inch deep, so large holes or voids must be filled in with some other material first. Rope caulk or foam fillers can be used on doors and windows to create a buffer between the frame and the wall. They work well in unusually shaped gaps and can be made to fit in any enclosed area. These products come in coils and are measured to fit, then stuffed in the gap to seal it. Fiberglass insulation can also be used to fill larger gaps; the caulk can then be applied on the surface as a sealant.

Using a Caulk Gun

Use a cutting tool to snip off the end of a new tube of caulk. Insert a thin metal rod or long nail inside the spout to puncture the seal. Put the cylinder of caulk in the caulk gun and use the trigger to pump a thin "bead" of the product onto the surface of the project where desired. Applying caulk in this way is called "laying a bead." When the bead is in place, turn the L-shaped ratchet on the end of the caulk gun to stop the flow of material. Then use a damp rag to smooth out the surface of the caulk so that it will bond it to the project. Allow the area to dry before using.

Weather-stripping Basics and Tips

Weather stripping is a thin strip of insulating material, such as foam, rubber, or metal, that seals the area between the fixed and movable parts of a door or window and prevents air from leaking into or out of a closed environment. All operable windows and exterior doors, as well as doors leading to an attic or garage, should be weatherized.

Weather stripping comes in many forms and prices. The least expensive is an adhesive-backed foam that is best used for areas that aren't exposed to the elements, as it will degrade over time. Vinyl is

Andrea's Choice:
Caulk Talk

Sealants have changed over the years and are much better today than just a decade ago. Check out DAP's DYNAFLEX 230, an elastomeric latex sealant. It is perfect for sealing smaller gaps, cracks, and holes and comes with a 50-year durability guarantee. GE also makes a full line of caulks and sealants. Both companies spend countless dollars on research and development each year to create products that last longer and work better than just a few years ago.

more expensive than felt and foam, but is more durable. Metals such as bronze, copper, stainless steel, and aluminum are also popular weather stripping materials. Metal weather stripping tends to be low cost and durable and is often combined with other insulates, especially vinyl and rubber, which are moisture resistant.

You can install weather stripping yourself fairly easily with kits that are available at your local home improvement or hardware store. Here are some helpful tips.

▶ Metal weather stripping is not affected by moisture or temperature, is durable, and is best used in high-traffic areas, such as external doors. Make sure that bronze strips are tacked down with the flare positioned in the opposite direction from the way the door opens so that the door closes over it easily.

▶ Vinyl V-seal weather stripping has an adhesive back, requiring no extra tools or tacking. Measure the area to be sealed and cut the strips to size with normal household scissors. V-strips are best used in lower-traffic doors and windows and may have to be replaced every two to three years, depending on wear and tear.

▶ Much like the vinyl strip, foam weather stripping has a self-adhesive backing and is cut to measure with household scissors. It is, however, much less durable than vinyl and will not stand up to exposure to the elements. Use foam strips on doors and windows that aren't used very often. If possible, position the weather stripping where it won't get wet. While foam stripping is very inexpensive, it doesn't last as long as other types of weather stripping, so it may have to be replaced much more often, canceling out the savings on the original purchase.

▶ Thresholds are included in types of weather stripping. There are several kinds of thresholds: door sweeps, door shoes, vinyl gaskets, interlocking metal, and rubber garage door seals that affix to the bottom of the garage door. Door sweeps and shoes are mounted to the door itself, whereas vinyl and interlocking metal thresholds are attached to the floor beneath the door.

Appliance Energy Solutions

The appliances in our homes can use close to a fourth of our total energy costs. Keeping your appliances in good working order and cleaning all vents and air intakes can help reduce costs. Replacing older units with more energy-efficient models can save 40 percent or more. Household appliances are responsible for about 25 percent of a home's energy bill. When shopping for new appliances, it is important to watch for the ENERGY STAR label. It's also important to take design into consideration. For example, refrigerators with freezers on top use 10 to 15 percent less energy than side-by-side models. And doing a single large load of laundry in a large-capacity washer may consume less energy than multiple loads in a smaller washer. When shopping for a dryer, look for one that features a moisture sensor that automatically shuts off the machine when the clothes are dry.

If you don't want to buy new, follow these suggestions to ensure that you're getting the most out of your current appliances while paying less on your electric bill.

Clean Appliances

Make sure appliances are clean and free of dust and lint to ensure proper ventilation and to increase their efficiency. Defrost your freezer if ice buildup becomes thicker than ½ inch to increase cooling efficiency. In addition, make sure refrigerator and freezer doors are sealed tight to prevent cool air from escaping. Replace rubber gaskets around the door if they are worn and are allowing cold air to escape.

Consider a New Fridge

Your refrigerator probably uses more electricity than any other appliance in your home. If it's over ten years old, it may be time to go shopping for a new one. Newer ENERGY STAR–labeled models may use less than half of the energy of your old unit.

Use the Air-Dry Setting

When washing dishes, use the air-dry setting on automatic dishwashers rather than heated drying, or just open the dishwasher and allow dishes to dry naturally. Consider replacing older appliances with ENERGY STAR–labeled models that use less energy and save dollars.

Laundry Tips

Up to 90 percent of the cost of washing a load of laundry goes toward heating the water. Try washing clothes on the cold-water setting with a warm rinse. Reserve hot water for sheets, blankets, baby clothes, and towels to kill germs and dust mites. Always wash full loads or adjust the water level down for smaller loads. If replacing your washer, choose a front-loading, ENERGY STAR–labeled machine, which can use up to 40 percent less water and 50 percent less energy, plus can clean more effectively with less wear and tear on your clothes.

Encourage your family members to wear shirts and other garments twice before washing them. Do you really have to change your sheets each week? Try waiting two weeks or even a month between washings. Make sure everyone uses the same towel for a full week. Many families wash a load of towels every day. It's a terrible energy waster.

Adjust and Wrap Your Water Heater

Heating water alone accounts for approximately 17 percent of a household's energy bill, so it's a good idea to lower the temperature setting on the water heater to save energy. Also consider insulating it with a water heater wrapping or "jacket" that can be purchased at most hardware stores. It's a quick-and-easy project that can save you dollars right away. Also, turn the thermostat down a bit. Many water heaters have factory settings of 140 degrees or higher, but 115 degrees can provide comfortable hot water for most household uses.

It is recommended to replace your water heater if it is more than ten years old with an ENERGY STAR–rated unit. New technologies are emerging that have revolutionized water heating. Point-of-use or "tank-less" water heaters can be up to 30 percent more efficient and do not have the leakage problems that tank-style units can have. These are naturally more efficient because they heat the water instantly when it's needed. They also use less room, so they can be tucked into a smaller space in new construction or remodels. I have one in my own home. They are also much more efficient for heating a swimming pool or hot tub than conventional heaters.

Also, solar water-heating systems are becoming more popular each year. They usually cost more to purchase and install than conventional water-heating systems. However, a solar water heater can often save you money in the long run, especially if your family uses a lot of hot water. According to the U.S. Department of Energy, if you install a solar water heater, your water-heating bills should drop 50 percent to 80 percent, on average. Also, because the sun is free, you're protected from future fuel shortages and price hikes.

If you are building a new home or refinancing, the economics of energy-saving products can be even more attractive. Including the price of a solar water heater in a new thirty-year mortgage usually amounts to between $13 and $20 per month. Recent federal income tax deductions for mortgage interest attributable to the solar system might reduce that by about $3 to $5 per month. So if your fuel savings are more than $15 per month, the solar investment is immediately profitable. On a monthly basis, you're saving more than you're paying. Certain systems may also qualify for federal tax incentives. Visit www.energystar.gov for the latest information.

Fix Drippy Faucets

A hot-water faucet that leaks can waste over 200 gallons per month and also triggers the hot-water heater to run unnecessarily.

Turn Up the Temperature on the Air Conditioner

In the summer, wear less clothing in the home and turn the setting on the air conditioner up as high as you can while still being comfortable. Each week, try turning the thermostat up by 1 degree to allow everyone to adjust to a higher temperature. In cooler months, do the opposite.

Three to 5 percent more energy is used for each degree the air conditioner is set below 78. Just a few degrees can mean a lot in terms of dollars saved.

Circulate the Air

Use a ceiling fan or portable fan to circulate air in a room. A fan uses very little energy and can help maintain comfort at a higher temperature. Just be sure to turn it off when you leave the room.

Turn the Power Off

Shut down your computer, monitor, and other electronics when not in use. In addition to saving energy, electronics that are allowed to power down and cool off will often last longer.

However, even idle electronics often use a small amount of power when they are plugged in. Over time, this usage can cost big bucks. Idle appliances not only waste energy, but they also create heat, forcing your air conditioner to work harder.

In fact, in the average home, 40 percent of all electricity used to power home electronics is consumed while the products are turned off. Across the United States, this equals the annual output of seventeen power plants. To prevent this, keep appliances unplugged. Also, you can plug home electronics into a power strip and turn the whole strip off when you're done with them.

Buy ENERGY STAR

Another reason to consider purchasing ENERGY STAR products is that they cut down on the energy wasted when appliances are turned off. Home electronics use energy when they're off to power features such as clock displays and remote controls. Those who have earned the ENERGY STAR use as much as 50 percent less energy while providing the same features at the same price as less-efficient models. An ENERGY STAR–qualified computer in sleep mode consumes about 80 percent less electricity than it does in full-power mode. So if you're thinking of new equipment, look for the ENERGY STAR label.

Water: A Precious Commodity

In the last few years, we have all watched as gasoline prices have sky-rocketed. As this impacts our pocketbooks, we are learning to appreciate our natural resources more and more each day. But there are few resources in our world more precious than water. Sure, H_2O is the single most prevalent substance on Earth: it's everywhere and in every living thing. And it is a fact that nearly two-thirds of Earth's surface is covered by water. However, this is a misleading statistic because most of Earth's water (nearly 98 percent) is unusable salt water.

One might argue that Earth is a big planet—and if almost 2 percent of our water is fresh, then that's a lot of water. Well, the vast majority of that freshwater is frozen in the two polar ice caps, so the reality is that less than 1 percent of all the water on our planet is actually available for consumption (i.e., drinking, bathing, watering the lawn, doing laundry, etc.). In fact, according to the World Health Organization, the amount of freshwater available for Earth's population is less than 0.007 percent of all the water on Earth. That's seven one-thousandths of a percent! And remember, that's the water for everybody. We share that with the rest of the world, and the world's population is rapidly growing.

When we use water or waste it, the cost of cleaning it can be high, and that cost gets passed on to you by your local water utility. The water we use at home doesn't just magically appear. Treated water is a carefully manufactured product that arrives at your home only after traveling through many miles of pipeline and lengthy treatment processes. So water is not only a precious resource, but also an expensive one!

Most local water utility companies charge you for the amount of water you use and waste. So, the more you use and let run down the drain, the more expensive the water gets. If you are conscientious about saving water, you could end up paying the lowest rate per gallon. But if you use a lot of water, then each incremental gallon will be billed at a progressively higher rate. Paying for water at the highest rate tier means you will spend a lot more for your water than your conservation-minded neighbor does.

If you don't think any of this is your concern because you don't live in the Desert Southwest, bear in mind that drought affects more than half of the states in America, according to the National Drought Mitigation Center. But your water bill isn't very high, you say. Well, it wasn't long ago that we were paying only pennies per gallon for gasoline. How long will it be until we are paying dollars per gallon for water?

Water-Saving Tips

IN THE KITCHEN

When you go into the kitchen today, try to pay attention to how much water you use for simple tasks. When you wash or rinse fruits and vegetables, do so in a sieve over a bowl or in a salad spinner. Let the water collect in the bowl or tub part of the spinner and let the food dry off in the sieve or rack. The water you collect can be given to your indoor or outdoor plants. Here are a few more ideas.

▶ Thaw frozen food in the refrigerator instead of running water over it.

▶ Steam vegetables instead of boiling them. You'll use less water and the veggies will taste better and retain more of their nutrients.

▶ If you must prerinse dishes before putting them into the dishwasher, plug the sink and fill it with water rather than running water continuously. This can help you save 10 to 20 gallons of water.

▶ If you don't have a dishwasher, wash your dishes in one sink filled with soapy water and rinse them in another filled with hot water.

▶ Let those really hard-to-clean pots and pans soak in the sink overnight and wash them the following morning instead of running a lot of water over them after dinner.

▶ When running the dishwasher, never wash less than a full load.

▶ Avoid putting items down the garbage disposal that could be used for compost. You'll save water in the house, and the moisture-rich compost will keep water from evaporating in your garden, so you won't have to overwater during the hot summer months.

IN THE BATHROOM

It's no secret: the bathroom can be an outlet for wasting water. Sometimes, the simplest action, such as throwing a tissue into the trash instead of flushing it down the toilet, can save gallons of water per year. These tips from Fluidmaster and ConservCo, manufacturers of water-saving devices, can help, too. Visit www.fluidmaster.com or www.dripstop.com for more information.

▶ Replacing older, regular toilets with low-flow (1 to 1.6 gallons per flush) models saves up to 350 gallons per week. Check online to be sure that the toilets have a strong "flush-approval" rating from consumers' groups such as Consumer Reports.

▶ Repairing a leaking toilet saves up to 100 gallons per week.

▶ Repairing a dripping faucet can save up to 350 gallons per week.

▶ Installing a low-flow showerhead will save you as much as 500 gallons of water each week. You need one if your shower fills a 1-gallon bucket in less than 20 seconds.

▶ Taking shorter showers can easily save 20 gallons of water per day.

▶ Keep in mind that a short shower uses less water than a full tub bath, but a partly filled tub uses much less than a long shower.

▶ You can conserve even more water by using a bucket to collect the water that comes out of the tap or showerhead as you wait for it to heat up and use it later to water houseplants or to give to your pets.

▶ Installing a point-of-use hot-water heater (a model that uses a pump at your water heater to keep the water in your line hot from the moment you turn on the tap) can save several gallons daily.

▶ Don't let the water run when you brush your teeth or shave. Running water only while rinsing will save several gallons of water each week.

OUTDOORS

Inside or outside of our homes, it's very important to conserve water whenever possible. Here are a few simple outdoor water conservation tips.

▶ Sweep your driveway and sidewalk rather than using a hose, or use a water-saving device to keep the flow at a minimum.

▶ Water your lawn no more than twice a week. And when you do water, keep the sprinklers on for no more than 10 to 20 minutes at a time. Never water your lawn between 10:00 a.m. and 6:00 p.m. in the summer, as most of the water will just evaporate.

▶ Make sure your sprinklers are watering your lawn, not the sidewalk. Avoid watering your lawn when it's windy.

▶ Raise your mower blade: closely cropped grass dries out very quickly.

▶ Aerate your lawn for more efficient watering.

▶ When you wash your car by hand, use a bucket instead of the hose. This can save up to 300 gallons of water! If possible, drive your car onto your lawn so that you'll be watering it while you wash the car. Most soaps and detergents are actually good for your grass. Better yet, go to a commercial car wash that recycles the water it uses.

▶ When you do use the hose, make sure it has a nozzle that shuts off when you let go of it. This will reduce water flow and save you money.

▶ If you have a pool, use a cover to slow evaporation. A cover offers the added bonus of keeping pool water cleaner and cutting the need for chemicals. This can save up to 250 gallons weekly.

▶ Use collected rainwater for watering plants.

▶ Consider xeriscaping (using native plants that don't need much water) for all or a portion of your yard, especially if you live in the Southwest.

▶ Wash the dog outside on the lawn, instead of in the tub or the shower. Don't worry—an environmentally friendly shampoo won't hurt the grass. Just check the label to be sure it's safe for fish and wildlife.

▶ When you give the dog fresh water, dump the old water into a houseplant or pot outside.

One of the least expensive ways to increase your home's efficiency is to upgrade your attic insulation. Many homes were built with inferior amounts of insulation, before energy costs skyrocketed. Insufficient attic insulation may require your home's heating and cooling system to work harder to regulate the indoor temperature. Adding insulation to the attic is an effective and easy way to increase energy efficiency and provide an extended barrier against the elements.

Leave the kiddos out of this one. This project involves the use of a ladder and the handling of messy insulation. Coerce your brother-in-law instead. Just be sure to wear long pants and a long-sleeved shirt, a particulate mask, gloves, and a hair cover or hat. Insulation is very messy and the tiny fiberglass particles can cause lung damage as well as severe skin itching if you don't protect yourself. Included in this project are some other tip-top tips to stop energy loss up top.

You will need:

- ✓ Measuring tape or ruler
- ✓ Temporary flooring and lighting (if needed)
- ✓ Particulate mask
- ✓ Work gloves
- ✓ Hair cover or hat
- ✓ Insulation
- ✓ Scissors

Phase 1: Before You Insulate

1. CHECK YOUR ATTIC INSULATION. Before you add any insulation to your attic, you need to know how much insulation (R-value) is already there. This is simply done by measuring the thickness of your attic's existing insulation. Most older homes have between 3 and 6 inches of fiberglass blanket insulation. This is roughly equal to an R-value between R-9 and R-19. If the attic has less than 5 inches of insulation, it's a good idea to add more.

Subtract the amount of your attic's existing insulation from your area's recommended R-value to determine how much more should be installed.

If you are unsure how much insulation to add, the U.S. Department of Energy recommends amounts for homes in each area of the country to achieve optimum energy efficiency. Visit its Web site at www.eere.energy.gov to help determine your home's needs.

2. CHECK THE VAPOR BARRIER. While you are inspecting the attic, check to see if there is a vapor barrier under the insulation. The vapor barrier could be tar paper, kraft paper attached to fiberglass batts, or a plastic sheet. If there does not appear to be a vapor barrier, consider painting the inside of your attic ceiling with vapor barrier paint to reduce the amount of water vapor that can pass through the ceiling. Large amounts of moisture can reduce the effectiveness of insulation and promote structural damage. If your home is in a hot, dry climate, a vapor barrier is probably not necessary.

3. SEEK OUT POTENTIAL LEAKS. If the attic hatch is located above an air-conditioned area, be sure it has foam weather stripping and closes with a tight seal. In the attic, determine whether openings that lead into the house for items such as electrical boxes, pipes, ductwork, and chimneys are potential leaks. Fill gaps with an expanding foam caulk or some other permanent sealant. If you have attic vents, make sure they are not blocked by insulation, to allow for proper airflow.

4. BLOW IT OUT YOUR ATTIC VENTS. If you don't already have them, consider having attic vents (wind turbines) installed on your roof. They can lower summer attic temperatures by 10 to 20 degrees or more. Don't worry about covering them in the winter; your attic needs to breathe, no matter what the weather. Solar-powered attic vents are a great investment and do not require additional wiring. The area under your roof around the edge of your home is called the soffit. Many builders install soffit vents during a home's construction, but if your home doesn't have them, you can buy them at most lumberyards and install them yourself. Attic peak vents are also a big help. Also, cover attic windows, such as dormers, with heat-proof shades.

Phase 2: Let's Insulate!

1. START AT THE OUTER EDGES. Safety first: When you are ready to insulate, temporary flooring should be laid across the joists to provide some

Andrea's Choice: Radiant Barrier

If summer heat is driving your electric bills through the roof, consider installing a spray-on radiant barrier. Similar in application and appearance to ordinary house paint, radiant-barrier spray is actually a high-tech coating that was developed to make military vehicles invisible to heat-seeking missiles. A single thin coat of spray applied to the underside of a roof can block up to 75 percent of the sun's radiant heat. And in the winter, that same barrier will reflect back 75 percent of the heat that tries to escape from your home. Its remarkable heat-shielding properties, combined with its ease of application, make it the ideal radiant barrier for existing homes. If your roof is being reshingled, consider having radiant barrier panels applied under the shingles. Another option is to choose a shingle that has radiant-barrier properties, such as Gerard metal roofing or Owens Corning shingles.

footing and a work light should be used to offer adequate lighting. Make sure that you are wearing old clothes and safety glasses. Plan to shower and wash clothing as soon as you are finished.

Start installing the insulation at the outer edges of the attic space and work toward the center. This allows for more headroom in the center of the space, where cutting and fitting can be done. Avoid working yourself into a corner where it will be hard to get back to the attic entryway.

2. ADD PERPENDICULAR LAYERS. If the joist cavities are completely filled, lay the new insulation in long runs perpendicular to the direction of the joists and use leftover pieces for small spaces. If the cavity is not completely filled, use the appropriate thickness of insulation to fill it to the top and then add an additional layer of insulation in the perpendicular direction.

3. JUST STUFF IT. The insulation should extend far enough to cover the tops of the exterior walls, but should not block the flow of air from the eave vents. To make sure the eave vents aren't blocked, install attic vents or baffles to provide unrestricted airflow from the soffit to the attic.

Stuff spaces around masonry chimneys or other areas that have small openings with small pieces of nonflammable, unfaced insulation.

4. WATCH OUT FOR HEAT SOURCES. Insulation should be kept at least 3 inches away from recessed lighting fixtures unless they are marked "I.C." (Insulated Ceiling), indicating that the fixtures are designed for direct contact with the insulation. If insulation is placed over an unrated fixture, it may cause the fixture to overheat and start a fire. Also, the insulation should always be installed at least 3 inches away from any metal chimneys, gas water heater flues, or other heat-producing devices.

A Few More Tip-top Tips

Insufficient attic insulation may result in the home's heating and cooling system having to work harder to regulate the indoor temperature. If you have already added insulation to your attic but it just doesn't seem to be sufficient, you may want to consider upgrading to professionally installed spray-on polyurethane foam insulation, which affords the maximum energy efficiency available today.

While you're thinking up top . . . with high winds, snow, and ice, the winter months can be particularly strenuous on the roof of a house. Thus, spring and summer are good times to examine your roof to ensure all shingles are intact and flashings around chimneys, skylights, antennas, and vents are sealed. Be sure to replace broken, curled, or missing shingles and use roof caulking to patch any holes to prevent energy loss.

For additional energy savings, consider using ENERGY STAR–labeled roofing products, sometimes known as "cool roofs," which reflect the sun's rays to keep the roof and house cooler and decrease air-conditioning usage. These roofs may be subject to government tax incentives. They are also often tornado and hail proof and may save you money on your homeowner's insurance.

Also, make sure that your fireplace damper is closed for the summer, and also during the winter when it's not in use. Leaving it open is like leaving a window open continually. In the summer, invest in a fireplace plug. It's an inflatable balloon that helps to prevent cold-air loss.

Old-House Issue

Is your older home drafty even after boosting your attic insulation? You will probably want to add insulation to your walls as well, but you'll have to be able to access the inside of the walls first. Removing and replacing the wood siding is not the way to go, because on old homes it's often made from yellow pine, which becomes very hard, brittle, and sometimes crystalline with age. Even if you could get it off intact, it would be almost impossible to hammer nails through it to put it back up. It would probably all have to be replaced. This job could cost a small fortune, if you could even find someone to do it.

A better option is to hire an insulating company to blow insulation into your exterior walls. They do this by removing one strip of siding all around the house at the top of the wall and bore a hole so the insulation can be blown in. Then they cover the hole with replacement siding along that one strip. Inside the home, you can cover similar holes with decorative molding. If there is space beneath your home, the insulating company may also be able to put batt insulation under your floor between the joists to keep the floors warmer. There are many methods and products that work. Check with a reputable insulating company in your area. ■

Choose a Programmable Thermostat

Many homes were originally built with simple mechanical thermostats that you must manually turn up or down. Installing an automatic setback or programmable thermostat can afford you tremendous savings. There's no point in the air conditioner or heater running all day while you are at work. Programmable thermostats allow your air conditioner to cycle on when you are home and take a break when you're gone. They are easy to install, usually for under $100. Professionally installed models can range up to $400 and offer more features and benefits that may pay for the difference in cost. Some may qualify for tax incentives or rebates.

PROJECT: **INSTALLING WINDOW-TINTING FILM**

Level of difficulty: T T

Would you buy a car without tinted glass? Probably not. But most of us live in houses without any type of light-filtering material on the windows. Applying light-filtering window film is a simple process, with only a few basic steps, and it is relatively inexpensive. The payback is quick—on average, you can save about $100 or more on your electric bill per summer by applying film to major windows, especially south- and west-facing windows. For more info, visit www.gilafilms.com.

Note: Most residential window films are applied directly to the inside of the window. If you have a removable storm window, remove it and apply the film to the inside surface of the outermost window, then remount the storm pane.

You will need:

- ✓ Single-edged razor blades
- ✓ Spray-on application solution (sold with film)
- ✓ Squeegee
- ✓ Rags or paper coffee filters
- ✓ Window-tinting film
- ✓ Utility knife
- ✓ Scissors
- ✓ Transparent tape
- ✓ Ruler

Some special points to remember:

▶ Handle the film very carefully. As with aluminum foil, once creased, the film will remain creased.

▶ Avoid using concentrated or degreasing detergents. These can make the solution or the film dry and cloudy or fail to adhere.

▶ Larger windows (3- to 4-feet wide) usually are more easily filmed by two people working together to remove the liner and install and trim the film. (See steps 3 and 5).

▶ Apply film anytime other than in direct sunlight (the film may stick too quickly) or freezing weather (the film will not stick at all). The best temperature is between 45 and 90 degrees Fahrenheit. The best time is early morning or late evening, when the glass is cooler.

▶ Work in a dust-free area. Turn off fans. Apply the film to windows hung vertically. Do not lay windows down to film them or you will trap air bubbles under the film.

▶ Follow the manufacturer's directions.

1. MEASURE THE WINDOW. Measure the dimensions of your window carefully before unrolling and cutting the film. The film may be applied from side to side or top to bottom from the kit roll.

2. CLEAN THE WINDOW. Generously spray the window with solution. Then use your squeegee to clean the windows thoroughly. Respray the glass, and then use a razor blade to remove any caked dirt or paint. Use special care cleaning the corners. Rewet the window, then squeegee downward. Wipe off accumulated dirt from the window gasket with a soft cloth or paper coffee filters.

3. CUT THE FILM. Unroll the film on a clean, flat surface near the window. Use a ruler as a guide and cut the film 1 inch larger than the dimensions of the window to be sure that the film will fit. Or, if you choose, pretrim the film to the final dimensions of each window (including the $\frac{1}{16}$-inch gap described in step 8).

4. WET THE WINDOW THOROUGHLY. Generously spray the solution onto the inside surface of the window until beads of the soapy water run down the glass. If the window becomes dry, rewet it completely before applying the film.

5. REMOVE THE CLEAR FILM BACKING ("THE LINER"). Note: Usually the liner is on the outside surface of the film roll.

Remove the liner by attaching two pieces of transparent tape to the front and back surfaces of a corner of the film so that about 1 inch of tape is on the film, while the rest is centered and hanging over the pointed corner of the film. Press the two pieces of tape firmly together, then quickly pull them apart to begin separating the clear liner away from the adhesive side of the film.

Quick Tip:
French Doors Made Easy

I recommend pretrimming the film to final size for French panes, skylights, and arched windows. It makes the job go much faster.

Quick Tip:
An Easy Solution

Always wet the film with the solution before squeegeeing. You can remove any large bubbles by pushing them with the squeegee to the nearest film edge. Small bubbles (less than ⅛ inch in diameter) should disappear in a few days.

This process may require a quick, snapping pull, much like pressing together and quickly pulling apart two pieces of Velcro. As you carefully peel the liner away, generously spray the soapy solution onto the exposed adhesive. This spray helps break any static cling, reduces contamination, and makes the liner separation easier.

One other method is to wet the film and place on the window with the adhesive side out. This will hold the film while you remove the liner. Wet your hands with the solution before handling the film to avoid leaving fingerprints on the adhesive.

For small windows, remove the liner diagonally, from one corner toward the opposing corner. Try to keep the film from touching itself. For large windows and patio doors, removing the liner from a large sheet (i.e., patio door size) involves two people. Your helper faces the window and holds the film perpendicular to the floor. You face the liner side of the film, separate the corner of the liner, slide your finger along the top edge of the film to fully separate the liner, and then peel the liner down toward the floor in a smooth, even motion. After removing the liner completely, thoroughly spray the glass and then the adhesive side of the film.

6. PLACE THE FILM ON THE WET WINDOW. Completely remove the clear liner from the back of the film and thoroughly wet the exposed dry adhesive surface. Be sure the window is dripping wet; too much solution is better than not enough. Apply the adhesive side of the film to the wet glass. Start at the top of the window and then allow the film to gently lay down onto the glass. Handle the film carefully at the corners to avoid wrinkles or creases, which cannot be removed. Use your hands to smooth the film onto the glass. You can slide the film around and position it correctly while the window and film are thoroughly wet.

7. SQUEEGEE THE FILM IN PLACE. Spray the entire surface of the film facing you with the soapy solution to lubricate its surface. Begin squeegeeing the water and air out from under the film. To do this, start about 2 inches from the top and side and squeegee from left to right. Second, to set the film on the glass, lightly squeegee the rest of the film downward, but leave the 2-inch perimeter area unsqueegeed. If you need to remove large air pockets, rewet the top of the film and squeegee again. If the squeegee drags, respray the solution on the top of the film.

8. TRIM EDGES AND SQUEEGEE DRY. Use a sharp razor blade or utility knife and a 1/16-inch-wide guide to trim the film around the four perimeter edges of the film. This gap is essential for the proper thermal expansion of the glass and allows you to completely squeegee the water and air from under the film. Rewet the entire film surface and squeegee again. Press very firmly to remove all the water so that the adhesive can cure clearly.

This time, imagine an invisible line dividing the window from top to bottom. Starting at the top of the window, squeegee from the center to the left, then from the center to the right. Repeat this process until you reach the bottom of the window. ◾

Quick Tip: Troubleshooting

If your squeegee has a stiff blade, push it toward the sides. If it has a flexible rubber blade, pull the squeegee. If "fingers" or bubbles appear along any edge, wrap your squeegee with a few paper coffee filters (or soft, absorbent cloth) and carefully push the defects toward the edge of the film. Hold in place for a moment to absorb any excess water.

PROJECT: CHOOSING AND INSTALLING A CEILING FAN

Level of difficulty: 𝑇 𝑇 𝑇 𝑇

Quick Tip:
Certain Circuits

Since a fan draws about the same power as a ceiling fixture, the existing electrical circuit should be able to power the average ceiling fan. But if your fan includes lights, be sure the circuit has enough extra capacity. If not, you must run a new circuit with a new circuit breaker from the house's main service panel or subpanel to the fan. If you are not familiar with your house's electrical system, seek the help of a professional electrician.

Ceiling fans are one of the best appliance investments you can make and are versatile enough for just about any room in your home. Although ceiling fans don't actually lower the air temperature in the room, the flow of air over your skin makes you feel cooler. If there is a breeze or cooler air outside, a ceiling fan can help draw in that air through an open door or window. Using ceiling fans can help lower both heating and cooling bills significantly, by about 15 percent to 40 percent.

Whether you are replacing an old fan that has finally given out or installing one where only a light fixture exists now, it is definitely worth the investment and the few hours it takes to shop for and install it.

You will need:
✓ Phillips screwdriver
✓ Straight screwdriver
✓ Wire strippers (if necessary)
✓ Wire nuts

Phase 1: Selecting Your New Fan

1. CHOOSE THE RIGHT SIZE. Note the size of the room in which you will install your new fan. It's important to fit the size of the fan to the room for it to work effectively. For example, a fan with a 36-inch span will work well in a room up to 100 square feet. If the room is larger, you'll need more blade span.

2. CHOOSE THE CORRECT PITCH. Examine the angle of the blade, which is typically listed on the packaging or in the owner's manual. This indicates how efficiently the paddles move the air. A good range is between 11 and 16 degrees.

3. CHOOSE FEATURES THAT YOU NEED. First of all, look for the ENERGY STAR label. Also, decide whether you want a pull-chain model or one that comes with a remote. A good remote will include all functions—the fan speeds and the light (if included). Do you want or need a light? Lights are often added to the bottom of the ceiling fan for decoration as well as function. Also check the warranty. Some warranties only cover specific parts of the fan, while others are more comprehensive, covering the fan up to a year and the motor for a lifetime.

4. CHOOSE THE CORRECT MOUNTING. The type of mounting will depend on where you are installing the fan, the type of ceiling that you have, and if you want the fan to be a decorative accent or virtually unnoticeable. Measure your ceiling height, or from the floor to the blades on the existing unit. The minimum recommended height from manufacturers and most area building codes for any unit is 7 feet from the floor to the blades. Flush or hugging mounts are standard, but down rods can be used to extend the appliance from the ceiling between 4 and 24 inches.

If your ceiling is too low, check into a low-ceiling mount for your fan. On some models, the fan blade height can be increased by as much as 10 inches. Remember, you need at least 12 inches between the ceiling and the tops of the fan blades for proper airflow. Eighteen inches is even better if the space is available.

Phase 2: Installing Your New Fan

1. TURN OFF THE ELECTRICAL POWER. First, turn off the power to the light's circuit breaker or fuse. Only then should you remove the light fixture. Make sure to read all of the electrical safety tips.

2. CHECK YOUR ELECTRICAL BOX. Use only a metal junction box to support a ceiling fan; never hang the fan from a plastic box. Depending on the brand, style, and size of your ceiling fan and your electrical code, you may use a 4-inch or a 3-inch octagonal junction box. (Some local codes don't permit the use of 3-inch boxes.)

3. ASSEMBLE THE FAN. Fan assembly varies from brand to brand. Be sure to follow the specific instructions with the unit that you buy. Regardless of the manufacturer's instructions, if the fan blades are less than a screw-

Andrea's Choice:
A Cool Way to Stay Warm

Ceiling fans come in a variety of colors, finishes, and options with something for everyone. One brand, the Reiker Room Conditioner, is both a ceiling fan and a heater in one. It can reverse the airflow to circulate warmth and actually heat the room. (Visit www.reiker.com.)

driver's length away from the ceiling, it may be best to install the blades before hanging the fan.

4. INSTALL THE HANGER PIPE. The hanger pipe is usually placed into its hole on top of the motor. The wires are then drawn up in the center. A set-screw is tightened securely to make sure the pipe stays in place after it is threaded down.

Some fans have a separate motor hub into which the hanger pipe mounts. In this case, you will place the actual motor housing over the hub.

Other fans have a two-piece decorative ceiling cover to hide the hole in the ceiling. It is installed after the fan has been hung on the ceiling.

Other models use a hook, with the hanger bracket designed to accept it.

5. INSTALL THE HANGER BRACKET. Install the hanger bracket on the box with screws and lock washers. If no lock washers are supplied, purchase them at your local hardware store. They will help prevent fan vibration from loosening the screws over time.

The hanger bracket may accept either a half-ball hanger or a hook-type hanger, depending on which kind your fan uses. Either way, the hanger on the top of your fan should be carefully slipped into the bracket.

6. WIRE THE UNIT. Next, wire the unit. Be sure to connect the black house wires to the black fan wires and the white house wires to the white fan wires.

7. GROUND THE FAN. The fan should be electrically grounded to both the metal box and the fan. The grounding wires will be either green or bare copper. A green grounding pigtail attached to the box by a bonding screw will make your work easier. Wirenut the grounding wires from the box, connecting the fan and the power supply together. Slip the ceiling cover up to its full height and tighten it in place.

8. ATTACH THE FAN BLADES. Most fan blades have a two-pronged attachment, using screws that come through holes in the blades and into the flanges. Draw them up securely, but not so tightly that the threads are damaged or the laminated blade material is crushed. On many fans you'll find the flanges or prongs also need to be mounted to the motor housing. If this is the case, mount them before the flanges are mounted to the blades themselves.

9. INSTALL THE LIGHT KIT. Install the light kit if one is included, according to the manufacturer's directions.
(Resource: www.doityourself.com) ■

Quick Tip:
Setscrew Secrets

Tighten the setscrew well. Use thread lock or clear fingernail polish to keep the setscrew from loosening up over time.

8

if it's broke, fix it;
if it ain't broke,
fix it anyway!

Indoor Home Maintenance and Repairs

The major difference between a thing that might go wrong and a thing that
cannot possibly go wrong is that when a thing that cannot possibly go wrong
goes wrong it usually turns out to be impossible to get at or repair.

—DOUGLAS ADAMS,
AUTHOR OF *THE HITCHHIKER'S GUIDE TO THE GALAXY*

If you own a home, or even if you are renting, sometimes it seems like there is a
new repair to make every week or so. From doorknobs falling off to faucets that
drip, maintaining a home can be a challenge. As the quote above indicates, sometimes the best option is to fix something before it breaks; this is called preventive
maintenance.

In this chapter, we will cover some of the most common and sometimes challenging home repair and upkeep issues. Most of them, such as maintaining your
water heater, are much easier to tackle before they become big problems. Others,
such as repairing brick mortar joints, must be addressed when damage has become
more obvious. Here we go!

- ▶ Project: Replacing the Screen in a Door or a Window
- ▶ Refurbishing Historic Windows
- ▶ Project: Repairing Damaged Wood or Metal with Epoxy Filler
- ▶ Choosing, Placing, and Maintaining Smoke and Carbon Monoxide Alarms
- ▶ Improve Your Home's Air Quality
- ▶ Appliance Maintenance
- ▶ Project: Preventing a Water Heater Disaster
- ▶ Project: Home Electrical Safety

PROJECT: REPLACING THE SCREEN IN A DOOR OR A WINDOW

Level of difficulty: T

Have the kids or pets wreaked havoc on your screen door? Have flies taken up permanent residence in your kitchen from a tear in the window screen? Have you stitched a patch onto the old screen on your bedroom window? If you've been avoiding replacing your old screens because you don't know how, you'll be happy to discover that it's easy, inexpensive, and fun.

You will need:

- ✓ Measuring tape
- ✓ New window screen mesh
- ✓ New spline
- ✓ Spline roller
- ✓ Utility knife
- ✓ Wood blocks or clamps

1. MATCH THE COLOR AND TYPE OF EXISTING SCREEN. Fiberglass is the most common and economical type of screen mesh in today's homes. It is the easiest to install, durable, and resistant to the elements (even salt air). Aluminum mesh is suited to match existing screening in older homes. It is also a great choice for high-traffic areas.

2. MEASURE THE EXISTING SCREEN. Measure the width and height of the screen(s) you want to repair. When choosing a screen in the store, purchase the next size up from your measurements. Cut the new screen mesh at least 1 to 2 inches larger than the outside of the frame. With aluminum screening, measure ½ inch in from the corner and make a small cut at a 45-degree angle to make tucking in the corners easier.

3. CHOOSE THE RIGHT SPLINE. When you repair your screen, you will also need to replace the spline, the rubbery strip that holds the screen into its frame. It is a good idea to take the old spline into the store to make sure you are getting the correct match. Pay attention to its color and thickness.

4. SECURE THE INSIDE OF THE FRAME. Lay the screen frame or screen door on a clean, flat surface. Make sure that all of the old screen material has been removed from the frame and that the frame is clean and dust free. The secret to successful screens is to secure the inside of the frame with wooden blocks or clamps so that it cannot move. This allows you to roll the new mesh in tightly without bowing the frame. Most of the next steps for screen repair are common to both fiberglass and aluminum screening.

5. INSTALL THE NEW MATERIAL. Lay the new screen mesh over the frame and the exposed groove. Start at one corner, with the roller angled to the outside, and roll the spline down into the groove, pressing the screen mesh into place.

With aluminum screening, precrease the screen into the groove with a gentle back-and-forth motion of the roller. It may even help to run the roller into the groove over the mesh before inserting the spline. Make sure to center the aluminum screen mesh over the opening so that the little corner cuts that you made earlier line up evenly at each corner.

6. TRIM AND FINISH. At each corner, tuck the spline down into the frame. Use a sharp utility knife to cut off the excess screening.

To prevent damage to your new screen, keep the knife angled to the outside edge of the frame. Reinstall the frame into your window or door. No more flies!
(Resource: Saint-Gobain Technical Fabrics) ∎

Refurbishing Historic Windows

If you own an older home, you have probably agonized over your vintage windows. Should you replace them or try to save them? Here are four common problems with old windows.

▶ **THEY ARE DRAFTY.** Be careful to choose a weather-stripping option that will not ruin the historic value of your home. DAP makes a caulk-type sealer that can actually seal your windows closed when not in use and then simply be peeled off when you want to open them again. Also consider easy-to-install, clear-plastic window covers, available at most hardware stores. They can be installed on the inside of the windows, where they will not show.

▶ **THEY MAY BE PAINTED SHUT.** Removing paint from old windows is just like stripping a piece of furniture. It is a lot of work, but the finished product can be gorgeous. Try heat guns that are made for this purpose. They work well and may be less messy than chemical strippers.

▶ **THE BALANCE WEIGHT ROPES HAVE BROKEN.** Balance weight ropes are not hard to replace. If you carefully remove the side window casing on the inside of the windows, you can usually access the old weights. Choose a good-quality, braided-nylon rope to replace the old rope.

▶ **THE FRAME OR SILL IS ROTTED.** Rotten wood frames are usually the result of a moisture problem. You must first eliminate the cause and then repair or replace any rotten areas. The following project, using epoxy filler, is an excellent method for repairing window frames.

If you want to save your windows, just plan on some work. If you're having trouble finding the right parts, visit www.blainewindow.com or www.vandykesrestorers.com. If you decide to replace your historic windows, choose a brand that offers proper replacements, such as Andersen, Pella, or Marvin. Another option is to work with a company such as Hull Historical Restoration in Fort Worth, Texas, which can rebuild your windows for you or make custom replacements.

PROJECT: REPAIRING DAMAGED WOOD OR METAL WITH EPOXY FILLER

Level of difficulty: T T

Sometimes, due to wood rot or rust, a surface may become damaged and need a large amount of filler. Just as epoxy is an excellent adhesive for many materials, epoxy fillers can be used to bridge gaps in many items, too. It is strong enough to be used in areas such as torn-out hinges and faceplates, broken window rabbets, or mortise-and-tenon joints and is ideal for wood, metals, plastics, and ceramics. As long as the surrounding surface is strong, an epoxy repair should last indefinitely and be completely waterproof, so it's a good choice for outdoor or underwater use.

You'll need:
- ✓ TSP (Trisodium phosphate) or other cleaner
- ✓ Acetone (to clean metal surfaces)
- ✓ Steel brush or steel wool
- ✓ Bleach (if mold is present)
- ✓ Paint thinner (often labeled "mineral spirits")
- ✓ 2-part epoxy filler kit
- ✓ Disposable mixing surface
- ✓ Disposable putty knife (or popsicle stick)
- ✓ Sandpaper

1. PREPARE ALL SURFACES. All surfaces must be dry and free from oil, dust, dirt, etc. If working on metal, remove rust and oxidation (a white, chalky residue) from the surface and scrub with acetone using steel wool or a steel brush. Clean exotic woods (such as teak) with mineral spirits. If the wood has rotted, make sure that the cause of the original moisture has been eliminated. Sometimes this is tricky, especially if you do not know the source of the leak. But spend some time to eliminate the water infiltration or the wood will simply rot again. Then remove any damaged or softened wood and prep the remainder with a weak bleach solution (1 teaspoon of bleach in 1 cup of water) to kill residual mold and mildew.

2. MEASURE AND MIX THE EPOXY FILLER. Most epoxy fillers are a mixture of 2 parts resin to 1 part hardener, but read the manufacturer's directions for your specific brand. For most applications, apply 2 equal strips of resin and 1 strip of hardener on a disposable surface. Immediately replace caps to avoid drying out the remaining product. Mix thoroughly until the color is uniform.

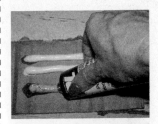

3. APPLY AND FILL. Apply with a disposable putty knife or popsicle stick. Press the mixture into the cavity, overfilling slightly. Most products allow 10 to 15 minutes of workable time. The product will thicken as you work it into the damaged area. If it begins to harden too quickly, you may be able to delay it a bit with mineral spirits, used sparingly.

4. CLEAN UP. Clean tools and any excess filler with mineral spirits at once, following the manufacturer's precautions.

5. FINISH THE SURFACE. Most epoxy wood fillers can be sanded, milled, drilled, planed, sawed, and screwed into after 4 to 6 hours. Wear a particulate mask when sanding to avoid ingesting the dust. Read the manufacturer's recommendations for staining or painting to match surrounding surfaces. (Resource: PL FI:X Wood Repair Products, by Henkel Consumer Adhesives/www.stickwithpl.com) ■

Choosing, Placing, and Maintaining Smoke and Carbon Monoxide Alarms

Installing smoke and carbon monoxide alarms in strategic areas of your home is one easy way to ensure your family's safety. When shopping for alarms, first of all, look for products listed by recognized testing agencies—specifically Underwriters Laboratories (UL). Then choose alarms based on the power in your home and the area of placement. Smoke and carbon monoxide alarms are powered in three ways.

▶ **HARDWIRED INTO YOUR HOME'S ELECTRICAL SYSTEM:** This type of alarm can also be interconnected, meaning that when one alarm sounds, all the other interconnected alarms sound, too.

Hardwired alarms are normally installed during a home's construction or major remodeling. Choose units that have a battery backup for power outages.

▶ **BATTERY POWERED (TYPICALLY 9 VOLT, AA, OR LITHIUM):** This type of alarm is used when hardwiring is not practical and can be added anywhere, anytime.

▶ **AC-POWERED CARBON MONOXIDE:** Installing this type of alarm is as simple as plugging it into any normal outlet.

There are two types of sensors used in smoke alarms. Some units combine both of these technologies:

▶ **IONIZATION:** These types of alarms are generally sensitive for detecting small particles that tend to be produced by flaming fires, which consume combustible materials rapidly and spread quickly. Sources of these fires may include paper burning in a wastebasket or a grease fire in the kitchen.

▶ **PHOTOELECTRIC:** These alarms are sensitive at detecting large particles that tend to be produced by fires that may smolder for hours before bursting into flame. Sources of these fires may include cigarettes burning on couches or bedding.

Placement

The National Fire Protection Association recommends installing a smoke alarm on each floor and one in each bedroom or sleeping area of a home. Many smoke alarms combine both types of detection; ionization and photoelectric. Some incorporate carbon monoxide detection as well. If not, add carbon monoxide alarms in areas where gas appliances are installed and in the garage. Most alarms should be placed out of children's reach, approximately 8 feet off the ground. Be sure to follow the manufacturer's directions.

Long-term Maintenance

To ensure the proper functioning of your alarms over time, implement the following basic maintenance procedures.

▶ Test alarms at least once a month by pressing and holding the Test/Silence button until the alarm sounds (alarms take up to 20 seconds to respond).

▶ Clean the smoke alarm monthly by gently vacuuming the outside of it using the soft-brush attachment on your vacuum. Never use water, cleaners, or solvents, since they may damage the unit. Test your alarm after cleaning.

▶ If the smoke alarm becomes contaminated by excessive dirt, dust, and/or grime and cannot be cleaned to avoid unwanted alarms, replace the unit immediately.

▶ Relocate the unit if it frequently sounds unwanted alarms. For example, if an alarm is located too close to your kitchen stove, cooking smoke may activate it even when there is no fire and desensitize residents to the sound.

▶ Never remove the battery or unplug the unit to silence the alarm.

▶ Replace batteries at least once a year or more frequently if needed.

▶ If the alarm signals a malfunction, first check to see if the battery is installed properly in battery-operated and battery-backup units. If this does not fix the malfunction, replace the alarm.

▶ Replace smoke alarms at least every 10 years and CO alarms every five years.

Carbon Monoxide Safety

Carbon monoxide (CO) is an invisible, odorless gas. When you inhale carbon monoxide, it bonds with the hemoglobin in your blood, displacing life-giving oxygen. This produces a toxic compound. Over time, exposure to CO can make you very sick with flulike symptoms.

Quick Tip: A Gift of Safety

When you think of home safety, consider older relatives, too. A friend of mine lost both elderly parents in a fire because there was no smoke alarm in the home. The couple had stored some newspapers in the heater closet, which caught on fire when they started up the heater for the first time that season. Avoid a tragedy by giving the gift of safety to older or mobility-limited relatives.

Victims can suffer brain damage or worse. For this reason, it's important to outfit your home with CO alarms.

CO is a common by-product of incomplete combustion, produced when fossil fuels such as wood, coal, charcoal, gasoline, kerosene, natural gas, and oil burn. Carbon monoxide can be produced by gas or oil appliances, such as furnaces, clothes dryers, ranges, ovens, water heaters, and space heaters. When appliances and vents work properly and there is enough fresh air in your home to allow complete combustion, the trace amounts of CO produced are typically not dangerous. However, conditions such as the ones listed below can cause CO gas levels to rise and become hazardous to your health.

▶ An appliance malfunction, such as a cracked heat exchanger on your furnace

▶ A vent, a flue, or a chimney that is blocked by debris or even snow

▶ A fireplace, a wood-burning stove, or a charcoal grill that is not vented properly

▶ A vehicle that is left running in an attached garage with the door open or shut

▶ Several appliances running at the same time and competing for limited fresh air, even if all appliances are in good working order

(Resource: First Alert)

Improve Your Home's Air Quality

If you live in a new home, you may not be getting the fresh air that you need. The same modern, airtight construction that is designed to improve energy efficiency permits less fresh air to enter the home. High-efficiency heating and cooling systems constantly recirculate indoor air, so particles and toxic emissions build up over time. Also, modern building materials contain higher levels of glues and other chemicals that contribute to indoor air pollution.

According to U. S. Environmental Protection Agency (EPA) studies, levels for many pollutants may be two to five times higher indoors than outdoors. The American Lung Association estimates that most people spend 90 percent of their time indoors, so clean indoor air is very important.

The American Academy of Allergy, Asthma & Immunology states that the number of people with allergies, asthma, and lung disease has nearly doubled over the last ten years. Experts at the Mayo Clinic have recently noted that almost all chronic sinus problems are related to indoor air quality. In fact, the EPA reports that indoor air pollution is among the top-five environmental risks to public health. If someone in your family suffers from asthma, allergies, or other respiratory problems, airborne particles in your home, such as dust mites, pollen, molds, pet dander, and insect debris, may be the culprits.

(Resource: Lennox Indoor Comfort Systems)

1. Determine If You Have a Problem

Have you been having trouble catching your breath lately? Does it seem worse when you are inside your home rather than outside? Does someone in your home suffer from nagging respiratory problems? Do you suspect indoor air pollution? If you answered yes to any of these questions, it is important to try to find the source of your indoor contaminants. Check your home for:

- ▶ Unusual and noticeable odors
- ▶ Stale or stuffy air; a noticeable lack of air movement
- ▶ Dirty or faulty central-heating or air-conditioning equipment
- ▶ Damaged flue pipes or chimneys
- ▶ Unvented combustion air sources for fossil fuel appliances
- ▶ Excessive humidity
- ▶ Presence of molds and mildew

▶ Health reaction after remodeling, weatherizing, using new furniture, using household or hobby products, or moving into a new home

2. Ventilate the Area

Unlike older homes that are not as airtight, today's modern homes are well insulated and sealed to conserve energy, which means airborne pollutants have no way to escape. Simply opening windows periodically and running fans to help exchange the stale air inside your home for fresh outdoor air can help.

3. Clean the Air

There are a variety of products available that can help clean and purify the air inside a home. Electronic air cleaners and high-efficiency particulate air (HEPA) filters capture small particles and biological pollutants, such as bacteria, while germicidal lights kill them. Some air purification systems go a step further, attacking all three classes of indoor air contaminants—particles, biological pollutants, and odors/chemical vapors. Before you pick an air cleaner, remember that electronic models require regular maintenance, including washing and/or vacuuming. If they are not maintained, they lose their effectiveness very quickly. The type of units with filters only requires periodic filter replacement. Be honest with yourself about how good you are at doing this maintenance.

If you live in a heavily polluted area or if your family's health problems persist, installing a ventilation filter or whole-house system can help remove particles and other contaminants by exchanging recirculated indoor air with filtered outside air.

4. Monitor and Adjust the Environment

Keep humidity levels low. Set the air conditioner at a lower temperature. The air conditioner can actually help to dehumidify the area. The humidity level in the home should stay below 50 percent. You can buy a humidity-level reader at most home supply stores. Installing a humidistat and a thermostat helps regulate moisture levels and temperatures to enhance overall comfort. These controls also may help prevent the growth of dust mites, bacteria, and mildew on an ongoing basis.

A Few More Clean Air Ideas

Most of us spend about 33 percent of our time in our bedrooms. While that sounds safe enough, if you have allergies, it can be the worst room in the home for attracting dust, dander, dirt, and dust mites. There are some basic things you can do to cut down on allergens and keep yourself sneeze free. Some of these tips may be contrary to other advice that I've given on lowering energy costs, but the payoff of a healthier home may be worth it.

▶ First, start at the front door by taking your shoes off. Up to 85 percent of all household dirt, dust, and allergens come from the bottom of shoes.

▶ Change the filter in your air ventilation system or heater regularly. Check to see if your system can accommodate HEPA-filter upgrades.

▶ Change your vacuum cleaner bag regularly and use a vacuum with a HEPA filter. In fact, buy the best vacuum cleaner that you can afford with state-of-the-art filtration.

▶ Next, dust regularly. Make sure you choose a duster that will actually pick up the dust rather than just move it around. When possible, vacuum areas that you might normally dust, such as the tops of curtains and doors or edges of moldings.

▶ Cover mattresses and pillows in zippered dustproof covers. These go underneath your normal bedding to help reduce allergens.

▶ Wash bedding, uncovered pillows, and stuffed toys in hot water (130 degrees Fahrenheit) weekly.

▶ Spray other soft surfaces in your home that cannot be easily washed, such as sofas, carpets, pet beds, bed comforters, and

Quick Tip:
Air Advice

People with chemical sensitivity can also experience symptoms when they are exposed to volatile organic compounds (VOCs) found in building materials, furniture, paints and solvents, household cleaners, and fragrances. Children, the sick, and the elderly can be particularly sensitive to these indoor air pollutants. If someone in your home is sensitive to these allergens, you may want to test VOC and particle levels in your home.

Many heating and air-conditioning contractors can perform monitored testing, which involves installing a monitor in your home for a few days to measure temperature, humidity, carbon dioxide, carbon monoxide, and airborne particles in one-minute cycles. Then, once a day, it transmits the data via the phone line to a lab for analysis. This process is relatively inexpensive, usually under $200, and is often included in a heating and air-conditioning replacement contract.

Contact AirAdvice at www.airadvice.com for a list of contractors in your area.

It's easy to forget about your washing machine until it is too late. One common problem is a split or leaking supply hose. Ignoring this issue can cause a water disaster costing thousands of dollars in damage. The good news is that replacing the old hoses is easy and very inexpensive. If you can't remember how old your washing machine is, it is probably time to check the hoses. You should do so at least every three to five years, regardless of whether there is a visible defect.

Fluidmaster NO-BURST hoses are more durable and are less susceptible to physical damage than rubber hoses and generally carry a longer guarantee. They cost a few bucks more but can save you thousands in repairs if your old-fashioned hose bursts. (Visit www.fluidmaster.com.)

floor rugs with allergen-reducing fabric refreshers and then vacuum thoroughly. This can reduce irritants up to 75 percent.

▶ As a dog lover, this one pains me to suggest, but it may be a big help with persistent allergies: keep pets off the bed or the sofa. Or at least encourage them to stay on a special blanket, such as a fleece pad, that can be shaken outside or washed frequently.

▶ Also, use alternatives to down for pillows, comforters, and featherbeds. Ask your local linen supplier for products that feel like down but do not cause the allergy problems that real feathers can.

Appliance Maintenance

Did you know that regular tuning and care may help your household appliances last twice as long and run more efficiently, which can save you energy dollars? My friends at RepairClinic.com offer some great advice on when and how to keep your devices in top running order.

Washing Machine

▶ Once each year, check your washer's water fill hoses for cracks, blisters, corroded fittings, and leaks and replace them if they have any of these conditions. Cracks are a sign that the rubber is aging. Blisters signal a rupture in the inner lining of the hose, which means the hose may burst at any time. Corroded fittings mean the hose has leaked or is leaking now. If you wait to replace it, you may find the corroded fitting is virtually impossible to remove from the faucet when you really need to remove it. Washer water fill hoses generally need to be replaced every three to five years, regardless of whether there is a visible defect. When replacing old hoses, I recommend using stainless steel fill hoses. They last virtually forever.

▶ Check that the washer is level and sitting on a well-supported subfloor. A leading cause of washer failure and customer complaints is a washer that bangs around unbalanced for many loads.

▶ Check to be sure no water is dripping into the washer when it's turned off. If water is dripping in, even a little, it's a sign that the water inlet valve is defective and should be replaced.

Dryer

▶ Dryer lint buildup is the leading cause of dryer failures and often dramatically increases drying times. Lint buildup is also responsible for thousands of house fires each year. Check and clean the lint filter after every drying cycle. If the lint filter has any rips or tears, replace it. If fabric softener residue or other debris clogs the filter, you can easily clean it with a soft-bristle brush and a little detergent.

▶ You can also clean the chute, the duct, or the area that the lint filter fits into. If necessary, use a vacuum cleaner to reach into the duct and clean out any lint. If the lint buildup is severe, it's important to disassemble the dryer and clean it out more thoroughly—but reserve this job for a qualified appliance repair technician to avoid injuring yourself or damaging the machine.

▶ Every couple of months, use a dryer vent brush to remove lint buildup in the vent that leads to the outside of your home. Remove the lint from the duct. Don't just push it back into the dryer or let it clog any part of the vent. A Shop-Vac works well for this purpose.

▶ If your dryer vent is white vinyl, replace it with a rigid or semirigid aluminum vent. White vinyl ducts no longer meet building codes and are flammable.

Air Conditioner

▶ In preparation for the cooling season, clean the condenser coils on your air conditioner. Remove the entire cover of the air conditioner to gain access to the coils. Watch out for wasp or bee nests inside the unit. Clean the coils by blowing compressed air (from an air compressor) at them or using a soft-bristle brush to wipe the dirt off. You can also reverse a Shop-Vac and use it as a blower for this purpose. While you have the unit open, be sure to clean any dirt or lint buildup in the bottom of the air conditioner and oil the motor if it is equipped with oil ports on the sides. Read the instructions that were supplied with your air conditioner for oiling specifics or search for your unit's manual online.

▶ When storing a window AC unit, keep it in a basement or utility room, not a garage. It might be best to wrap it in heavy-duty plastic. Mice and other small animals love to live in air conditioners, and they can cause serious damage to the unit by chewing on wiring and insulation. Also, wasps and birds like to nest in uncovered units left in windows. Avoid these problems by storing your window air conditioner in a protected area, away from small animals, or by installing a cover on the part of the air conditioner that sticks outside.

▶ At least twice each year, clean or replace the air conditioner filter. Depending on your indoor air quality, this may need to be done monthly throughout the cooling season.

Humidifier

▶ Take time to replace your humidifier filter, wick, or pad at least twice per year. As water is evaporated through these components, they tend to get clogged with calcium, lime, and other deposits. This buildup is nearly impossible to remove and greatly reduces the humidifier's effectiveness. Many humidifiers can evaporate at only half their stated rate when the pad or filter gets clogged.

▶ If you have a reservoir-type humidifier, inspect and clean the float assembly quarterly to prevent overfilling. Also, add a bit of bacteriostatic solution to prevent bacterial growth.

▶ If you have a flow-through type of humidifier, check the drain to be sure the water is flowing properly.

Dehumidifier

▶ Get your dehumidifier ready for the cooling season. Make sure the humidistat is set correctly. If you set it too high (low humidity), the unit may run continuously, which is unnecessary. Purchase a hygrometer to determine the correct setting for your humidistat.

▶ Clean your dehumidifier water container.

▶ Replace your dehumidifier filter.

PROJECT: PREVENTING A WATER HEATER DISASTER

Level of difficulty: 𝏉 𝏉

Even when certain systems in your home appear to be functioning, they can become trouble spots as they slowly wear out. One such area is the water heater. A leaking water heater tank has the potential to do a lot of damage to your home. Even a small, slow leak can soak into the subfloor and cause it to decay. Leaking water may also destroy your carpeting, create mildew, and permanently stain your walls.

Fortunately, most water heater problems can be avoided with proper maintenance. Follow these few simple steps to keep your water, not your temper, well heated.

You will need:
- ✓ Water bucket
- ✓ Flashlight
- ✓ Water sealant
- ✓ Paintbrush
- ✓ Water heater drip pan
- ✓ Painted plywood (if necessary)

1. CHECK PRESSURE RELEASE VALVE. Take time to test the temperature/pressure relief valve once each year to make sure it's working. Use caution. The water in the tank is hot and can cause scalding burns. When you pull up or push down on the valve handle, hot water should come out of the overflow pipe. If it does not, it may need replacing. My recommendation in this case is to call a professional plumber.

2. DRAIN WATER. Periodically, every year or so, drain a bucket of water from the drain faucet at the bottom of the water tank in order to remove sediment that could corrode the unit and reduce its heating efficiency. Again, take care not to get burned by the hot water.

3. **CHECK WATER LINES.** Check all water lines, connections, and valves for signs of leakage. Using a flashlight, check under the tank for small leaks that could be caused by rust and corrosion.

4. **PROTECT FLOORING.** Protect the floor under the water heater from water damage by painting the area with a water sealant—but be sure to turn off the heat source to the water heater first to avoid a fire hazard.

5. **REPLACE PARTICLEBOARD.** Since the particleboard may be damaged if it's soaked, consider replacing it with a specially designed drip pan under the water heater. If the heater is sitting on unpainted particleboard, it will collapse if it gets wet. Replace the particleboard with painted plywood and place the pan on top of that. These pans are available at most building supply stores for about $10. Make sure the pan you select has a drain out of the bottom.

6. **CONSIDER A NEW WATER HEATER.** If your water heater is more than 10 years old, you may want to replace it to avoid potential leaks and to save energy. If you want to stick with a tank-style model, choose one with the best ENERGY STAR rating possible for greater efficiency. If you want to spend a bit extra to save in the long run, consider upgrading to a "tank-less" hot-water heater or even a solar unit. You might also want to visit www.energystar.gov for current statistics. ■
(Resource: Warrantech Corporation)

Andrea's Choice:
WAGS

If you are concerned about potential problems with your water heater, consider having a WAGS (water and gas shutoff) valve installed on your water heater. These automatically shut off explosive gas and water lines in the event of a leak.

Level of difficulty: T

Electricity is a wonderful invention that makes our lives easier and more comfortable. But, if taken for granted, it can be dangerous. Each year, many people are hurt or killed at home. Bad cords on appliances, improper use of extension cords, overloaded circuits, and damaged wiring represent a few of the conditions that cause fires, shocks, and even electrocution. Here are some valuable safety tips from my buddies at Square D, a manufacturer of electrical parts, and the Electrical Safety Foundation International (ESFI).

1. LOOK FOR ELECTRICAL HAZARDS. Take just a few minutes on a regular basis to look for electrical safety hazards in your home.

▶ Inspect the insulation on all electric appliances.
▶ Be sure all lamps/light fixtures have the correct-wattage bulb.
▶ Keep appliances away from water.
▶ Be sure all outlets near water have ground fault circuit interrupters (GFCIs).
▶ Test ground fault circuit interrupters.

Ground fault circuit interrupters are required on outlets that are within 6 feet of water, such as near the bathroom sink. They protect against accidental shock by turning off the circuit if there is a power "leak" from the circuit. This can prevent accidental electrocution, such as when a hair dryer is dropped into a bathtub. There are different types of GFCIs that provide protection for an individual outlet or a circuit breaker, or are portable. The normal home unit looks like a normal outlet, except it is usually squared off and has a test and a reset button in the middle. It is important to test GFCIs regularly, especially after an electrical storm, to make sure that they are working properly and still providing optimal shock protection.

To test GFCIs:

1. Press the Reset button on the outlet.
2. Plug in a night-light and turn it on.
3. Press the Test button on the GFCI outlet. The light should go off.

If it does not, the unit is not working properly or has not been properly installed.

4. Press the Reset button again and the light should go on.

If your unit fails the test, it may be damaged or incorrectly installed. In either case, it is not providing the protection against electrical shocks/electrocution that it should. Have it inspected by a licensed electrician.

2. DETERMINE IF YOU NEED TO CALL IN THE PROS. It is important to inspect your home on a regular basis. Just like any other product or appliance, the electrical system in your house ages and gradually deteriorates. Increased electrical demands also place stress on older systems that were not designed to handle such heavy loads.

Guidelines created by the Electrical Safety Foundation International suggest that if you can say yes to one or more of the following questions, you should have a licensed electrician or electrical inspector check your home.

▶ Is your home 40 years old or more?

▶ Has your home had a major addition or renovation in the last 10 years?

▶ Have you added a major new appliance in the last 10 years, such as a freezer, an air conditioner, or an electric furnace?

▶ Do your lights often dim or flicker?

▶ Do you blow a fuse or trip circuit breakers often?

▶ Are outlet and light switch faceplates discolored or hot to the touch?

▶ Do you hear noise from your outlets, such as a buzzing, crackling, or sizzling?

▶ Are you permanently using extension cords and several power strips throughout the house?

3. CHECK YOUR POWER CORDS. The lowly power cord carries the necessary power from the outlet to the appliance that makes it work, and as long as it works when we turn it on, it usually doesn't draw much attention. Your radio or computer will probably work even if the cord is damaged, but a nicked or frayed cord increases the risk of electrical shocks and fire.

Also remember that extension cords are made to be a temporary fix,

Never tuck an electric blanket in or put other blankets on top. This can cause the wiring to overheat and start a fire. Avoid using electric blankets on children, and do not fall asleep with a heating pad. Older models can cause burns. Newer models have an automatic shutoff switch.

but many people use them as a regular part of their home's electrical system. When a cord is used constantly, it will deteriorate. Unplug and store extension cords after each use. Too many extension cords are a sign that you don't have enough outlets. Have a qualified electrician install additional ones where you need them. Also check the rating on cords and use them appropriately. Some are meant only for indoor use, others for outdoor.

▶ Regularly check power cords to make sure they are not cracked or otherwise damaged.

▶ Keep telephone, lamp, and extension cords out of the way to avoid tripping.

▶ Try to plug lamps and items directly into outlets and avoid extension cords whenever possible.

▶ Be sure that furniture legs are not sitting directly on any cords.

▶ Make sure cords are not under furniture or carpeting or behind baseboards. Electric cords need to breathe. Cords placed under carpeting or behind baseboards can overheat and cause a fire.

▶ Do not attach electrical cords to the wall with nails or staples. Be sure to turn off the power before trying to remove them.

▶ Never try to repair cords. It's not a DIY project! Take it to an authorized repair center or cut the cord and dispose of the item properly.

▶ Check if the power load of the cord is suitable for how you want to use it. Figure 125 watts per amp to determine if the wattage is appropriate.

▶ Replace old extension cords. Those made with 18-gauge cords can overheat at 15 or 20 amps. Newer models feature 16-gauge wires.

▶ Make sure the plug is polarized and/or has three-prong plugs.

▶ Be sure that cords carry approvals from an independent testing facility, such as Underwriters Laboratories (UL), ETL SEMKO (ETL), or Canadian Standards Association (CSA).

4. MAKE SURE YOU ARE USING POWER STRIPS AND SURGE PROTECTION CORRECTLY. It is critical to remember that power strips do not increase the total amount of power provided by an outlet or circuit, just more opportunities to plug in to it. Be sure to use them safely, and remember that surge protectors come in varying types. It is important to purchase one suited for the appliances you are trying to protect. If you live in an area with a lot of lightning, you should consider a surge arrester. These are available at your local appliance or electronics retailer and can help keep power surges from damaging appliances and electronics. ■

MORE SAFETY GUIDELINES

▶ Never overload circuits. Remember to account for all items plugged into them, even light fixtures.

▶ Surge protectors only protect the items that are plugged into them, not the rest of the circuit.

▶ If a home circuit does experience a large spike or power surge, like a lightning strike, the surge protector will have to be replaced. If the light on your surge protector dims or if the unit does not work properly, replace it.

▶ A power strip does not necessarily offer surge protection, and not all are rated for the same type of appliances and/or uses. Match your needs to the right product.

▶ Surge protectors are now available with phone and cable jacks to protect your phone, fax, modem, and TV.

5. Look Out for Lightbulbs

There are a wide variety of lightbulbs on the market that offer different levels of power and types of light. It is important that no matter what type you select, the power rating is appropriate for the lamp or fixture that you are using.

▶ Read the bulb manufacturer's safety instructions.

▶ Always use the correct power of bulb. If you are not sure, contact the manufacturer of your light fixture. Using a bulb that is too much for the fixture is a fire hazard, because it can easily overheat. Also, oil and tannic acid from your fingers can create

Quick Tip:
New Arc Technology

Arc fault circuit interrupters (AFCIs) are a newer technology that identifies particular arcs when electricity jumps through an insulator and immediately shuts down the circuit. The National Electrical Code requires all new homes to have an AFCI installed in all bedrooms. They help prevent fires that originate in outlets, switches, and damaged cords connected to the circuits.

Newer electrical products feature other safety technologies. One is immersion detection circuit interrupters (IDCIs) and another is appliance leakage current interrupters (ALCIs). These devices work to prevent fires due to damage to appliances and/or cords. Be sure to check the manufacturer's information when shopping for new items to be aware of the latest safety features.

"hot spots" on lightbulbs (especially incandescent) that cause them to burn out sooner—so handle and install them with gloves or a cloth.

▶ Be sure that bulbs are securely screwed into place. Loose bulbs can overheat.

▶ Make sure that halogen floor lamps are far from curtains, beds, rugs, or other items that could catch fire. This type of lamp gets very hot and can present a fire hazard.

▶ Never hang anything such as a hat or a blanket on a lamp to diffuse the light. This can be very dangerous.

6. Keep Your Batteries Going and Going, Safely

Batteries are tremendous small and portable sources of power, but, like electricity, they can also overheat and cause fires.

▶ As with lightbulbs, be sure to use the right size and type.

▶ Make sure the contacts on the appliance and the battery are clean.

▶ Always check to make sure the batteries are installed correctly with + to + and – to –.

▶ Always replace all batteries at the same time with the same brand. Never mix old and new.

▶ Loose batteries can short-circuit if kept in a pocket with keys or tools that connect the opposite poles.

▶ Never charge alkaline batteries.

▶ Never heat, damage, or crush batteries.

▶ Remove and properly dispose of dead batteries.

7. Be Careful with Small Appliances and Tools

▶ Use only electrical items that are approved by an independent testing lab like UL, ETL, or CSA.

▶ Always follow the manufacturer's instructions.

▶ Remember to unplug items—curling irons, clothes irons, toasters, hair dryers, etc.—when not in use.

▶ Have a damaged electrical item professionally fixed, or safely dispose of it.

▶ Never leave an appliance near water or a sink where it could fall in. If it should, do not touch it unless the circuit has been shut off.

▶ Power tools should have a three-pronged plug or a double-insulated cord. Always use a grounded adapter when using a three-pronged plug in two-hole outlet.

▶ Always check tools prior to use for damaged cords and plugs.

9

get outta here!

Outdoor Repairs and Maintenance Projects

The time to repair the roof is when the sun is shining.
—JOHN F. KENNEDY

It's Saturday afternoon, and you just can't think of anything to do. Hey, let's clean those gutters. Sure, nobody really likes to do it, but it's a necessary chore around most homes. And while you're in the mood, spruce up the deck, prune some trees, water the foundation, and fix the cracked brick on the front wall. Turn on some old John Denver tunes, grab a cold soda, and get on it. Just think—when you're done, you can go take a nap. But first you have to install that hammock! Oh well, there's always next Saturday.

- ▶ Project: Doctoring Your Deck
- ▶ Terrific Tree Trimming
- ▶ To Roof or Not to Roof?
- ▶ Project: Gutters and Drainage, Oh My!
- ▶ Choosing New Gutters
- ▶ Fun Foundation Facts
- ▶ Project: Mud Pies and Brick Joints

PROJECT: DOCTORING YOUR DECK

Level of difficulty: T T T

You don't have to have a contractor's license to give your deck a face-lift. Just do a little research first. A beautiful wood deck can directly increase your home's value and your family's quality of life. Whether the deck is 200 square feet or 2,000 square feet, keeping your deck in good condition can amount to no more than an afternoon or two every couple of years, depending on factors such as climate and the type of products you use. In fact, even a complete deck makeover can be relatively quick.

The best way to clean and protect your deck depends on several variables. What kind of wood is the deck made of? What kind of deck coating have you used before? Do you want a very natural look, or would you like to add more color? Carefully assessing your deck's condition and knowing what you need to fix it, as well as knowing how you want your deck to look when you are done, goes a long way toward a smooth and satisfactory job.

So where to start? Deck care involves two related steps: cleaning and waterproofing. Sometimes, you may need to replace a board or hammer nails back in, but cleaning and waterproofing in a timely manner actually helps reduce the need for this kind of structural repair.

You will need:

- ✓ Deck cleaner or deck wash
- ✓ Water hose
- ✓ Synthetic broom
- ✓ Plastic tarp (or shower curtain)
- ✓ Pressure washer (optional)
- ✓ Choice of deck coating

1. FIGHT DECK DESTRUCTION. Water took down the *Titanic,* and it can take down your deck, too. Outdoors, water is wood's worst enemy. Wood that has not been waterproofed will absorb rain or even water from a sprinkler, causing it to swell. As the water evaporates, the wood cells shrink. This "dimensional instability," repeated over time, is what causes boards to crack or split and nails to loosen. Sunlight and mildew may cause cosmetic or surface changes, but they don't affect the structural integrity of the wood. Water does.

A common myth is that pressure-treated lumber, the most common deck wood, is waterproof. False! Most pressure-treated lumber resists termites and wood rot, but not water damage. What about premium woods like cedar and redwood or even teak and mahogany? Nope. The bottom line is that any wood you might use for deck building is vulnerable to water damage and needs to be protected. Even check the premium woods to be sure that they will repel moisture and stay in good shape.

One of the most common questions is "How often should I waterproof my deck?" Again, there is no one-size-fits-all answer. It depends on a number of factors, from the type of coating that was on the wood originally to the environment in your part of the country to the amount of foot traffic on the deck. You might need to reapply the waterproofing coating after just one year, but in many cases you can let several years go by between sessions of deck cleaning and waterproofing.

More good news: it is easy to determine when it's time to waterproof your deck. Just try the "splash" test. Splash water on your deck from a hose, a bucket, or a cup. If it is quickly and noticeably absorbed and the surface darkens, then the wood isn't waterproof. If the water beads, sits on the surface, or runs off, then you're covered. Over time, the water beading may diminish while the waterproof coating is still working. So if you don't see beading, definitely watch for water absorption.

2. START WITH A CLEAN DECK. Cleaning your deck is a critical part of the restoration process for several reasons. Aesthetically, it can make a dramatic difference in your finished results by removing years of dirt, surface wood cells that have grayed over time due to sunlight, mildew, and dark mold, and worn coatings. While algae is green, other biological organisms, such as mold and mildew, are dark in color and discolor decks. Cleaning is also essential before applying a new coat of waterproofing, because soils and previous coatings can keep the new coating from being absorbed properly, decreasing its effectiveness, and potentially leaving the surface sticky and preventing a nice, even finish.

Even a brand-new deck should be cleaned to remove dirt and possible mill glaze, which may not be visible to the eye. Another common myth is that new wood should be allowed to "season" for six months to a year before being waterproofed. This is a recipe for damage. New lumber should be treated within the first month, unless you're using a premium type of waterproofed lumber.

Cleaning your deck is a lot easier if you choose the right method from the start. As the variety of exterior waterproofing products has increased and formulas have changed, manufacturers have also introduced new types of cleaners to handle different needs. The product decision should be based on what you need to remove.

▶ A general "cleaner" will remove dirt, mold, mildew, or a clear, oil-based waterproof coating that has weathered (if applied at least 2 years ago).

▶ A more powerful cleaner, such as Thompson's WaterSeal Heavy Duty Deck Cleaner, is needed to remove a weathered tinted waterproof coating or a semitransparent stain, along with the dirt and mildew.

▶ Redwood and cedar have natural characteristics that require special treatment to enhance beauty and waterproofing efficiency. These types of wood can darken if cleaned with certain products, so look for a product formulated specifically for redwood and cedar.

▶ Solid stains will need to be removed by a product labeled "stain remover" or "stripper."

After the selection, the actual application of the deck cleaner is relatively straightforward. Most products are premixed and can be sprayed on. After waiting a short time (usually 5 to 15 minutes), either spray off the deck with a garden hose or scrub lightly with a synthetic broom (necessary to remove tinted waterproof coating or stains), then rinse off. Read and follow label directions. In some cases, you'll be advised to work in small sections at a time to prevent the product from drying on the wood. If you missed any spots or if there are stubborn areas, you can usually go back and spot treat that section.

To safeguard plants and landscaping around the deck, thoroughly saturate them with water before applying any deck cleaner. Cover them with heavy plastic while you're working, then, after removing the plastic, spray the area again with clean water. This will effectively dilute any residual chemicals. (Follow this same procedure when spraying on a waterproof product, to avoid overspray affecting your plants.)

Another option for cleaning a deck is pressure washing; using a gas- or electric-powered machine to deliver water in highly concentrated jets that power-off dirt. Since pressure washers can be used on a variety of structures, from cars and boats to decks and siding, cleaning solutions for specific materials can be added for even more effective cleaning. Pressure washers will remove dirt, mildew, grayed cells, and all types of waterproofing or stains, but they can damage wood if the water pressure (pounds per square inch, or psi) is too high and if you hold the wand too closely to the surface. It's possible to literally "carve" into the wood with the water. For most woods, 1,500 to 2,500 psi should be sufficient, but for softer woods like cedar, keep the psi at 1,200 to 1,500.

3. TOP IT OFF. The final step in your deck's revival involves decisions based on questions of both beauty and protection. At this point, consider how you would like the deck to look when you're finished and how you'd like it to look a year or two from now. Based on these decisions, you can choose the best waterproof coating for your deck. Do you want your deck's color to weather naturally to a "driftwood" kind of silver-gray or keep the "like-new" wood color for as long as possible? Or do you want to add color?

There are four different categories of deck coatings, each of which will give you different looks and types of protection for your deck. In the following breakdown, I've included estimates for the length of time that the coating will remain effective before reapplication is needed. Keep in mind that these are only general guidelines; many different factors influence the life of a coating, from the product's formulation and proper application to weather exposure and how you use the deck. Use the splash test described on page 219 to decide if your deck is still waterproofed.

Clear, Multipurpose Waterproofers

These products can be used on wood, brick, concrete, and other masonry surfaces. They are primarily designed to stop water damage, but they don't contain mildewcides, pigments, or UV absorbers. Wood treated with this type of waterproofer will weather over time to a silver-gray color. This type of product will need to be reapplied every 1 to 2 years.

Quick Tip: Do Your Homework

When it comes to selecting and using a deck cleaner and a waterproofing agent, there is one critical point that cannot be stressed enough: read the label and follow the directions listed. To save time in the store, many manufacturers have detailed product information on their Web sites, making it easier to decide on what you need beforehand. For instance, the Thompson's WaterSeal products Web site (www.thompsonsonline.com) offers a variety of helpful features, from detailed product information to a five-day weather forecast for your zip code to a few short questions about your deck that will yield a "shopping" list you can print and take to the store. A little advance planning will pay off tremendously in the end.

Clear Waterproofers

These products are specially formulated to protect wood and will usually include agents to resist mildew and color fading in addition to waterproofing. They may subtly enhance the existing color of the wood, but they won't change it, so if you love the natural color of your wood, these are good choices. These types of waterproofers typically need to be reapplied every 1 to 2 years.

Tinted Waterproofers

These products usually offer the same combination of waterproofing and fade and mildew resistance, but they let you add a very sheer, natural-wood color at the same time. The subtle color allows most of the wood's grain and character to show through. Reapplication is usually needed within 2 to 3 years.

Wood Stains

Exterior wood stains are more pigmented than tinted waterproofers and come in a wider range of colors: well over 100 shades are available, ranging from natural-wood colors to pastel whites, greens, blues, yellows, and more. These stains are available in semitransparent formulas, which allow some of the woodgrain to show through, and solid formulas, which completely cover the woodgrain but allow some of the wood texture to come through. Semitransparent stains will typically need reapplication after 3 years. Solid formulas can remain in good shape for up to 5 years.

A Few More Tips

Many people think that "stains" and "waterproofers" are mutually exclusive and wonder if they should apply a clear waterproofer over an exterior stain. The good news is that many quality exterior stains will have effective waterproofing properties and no additional product is normally needed. Read the package copy to see if the stain you're considering also offers mildew and fade resistance.

Paints usually aren't considered a deck coating. Technically, you could paint a deck as long as you make sure that the label says the product will withstand foot traffic. Not all paints will withstand that kind of stress. However, paint negates most of the natural look and feel of the wood, and once you've committed to paint on a deck, removing it can be a big chore.

No matter what look you want, check the label of any waterproofing product that you buy to be sure it says it passes ASTM standards for waterproofing. Not all products labeled as waterproofers provide the same level of protection. In fact, some products on the shelf actually fail industry measurements for effective waterproofing.

Oil and Water

The different kinds of deck coatings, from clear to solid stain, can all be found in either oil- or water-based formulas, which can be more environmentally friendly. Manufacturers have made great strides in formulating water-based coatings to offer the same or better protection than their oil-based counterparts. New regulations involving air quality and emissions from paints and related coatings are also furthering the drive to more environmentally friendly water-based coatings. Best of all, water-based formulas can be applied to damp wood. (Most waterproofers require a 48- to 72-hour wait between cleaning the wood and applying the waterproofer.) Water-based coatings can be applied 2 hours after cleaning is complete, meaning that a 1-day deck makeover is now a real possibility.

More Waterproofing Words of Wisdom

Most deck coatings today only require one coat, but you can choose different ways to get that coat on your wood. Most clear and tinted waterproofers can be applied with a brush, a roller, or a pump-up garden sprayer. Obviously, the sprayer greatly reduces your bending and stooping and speeds up the application process. Stains should not be applied in a pump-up garden sprayer, as the higher pigment loads can cause clogging. For most formulas, you can also use a compression-driven sprayer at a low setting. With any type of sprayer, backbrushing (with paint pad or brush) may be required to even out the finish.

A great tool for applying any kind of deck coating, from clear to solid

Quick Tip:
Wonky Waterproofing

If you want to spend a little extra time applying your waterproofer, it is possible to create fun patterns and distinctive designs. It can be as simple as leaving the center of the deck "clear" (protected by a clear waterproofer) and creating a border with one of the tinted shades, or as elaborate as creating a faux "rug" using three (or more) shades of waterproofer applied in alternating blocks. Just don't attempt to coat the entire deck with one waterproofer and then apply a second color over it. Apply each different type/color of waterproofer to bare wood.

stains, is a paint pad. A paint pad goes on the end of a long handle, much like a mop. It eliminates the bending needed for a brush or a roller, while giving you a great deal of control and precision over the product application for the best finish and performance.

All Hands on Deck!

The point of a deck is to help you forget your cares and relax. It's a great place to reconnect with friends, family, and nature. I'll leave it up to you on how best to take advantage of the joys of your beautiful and well-protected deck. Put out some potted plants, add some seating and outdoor decor, and make plans for your next cookout! ■

Terrific Tree Trimming

First of all, why should you prune at all? By clipping away dead or unattractive foliage, you can produce a healthier and more attractive plant. Pruning fruit trees can also help to create a higher yield.

Safety is also a factor. A jutting tree limb that may end up falling on someone or on your property should be removed before it becomes a threat. Shrubs and trees that block vision, such as while exiting a driveway, should also be pruned regularly. Caution should always be exercised, however, when trimming trees that grow close to utility lines. This is a job best left to your local power company.

"Many homeowners put themselves in harm's way by trying to trim large branches which grow over or near power lines," says Steve Houser, my buddy at Arborilogical Services, a Texas-based tree-care company. "It is risky and can end in injury or even death."

Sometimes, plants need to be pruned to encourage healthy growth, especially if a tree or a shrub has become diseased or insect infested. The best strategy is often to thin the crown slightly to increase airflow and reduce the end weight on longer limbs and to remove any branches that rub against each other. Strong plants can better resist damage during harsh storms and high winds. Any broken limbs should also be removed to minimize stress on a damaged plant.

Many homeowners trim their trees to achieve an optimal shape to accent their home. When trimming, try to follow the tree's natural shape. The more you can respect a tree's natural lines, the easier the shape will be to maintain long term. Take care not to overprune for aesthetic reasons. No more than a quarter of the tree's natural growth should ever be removed at one time or the tree may sustain irreparable damage. Just as proper pruning can enhance the form or character of plants, improper pruning can destroy them.

A few more tree pruning tips:

▶ Most trees can be pruned at anytime; however, maples, walnuts, and birches should be trimmed in the summer because they "bleed" sap if pruned in the winter. The spring is a good time to trim oak trees, plus treat them for a common disease called oak wilt (*Ceratocystis fagacearum*).

▶ Think twice before pruning branches that are larger than 2 inches in diameter.

▶ Consult an expert before pruning anything larger than 4 inches in diameter.

▶ When trimming branches, choose those with weak, V-shaped angles of attachment. Do not remove those with a strong, U-shaped angle of attachment unless it's absolutely necessary.

▶ When pruning small branches, make your cut just outside of the branch bark ridge (a wrinkle on the inside of the "elbow") and the branch collar (a raised ring that runs around the branch near the stem).

▶ Cut the wood as it smoothes out, away from the stem, but not too far out or healing may be impaired. A vertical cut, angled slightly back toward the stem, is best. Avoid making the cut too horizontal or water can collect in it and cause rotting.

▶ If a tree requires extensive trimming or if branches are larger than 4 inches in diameter, consult an expert. Not only is your tree's health a factor, but your own safety may be as well. Make sure your experts use multiple anchors to secure a branch before cutting it, ensuring safety for people and property.

To Roof or Not to Roof?

That is the question. Although there are many jobs around the home that most folks can tackle, roofing repairs and replacement are often best left to the pros. Falls from roofs and ladders are among the most common causes of serious injury to homeowners. Unless you are completely comfortable doing roof work yourself, bring in a pro. In any case, here are some tips to help you decide what level of job needs to be done.

Whether you need a complete replacement or just repairs depends on several factors. Obviously, if your roof is leaking, something needs to be done, but sometimes just a patch or some proper sealing can solve the problem. Check to see if your roof shows any of these symptoms.

▶ Missing and/or torn shingles or other roofing materials

▶ Dents in metal accessories on the roof (vents, flashing, gutters, etc.)

▶ Indentations or slight pitting in the roofing material

▶ Exposed areas of asphalt roofing shingles

▶ Water leaks or visible staining in the interior of your home

Older roofs made from slate or tile can last for generations, but if you have a more conventional roof that is fifteen years old or older that is starting to show signs of deterioration or produce leaks, it is time to call a pro for an inspection and consultation. Most reputable roofing companies will provide this service at no charge, and they will also usually supply a bid for replacement.

Getting a new roof or even having repairs done can be a major investment, so it's important that you choose the right contractor and materials. We've all heard horror stories about fly-by-night roofers who abscond with a neighbor's hard-earned cash and leave a partially finished job or substitute shoddy materials that wear out quickly. Spring and summer storms seem to bring these "instant" roofing experts out of the shadows and onto your front porch with a quick smile and a briefcase full of promises.

In truth, storm damage can compromise the performance of a roof, thereby putting your home in danger of leaks, rotting, mold, or other serious problems. If your home has been subjected to severe weather conditions, you should have the roof inspected for damage that could lead to future problems.

A professional can best handle a comprehensive roof inspection. Homeowners should always put personal safety first and never get on a damaged roof. While some storm damage is visible from the ground, much of it may not be.

Selecting the Right Roofing Material

Although you may want to choose the type and color of the roofing materials for your home, you may opt to leave the specific brand choice to the contractor. Your roofing installer will know which products have held up well for past clients. Feel free to call a few of your installer's references to check on their satisfaction with a particular product and the installation process.

Choose the best roof that you can afford; not only will it last longer, but it could also increase your home's value. Also, certain roofing products may help to lower your homeowner's insurance and be eligible for federal tax credits.

When choosing a new roof, consider the following four things.

1. The color and style of the material in relation to your home and neighborhood. Think long-term, as most roofs will last for at least ten to twenty years. Also consider resale value. Will a blue roof sell your home, or make it more difficult to sell?

2. The roofing materials' resistance to the elements—weathering, hail impact, wind, and fire. Certain roofs can help to lower your homeowner's insurance cost.

3. The written details of the manufacturer's warranty for various roofing products. The installer's ability to back up his work is also important.

4. Selecting the right contractor with impeccable references. Consider what type of certification the company has. Also be sure

Companies such as Owens
Corning and Gerard Roofing
Technologies have recently
developed roofing materials
that can withstand hurricane-
and tornado-force winds.
Visit the resources section at
the back of the book for
contact information.

that the company carries its own liability insurance in case an accident occurs on your job!

Material Options

COMPOSITION SHINGLES

Composition shingles are the most common roofing products in the United States. A large variety of styles and colors are available, in addition to a wide range of quality and length of warranty. Traditional "three-tab" classic asphalt shingles are often being replaced by "laminate" or "dimensional" shingles that can look much more like cedar shakes or slate.

Composition shingles are rated by the years that an average roof should last under normal conditions. You may wonder why your twenty-year roof only lasted ten years. In some regions, weather conditions can be considered outside the spectrum of "normal," which is why you should buy the best material that you can afford.

METAL ROOFING

Do you admire country-style roofs with their shiny, green, or silver metallic look? If your home lends itself to this fun style, you can choose from metal-paneled products or the heavier-duty standing-seam metal roofing. Metallics are available in a rainbow of vibrant colors.

Want top-of-the-line? Check out stone-coated steel, which can last fifty years or more. Developed to withstand tornado- and hurricane-force winds as well as resist hail damage, steel roofs are offered in a range of profiles and colors that imitate clay tile, wood shakes, or heavy-duty composition roofs. In the aftermath of hurricanes and wildfires, many metal-roofed homes have survived where conventionally roofed homes have been destroyed. In addition, steel roofs are lighter in weight than most other materials and can actually add an insulating factor to your home.

WOOD SHINGLES

Wood shingles and shakes have fallen out of favor in recent years as more durable products have become affordable. In recent years, some municipalities have stopped accepting wood shingles. Insurance rates can be higher for wood roofs due to the obvious fire hazard. Wood roofs are also more easily damaged by wind and hail and can be prone to the growth of moss, which can lead to moisture retention and damage. If you decide that wood is what you want, for aesthetic reasons, ask your installer about fire-resistant options.

SLATE

Slate is a natural material that was often used on higher-end homes in the early part of the twentieth century. It tends to be a bit pricey, but lasts virtually forever. If you have an older home with a slate roof, consider repairing it before replacing it. You'll probably come out ahead while preserving the historic value of your home.

Many other materials are available for roofs, such as tile and synthetics. Certain materials are recommended for select climates and conditions. Ask your local roofing installers for popular options in your area.

PROJECT: **GUTTERS AND DRAINAGE, OH MY!**

Level of difficulty: T T

One area of your home that needs periodic attention is your gutter and drainage system. Since gutters control the flow of water from your roof, even small leaks can seriously damage your home over time, causing water to collect in your basement or creating uneven drainage around your home's foundation. Here are some reasons to keep your gutters in good shape.

▶ Proper drainage control helps prevent unwanted moisture damage.

▶ Gutters can help prevent water from staining your walls.

▶ Gutters and downspouts prevent a "waterfall" effect during storms, which can douse you or guests when entering or leaving your home.

▶ Gutters also help prevent soil erosion along the roof edge of your home and redirect excessive moisture away from your foundation.

▶ Gutters add resale value to your home.

▶ Taking the time to maintain and repair downspouts and gutters can double or even triple the life of your roof drainage system. This can save you a lot of money on repair costs.

▶ Leaks in the system can damage not only the siding on a home, but also get into the structure, causing rot and mold and inviting termite infestation. Also, gutters that do not empty completely after each rain can create breeding grounds for mosquitoes.

▶ A properly working gutter system is an insurance policy for your home, providing protection by controlling roof runoff.

You will need:
- ✓ Tube(s) of gutter seal
- ✓ Antifungal agent
- ✓ Hose bladder
- ✓ Vacuum
- ✓ Drop cloth
- ✓ Level or bucket of water (to check the gutter pitch)
- ✓ Plastic drainage trays
- ✓ Short flexible pipe
- ✓ Steel brush

- ✓ Ladder
- ✓ Gloves
- ✓ Broom, scoop, and/or tongs
- ✓ Water hose
- ✓ Power drill
- ✓ Weakened bleach solution
- ✓ Oxylic acid mixture

1. EXAMINE THE DOWNSPOUT SYSTEM. During the next downpour, have a look at your existing gutter and downspout system. Is everything draining properly? If it hasn't rained in a while, use a water hose to fill the gutters and check for problems.

2. SEAL AND REPAIR. Make sure the gutters are attached firmly to the house by checking the attaching hardware. Seal any leaks with a tube of gutter seal.

3. ADJUST THE GUTTER PITCH. Improper drainage due to poor gutter pitch is one of the biggest causes of roof drainage problems. Improper drainage causes water to accumulate in certain spots, which creates a buildup of debris and accelerates rusting.

There should be a drop of approximately 1/16 inch for each foot of length of guttering. You can use a chalk line and a level to take a reading and mark the slope of your gutters. Another way is to pour a bucket of water into the gutter and observe the flow. If it runs off without leaving pools of water in the gutter, the gutter is set properly. If there are low spots, the water will sit in the gutter, allowing you to locate the trouble spots.

Ordinarily, the pitch of a gutter can be set in only one direction. However, gutter runs of more than 35 feet should slant in each direction from the center. Again, the drop should be set at a rate of 1/16 inch of fall for each foot of gutter.

High or low spots detected in the gutter run can often be corrected by slightly bending the hanger that supports the gutter up or down. If this doesn't work, you can add gutter hangers and braces (use ones that match those already in use) to correct high or low spots.

---

*T*Andrea's Choice:
Outdoor Repairs Made Easier

Permanent Patch is like an adhesive bandage for home repairs. It creates a superstrong bond on almost any surface: wood, metal, concrete, fiberglass, PVC, plastic, and more. Fix the cracked housing on a mower, loose vinyl siding, a hole in the gutter, a weak joint in a pipe, or a leak on a boat. Cured by the sun, it is waterproof and durable. Just trim the 6- by 3-inch patch to size with a scissors or a razor knife, then peel and stick it on. Once cured, it can be sanded, drilled, and painted. (Visit www.supergluecorp.com.)

Some gutters are installed with spikes and sleeves (sometimes called spikes and ferrules). You may need to add an additional spike or sleeve to raise or lower the fall of the gutter at any specific point. Use a power drill to make a hole through the gutter before inserting the extra spike and sleeve.

4. REMOVE RUST. Keep the gutters properly cleaned and the pitch set correctly to slow down the rusting process. Once those faults have been corrected, if you notice rust, use a steel brush to remove any loose scale and then coat the area with a rust-inhibiting paint.

5. EXAMINE DRAINAGE PATTERNS. Once you've got the system on the house in working order, look at how the water drains onto the ground. It's important to get the water as far away from the foundation as possible, so that it can't leak back into the basement or soak your foundation unevenly. Make sure that the grade slopes away from the foundation and down-spouts are routed 3 to 5 feet out from the house. Simple plastic drainage trays or short flexible pipe can help. The pipe is widely available at home centers and needs to be installed at a slight slope, so that the water will drain down and out of the pipe.

6. REMOVE LEAVES AND OBSTRUCTIONS. If trees surround your home, leaves, pine needles, bird nests, and other debris can clog your gutters, which can interfere with their function and can cause wood fascia to rot and mildew. It is important to remove debris periodically. There are a number of ways to clean gutters, but for most methods, you will have to climb a ladder.

The most basic method for gutter cleaning is to dig the debris out with your hands—while wearing gloves, of course. Use a whisk broom or scoop to make it easier. Large tongs can also be used. Some are even made just for this purpose. Wash the rest of the debris out with a water hose. To dispose of the debris, spread a disposable drop cloth underneath you and allow the leaves to fall onto it. When you're done, just roll up the whole mess and throw it into the trash or empty the debris onto your compost heap.

Another method is to use a wet/dry shop vacuum and a long hose to suck up the leaves. To clean out a downspout, stick the end of a water hose approximately halfway down into the spout and turn the water on. The force of the water should push out the debris. If this does not work, you can purchase a hose bladder at most hardware stores or home centers. This creates additional pressure, which helps to blast out stubborn clogs. A long piece of wire or plumber's snake can also help to break up clogs.

If you notice mold or mildew growth on your home behind your gutters, apply an antifungal agent, following the manufacturer's directions. A weakened bleach solution or oxylic acid mixture can also be used to kill mold and mildew.

Clogged gutters are such a common problem that many companies have created solutions to try to fight it. Gutter protection devices include from strainers, snap-in metal and plastic gutter guards, filtered gutter guards, stainless steel gutter guards, hinged gutter guards, plastic and metal total gutter covers, and even gutter brushes that look like hairy caterpillars.

Regardless of the gutter guard protection used, all gutter systems should be examined for cleaning and repair twice every year. If clogging is a constant problem for your home, you may want to consider upgrading to hooded gutters. ■

Choosing New Gutters

Most hardware retailers and lumberyards carry bulk gutters and can advise you on proper installation. An online resource for gutter information is www.amerimax.com. Here's a basic primer on the two major types of gutters.

▶ If your home does not have gutters at all and if your budget is extremely tight, vinyl gutters offer an inexpensive water control system.

▶ Installing metal gutters, such as those seen on most homes, can be a do-it-yourself project, if you are reasonably skilled with tools and comfortable going up and down a ladder. Metal gutters tend to last longer than vinyl and hold up better under temperature fluctuations and in high winds. Metal can also be painted to match your home.

Andrea's Choice:
Hooded Gutters

You may want to opt for a permanent solution to frequent clogs: hooded gutters. Featuring a special covering that sheds debris but allows water to drain through, GutterMaxx is one of the companies marketing this newer technology. Hooded gutters can be a bit pricey, but the company guarantees that you will never have to clean your gutters again. (Visit www. guttermaxx.com.)

Fun Foundation Facts

When you think of home maintenance, sometimes you have to start at the bottom and work your way up. If the soil beneath your foundation expands when it's wet or contracts when it's dry, the foundation can shift, causing fractures and misalignment. In some areas of the country, due to expansive soils and periods of rain versus drought conditions, these issues are commonplace. If you've been wondering if your bottom needs a boost, read on for a basic primer on foundation care and repair.

Common Signs of a Damaged Foundation or Basement

- ▶ Doors that won't close or open easily
- ▶ Windows that bind when you try to open them
- ▶ Cracks in the Sheetrock, especially near the corners of doors and windows
- ▶ Nails popping out of the Sheetrock
- ▶ Cracks in a brick or stone fireplace wall
- ▶ A garage door that won't open or close properly
- ▶ Cracks or raised areas of floor
- ▶ Raised ceiling joints (visible in the attic or the basement)
- ▶ Curling or loose wallpaper
- ▶ Cracks in the exposed foundation around the house
- ▶ Caulking that pulls away from exterior surfaces or around tubs or fixtures
- ▶ Obvious cracks in brick and mortar
- ▶ Cracks and uneven elevations in structures attached to the home
- ▶ Termites or ants in or around the home

Common Causes of Shifting Foundations

▶ Water is the main culprit in most foundation problems. There is either too much, causing the soil to swell, or not enough, causing the soil to shrink. If the ground beneath a foundation moves evenly, it is unlikely to cause a problem. But when only part of the soil heaves or settles, it can cause cracks and other damage. Also, drippy outdoor faucets or other water sources near the home can cause water damage as well.

▶ Poor drainage can be a major contributor to foundation and basement problems. Make sure that your gutters and downspouts direct any roof runoff away from the house. Use gutter extensions to direct water at least 3 to 5 feet from the foundation. The ground next to the home should also slope away from the house about a quarter inch per foot to encourage proper runoff.

▶ Underground water from a spring or nearby creek can cause problems for your foundation. Broken or leaking plumbing can also wreak havoc, even under your home. If you suspect such a problem exists, contact a local inspector or your municipality to check for subterranean water sources.

▶ Soil in areas where trees were removed during construction can undergo eventual sinking.

▶ Trees that have grown over a period of years, with roots too close to the home can damage the foundation and can clog gutters with debris.

▶ A home built on fill dirt instead of heavily compacted soil.

▶ A structure that has been added to the original home.

Foundation Preventive Maintenance

Proper care of any concrete foundation or basement can help you avoid future problems. It is imperative to ensure that the moisture content around your home remains as even and consistent as possible, avoiding periods of excess moisture or dryness.

▶ To discourage excess moisture, be sure that gutter downspouts carry water well away from the foundation and that water doesn't puddle anywhere near the house during or after rainfalls. If you are adding new gutters to your home, be sure that they do not affect the normal moisture content by creating dry or moist spots near the foundation. Also make sure that water drains from around the house at an even rate.

▶ Regular foundation and lawn watering during dry periods can often help to prevent soil shrinkage, which is one potential cause of foundation problems. If you choose to hydrate the soil supporting your foundation, never water the space between dried soil and the actual wall of the foundation. Rather, use a soaking hose placed approximately 2 to 3 feet from the house for several hours a day to keep the soil moist. Don't wait too long before cracks occur in the soil, but rather begin soaking as the spring rainy season is ending and continue it until the weather turns cooler in the fall.

▶ Plants with shallow, strong roots can actually damage your foundation, so it's important to enjoy them at a distance. Some types of trees have fingerlike root systems that stay near the surface and can starve the soil of water. Check with the nursery you buy your trees from on how their root systems grow. A good rule of thumb is to place new trees the same distance from your house as you expect them to grow in height. In other words, a tree that will grow to 30 feet should be planted at least 30 feet from your home's foundation. Always water the trees on the side opposite your home to encourage root growth in that direction.

PROJECT: MUD PIES AND BRICK JOINTS

Level of difficulty: T T T

The cutting out and "repointing," or touching up, of mortar joints in brick, concrete block, and stone is a repair that most homeowners can tackle themselves. Believe it or not, it's actually pretty fun. Cracked, loose mortar can allow water to seep in and cause interior wall damage, but professional repairs can be costly. You don't have to be a bricklayer to master this technique. And unlike with some projects, if you try this one and are not satisfied with the results, the worst problem is usually that you will have to clean up a mess.

To ensure the best possible results, invest in a few inexpensive masonry tools, available at your local hardware store or home center.

You will need:
- ✓ Mortar mix or masonry mix, or vinyl concrete patch for concrete repairs
- ✓ Old clothes and shoes
- ✓ Safety glasses
- ✓ Drop cloth
- ✓ Plugging or joint chisel
- ✓ Bricklayer's hammer
- ✓ Wire brush or bristle brush
- ✓ Jointer
- ✓ Pointing trowel
- ✓ Garden hose with spray attachment
- ✓ Bucket of water
- ✓ Wheelbarrow or mortarboard

1. CHOOSE THE RIGHT MIX. While mortar mix or masonry mix is the product of choice for most applications, especially larger jobs, other products can also yield excellent repointing results. If you plan to make a number of concrete repairs, such as filling cracks, repairing chipped edges, and resurfacing scaled areas, as well as doing some repointing, vinyl concrete patch can handle all these jobs. If you plan to patch leaks in block or brick walls with water-stop cement, repoint the surrounding joints as well. Always follow the directions listed on the individual product package.

2. PREHYDRATE THE MIX. When using mortar mix or masonry mix for brick repair, it is recommended that you "prehydrate" the mortar prior to pointing the joints. *Prehydrate* is a fancy word that means that you get the mortar wet and then let it sit to fully absorb the moisture. This step will greatly reduce the shrinkage of any of the joints away from the edge of the bricks and cut down on the number of hairline cracks that occur when the mortar begins to dry against the old bricks.

To prehydrate the mortar, mix the required amount of mortar mix or mason mix with just enough water to form a damp mix that retains its form when pressed into a ball in your hand. Let the mortar set for about 30 to 45 minutes and then add enough water to make the mortar workable. The end result will be a mix slightly drier than what is normally used to lay new brick. Never make large batches of mortar for repairs; mix an amount you can use in about 45 minutes.

3. PREPARE THE JOINTS. Be sure to wear old clothes and safety glasses. You may also want to spread out a drop cloth to protect the surrounding area. You're going to make a mess. Cut out the mortar joints to an approximate depth of ¾ to 1 inch. Using the special plugging or joint chisel will help prevent binding in the joint and chipping of the brick edges. A clean surface is needed for good bonding. Use the jointer tool to rake out excess mortar or grit and brush or vacuum out the joints to remove loose mortar or sand. Flush out any remaining particles with a garden hose equipped with a spray attachment.

4. REPLACE BAD BRICKS. Any bricks in the wall that are badly broken or deteriorated should be cut out and replaced prior to repointing and repairing. Select new bricks that match the old bricks as closely as possible.

- ▶ Cut the old brick completely out of the wall.
- ▶ Clean out the recess carefully.
- ▶ Wet the cavity and the replacement unit with a brush or a fine spray of water. When the cavity is damp, but not wet, apply a thick layer of mortar mix or masonry mix to the bottom and sides of the cavity.
- ▶ Butter the top of the replacement brick, just as if you were buttering a slice of bread, and slide it into the cavity. Mortar should squeeze out from the joints. If it does not, rebutter the joint, adding more mortar.

5. REPOINT. Now we get down to the nitty-gritty. Practice a bit on some spare bricks to perfect your technique.

▶ Dampen the cleaned joints with a brush and water.

▶ Load the trowel with mortar. Pick up the mortar from the trowel with the jointer tool and press it into the joints. Pack the mortar firmly into the joints. Repoint the vertical (head) joints first and the horizontal (bed) joints second. This sequence allows you to make unbroken horizontal strokes with the jointer to form straight, even bed joints.

▶ In most cases, joints are filled flush to the wall face, then slightly depressed with the jointer and brushed clean. If concave or V joints were used in the original work, use the proper tool for these finishes after the repointing is done and before the mortar gets too hard to work.

▶ To reduce the possibility of cracking or sagging in extremely deep joints, fill in about half of the joint depth, wait until the mortar is thumbprint hard, and then repoint the remainder of the joint.

▶ In hot or windy conditions, dampen the repointed joints to prevent the mortar from drying too fast. Spray the finished job with a fine water mist to aid in the curing process.

▶ Repointing of stonework and block is essentially the same as brickwork. Tool the joints to match those in the sound sections of the wall.

Now go get the neighbors and show off your handiwork. But watch out, you may be doing more brick repair jobs before you know it! ■

10

where flowers bloom, so does hope

Making the Outside of Your Home as Beautiful as the Inside

The grass is not, in fact, always greener on the other side of the fence. Fences have nothing to do with it. The grass is greenest where it is watered. When crossing over fences, carry water with you and tend the grass wherever you may be.

—ROBERT FULGHUM, AUTHOR OF *ALL I REALLY NEED TO KNOW I LEARNED IN KINDERGARTEN*

Did you know that gardening is one of the most popular hobbies in the United States? It makes sense if you think about it: gardening not only helps to create a beautiful home environment, but it is therapeutic as well. There are few activities as relaxing and rewarding as tilling the soil and watching your labor come to life. Get the kids involved. The pattern of life in a garden can teach our young many lessons about their own world. Plus, it's fun!

In this chapter, we'll explore our outdoor universe, starting with some ways to make your home more appealing from the street view. We'll create a memory lane to be shared for generations. Then we'll delve into the earth and make things grow.

Level of difficulty: 𝑇 𝑇 𝑇 *to* 𝑇 𝑇 𝑇 𝑇 𝑇

Does your porch pale in comparison to your neighbor's? Do your shutters sag? Is your door a drag? If so, it's time to power up your porch and update your entryway.

1. DETERMINE YOUR STYLE. If your home was built before 1970, it may have a distinctive architectural style, such as Colonial, Greek Revival, Victorian, or Arts and Crafts. To preserve its historic value, your entryway should match the rest of the house. If you have a modern, ranch, or suburban home, you have more flexibility to follow your own tastes.

2. START WITH YOUR STRUCTURE. Assess your home's structural elements. If you already have a porch that's in good shape, you can build from that. Check the railings, the balusters, the columns, and the roof overhang to make sure they are not subject to rot or insect damage. If so, consider replacing them with materials that offer more durability, such as modern composites or cedar, which is naturally water resistant.

3. MAKE NECESSARY REPAIRS. Before you move on to painting or decor, fix any rotted wood or other damage. My own home had some dry rot on the pine porch planking, so I used a 2-part epoxy filler to repair the damaged area. Then I sanded and painted it white to match the trim on my home.

4. UPDATE YOUR ARCHITECTURAL ELEMENTS. A worn-out front door and old hardware can make your home look dated. Spending a few hundred dollars to revitalize the entryway's "curb appeal" can potentially increase your home's resale value by thousands of dollars, not to mention pleasing you and your guests.

When I updated my porch, I replaced the simple wooden slab door with an Arts and Crafts fiberglass model. Due to afternoon sun exposure, the old wooden door had split and was warping, making it drafty and less secure. Fiberglass is totally weather resistant as well as five times more energy efficient than wood. I stained the new door with a medium oak tint and then topcoated it with a satin polyurethane varnish for maximum weather and UV resistance. Decorative hardware and fixtures are a must for any porch makeover. For my project, I chose an oil-rubbed bronze lever set in a simple design to blend with the style of the door. A door knocker, a kickplate, and house numbers were coordinated in the same finish. Don't forget new lighting for creating a mood and adding security.

5. ADD PIZZAZZ WITH LANDSCAPING. Decorative stone and foliage can change even a challenging area from boring to brilliant. In the front of my home, I had difficulty growing grass due to heavy sun exposure, so I removed all of the grass, replaced it with flagstone, added a potted fern and a solar-lighted address plaque. It's now the highlight of my front yard.

6. ACCESSORIZE WITH FURNITURE AND ART. Now it's time to accessorize. For a casual effect, consider faux wicker that looks real but stands up to weather and insects. Include floral-printed cushions to provide color and comfort. For a more rustic look, try split-hewn furniture, rough twig chairs, and western-motif fabrics.

Whatever your style, you'll want to include some seating for relaxing afternoons, such as a rocking chair, a hammock, or a chaise longue. Even a small porch can accommodate a corner seat. Add a basket of weather-proof collectibles, a coordinating throw, a welcoming wreath, and flowers to complete the cozy effect. ■

PROJECT: MAKE A MEMORY LANE

Level of difficulty: T T T

Want a little walkway but don't know how to make it? Now you can construct a cobblestone path in no time using plastic forms, concrete mix, and a little creativity. It's a bit like making a really big mud pie. Grab a buddy and get to work. It's much more fun with a helper. This is also a terrific project for getting the kids involved. You can construct your path over old concrete, grass, or dirt, so it's a great project for "difficult" areas, too, where laying a normal walkway would present a challenge.

You will need:

✓ Power washer and degreaser (if needed for old concrete)
✓ Concrete bonding agent (if laying over old concrete)
✓ Sand (if laying over grass or dirt)
✓ Bags of powdered concrete
✓ Water for mixing concrete
✓ Concrete stain (optional)
✓ Large 3- by 5-foot tray or wheelbarrow for mixing concrete
✓ 2 trowels (1 small, 1 large)
✓ Bucket of water for cleanup and wetting trowels
✓ Cotton or leather work gloves
✓ Safety goggles or glasses
✓ Concrete cobblestone forms
✓ Shovel
✓ Clothes that can get dirty and stained
✓ Portland cement

1A. PREPARE OLD CONCRETE. If you are laying your cobblestones over concrete, power-wash the surface to remove dirt and oil. Allow it to dry, and then coat the whole area with concrete bonding agent to help the new concrete stick to the original surface. Keep in mind that the new stones will raise the surface approximately 2 to 3 inches.

T Andrea's Choice:
Fun Forms

If you're having trouble finding concrete forms that you like, check out Quikrete's versions. They make several styles, from cobblestone to brick. Each heavy-duty plastic form can be used over and over. (Visit www. Quikrete.com.)

Quick Tip:
Concrete Sense

What's the number one mistake that folks make when laying concrete? They add too much water, creating a concrete soup that does not set up properly. The second mistake is not buying enough bags of concrete. Concrete actually shrinks as it dries, so it's best to slightly overestimate your needs. You may even want to buy a stepping-stone form for using up any excess concrete mix.

1B. PREPARE GRASS OR DIRT. If you are laying your cobblestones over grass or dirt, smooth out the area with a thin layer of coarse sand.

2. MIX THE CONCRETE. Each 80-pound bag of concrete mix will form approximately 4 square feet of finished concrete (2 inches thick), so if your walkway will be 2 feet by 20 feet (40 square feet), you'll need about 10 bags of concrete. If you want your walkway to have color, such as adobe or brown, pick up the recommended amount of concrete stain at your masonry supplier, home center, or hardware store.

Mix an 80-bound bag of powdered concrete, 1 gallon of water, and, if desired, concrete stain (which will not wash out of your clothes). It's important to blend all of the ingredients thoroughly. Think of it as a big brownie mix. Then place the cobblestone form where you want it and pour the "batter" right in. If necessary, have an assistant hold the form in place as you shovel in the wet concrete.

3. SMOOTH THE SURFACE. It can take a bit of work to trowel the mix into each nook and cranny. I've found it to be helpful to have both a large and a small trowel and to keep them nice and wet for smoothing out the surface. Shimmy the form several times to help settle bubbles and voids. After smoothing off the tops, simply lift the form from the damp concrete and voilà—you have cobblestones!

The first form will take you about 30 minutes to make, including mixing, pouring, and smoothing. By the time you have made 3 to 4 forms, you should be finishing each one in 15 minutes or less. Create a meandering trail through your yard or simply a small play platform; you can do as much or as little as you choose.

For decoration, after you have formed up the walkway, you might enlist the help of younger children to press leaves into the concrete as it's drying. When you peel each leaf away, the design will dry into the stone, creating a virtual fossil. Also try imbedding waterproof family keepsakes such as tiles, keys, seashells, or old coins into your walkway. Older children can design their own stone "album." Just make sure everyone wears gloves and eye protection while they're working around concrete to avoid irritating skin or damaging those peepers.

Allow 24 hours for the stones to dry.

4. ADD THE FINISHING TOUCHES. After the concrete has thoroughly dried, fill the joints between the cobblestones with a mixture of sand and portland cement and then simply wet it with the garden hose to make the mortar. Now just add a few plants and a relaxing bench and serve some mint juleps! ■

Quick Tip: Easy Garden Accents

Want to create some romantic garden stones or bricks? A slight modification to the previous project produces loose stones instead of a solid walkway. Simply lay the concrete forms on top of a sheet of plastic (an old shower curtain works great) and pour. When the concrete dries, you just peel away and discard the plastic and distribute your creations for garden accents or edging. This is a great way to use up excess concrete.

PROJECT: CRAZY CONCRETE COATINGS

Level of difficulty: T T T T T

One of the best surfaces for home decorating may be just outside your front or back door: concrete! Much of the flatwork outside of a home is gray and distinctly drab, but there's no reason it has to be that way. Driveways, patios, walkways, pool decks, birdbaths, and outdoor furniture can all be transformed to help define and accessorize a home and the surrounding landscaping. Here are a few ways to turn concrete from dull to dramatic.

You will need:

- ✓ Clear waterproofer or concrete stain
- ✓ Concrete cleaner and degreaser (TSP [Trisodium phosphate] works well)
- ✓ Concrete caulk (for small cracks)
- ✓ Concrete patching compound (for larger cracks)
- ✓ Concrete sealer
- ✓ Concrete stamps or objects of your choice
- ✓ Concrete prestain etch (for smooth concrete)
- ✓ Concrete stain
- ✓ Brush

1. COME CLEAN. Concrete can get dirty, mildewed, and stained over time. A good cleaning can make it look fresh again. Apply the cleaner to the concrete, allow it 10 to 15 minutes to work, scrub lightly with a stiff-bristle brush, and rinse with a garden hose. If your concrete is heavily stained, rinsing with a pressure washer and repeating the application of cleaner can help speed up the process.

2. PATCH THINGS UP. Fill in relatively small cracks with a caulk designed for concrete. Fill in the areas with more damage with a concrete patching compound. This is similar to wood filler except that it repairs damage in masonry.

If your surface is too dirty and broken for spot repairs, consider resurfacing the entire area. Instead of tearing out the original structure and pouring new concrete, you can apply a specially formulated top layer over the existing surface. You can do this yourself or work with a contractor who specializes in concrete repair.

3. PUT YOUR STAMP ON IT. If you are pouring new concrete or resurfacing, you have the option to "stamp" decorative patterns into the surface before it dries. This can be as simple as using an object like a seashell to make a few imprints in the corners. Also, there are stamping forms made specifically for concrete, available in a wide variety of designs. You can use these to make an entire surface resemble brick, stone, or something even more exotic. (You can rent or buy these concrete stamps. Check local home centers, specialty stores, and even the Internet.)

4. APPLY SEALERS AND COLOR. Once the surface is clean and smooth, it's time to think about protecting the surface and the overall look you want to achieve. Concrete is actually very porous. Water causes a variety of problems when it penetrates concrete and masonry surfaces, including cracking and chipping. Salt and pool chemicals can also negatively affect concrete. A clear waterproofer or concrete stain will protect concrete against damage. There are many different sealers and waterproofers on the market. Do a bit of research to find the one that meets your needs. Visit your local hardware store or home center to familiarize yourself with various products that can help make your project a success. Most sealers can be applied with a brush, a roller, or a plastic pump-up sprayer.

And whoever said concrete had to be gray? If you're pouring new concrete, you can have powdered pigments mixed throughout the concrete, or you can dust on colored hardeners and then work the color into the top layer of the concrete with a trowel. Both methods create permanent color.

Acid staining is another option that do-it-yourselfers or professionals use to add permanent color to concrete. In this approach, metallic salt pigments penetrate the concrete and chemically react with it to produce mottled, natural color. The results can be beautiful, but the color choices are limited and the process should be done with care since it involves acid to help "etch" the concrete so the salts can penetrate.

Andrea's Choice:
Concrete Care
Cleaner & Degreaser

Trisodium phosphate (TSP) is a heavy-duty all-purpose cleaner that cuts through and removes heavy deposits of greasy dirt and grime from interior and exterior surfaces, such as concrete, siding, brick, and painted surfaces. It's also good for removing heavy deposits of greasy grime, smoke, soot stains, and chalked paint from walls, woodwork, and floors. It removes mildew and mildew stains when mixed with bleach. Be sure to follow the label directions and wear protective gear when using this or any chemicals. Ready-to-use cleaners like Thompson's WaterSeal Concrete Care Cleaner & Degreaser work much like a deck cleaner. In fact, Thompson's makes a full line of products to help make concrete jobs easier. (Visit www.thompsons.com.)

The easiest way to add beautiful, rich color to concrete is with a concrete stain. Most can be used indoors and out. Acrylic latex stains are easy to work with since they offer great convenience features, such as low odor and soap-and-water cleanup. (Smooth concrete will need to be treated first with prestain etch.) This stain waterproofs and resists fading and damage from mildew, algae, and mold without the need for an additional sealer. For even more decorative flair, consider using more than one color or creating fun patterns, such as simple squares or other geometric shapes. For more ideas, check out the concrete painting project in chapter 4. ■

PROJECT: PEP UP PATIO FURNITURE

Level of difficulty: T T T

Thinking of throwing out those old resin patio chairs? Don't do it. Color them fun and keep them for the poolside, parties, and other occasions. Special outdoor paints that adhere to plastic offer an easy and inexpensive way to change the look and color coordination of your patio set, all in just a weekend. These paints are great for a kid's plastic furniture, too.

For this project, choose two or more colors that coordinate with your outdoor decor.

You will need:

✓ Sandpaper, medium to fine grain (if working with wood)
✓ Wire brush or chemical rust remover (if working with rusted metal)
✓ Degreaser or denatured alcohol (if working with metal)
✓ White paint or primer
✓ Spray paint for outdoor use, in at least 2 coordinating colors of your choice
✓ Tack cloth
✓ Blue painter's tape
✓ Newspaper
✓ Drop cloth

1. PREP THE SURFACE. Completely tape off any area that you do not want painted. A low-tack blue painter's tape is best. Spread a drop cloth or a newspaper beneath the furniture in a well-ventilated area. If spraying outdoors, watch out for overspray or wind-borne mist.

If your surface is wood, sand it smooth with a medium to fine grain sandpaper, then wipe it clean with a tack cloth to remove dust. Spray it with a primer or a base coat of paint to hide the woodgrain, if desired. If your surface is metal, remove any loose rust or scale with a wire brush, sandpaper, or a chemical rust remover, then remove the oil with a degreaser or denatured alcohol.

2. APPLY THE BASE COAT. Shake the paint can for 2 minutes or more, according to the instructions. Apply a base coat of white paint or white primer to achieve a deep finished color. Spray in a well-ventilated area. Hold the can 8 to 10 inches from the surface and spray in a sweeping motion from side to side. Some spray paints have a special tip that can be adjusted to spray vertically or horizontally. Check the can label instructions. Apply a thin coat and allow it to dry for 30 seconds. Apply 3 or 4 thin coats until the surface is completely and evenly covered.

3. DECIDE ON A PATTERN. The trick with this project is to transform your furniture to reflect your tastes and outdoor decor. Simple lines create a more classic appearance. A lively stenciled pattern can mean fun, fun, fun. Examine your furniture and design a pattern that suits you, perhaps following concentric lines or shapes in the surface. You will use this pattern for masking and color placement. It may help to sketch out your idea on a piece of paper first. If you desire a pattern such as the leaves in our example, make stencils to create the desired effect. An easy method is to make peel-off stencils from removable contact paper, available at most craft stores. Wide blue painter's tape also works well for this purpose.

4. APPLY COLOR 1. Mask off the desired pattern on your project to create the look that you want. Then spray each with color 1, following directions on the paint can. Set it aside to dry. When the paint is dry to the touch, carefully remove the masking materials. Let the furniture dry completely overnight.

5. APPLY COLOR 2. Mask the top borders of your project with newspaper and blue painter's tape. Spray-paint the center tops of the tables and then the sides and legs with color 2. Set aside to dry. When the paint is dry to the touch, carefully remove the masking materials. Let the furniture dry completely overnight. Check the label for specific curing times, but it will most likely take a full 7 days to become chip and scratch resistant. Then have a party and invite all of the neighbors. They'll think you got a big raise.

The Sky's the Limit!

Looking for more ways to add some color and fun to items you already have? Check out these ideas from my friends at Krylon.

▶ *Playhouse makeover:* Transform an ordinary playhouse into a bright-red fire station or a pastel palace.

▶ *Around the house:* From dingy toy chests to uninspired storage containers, you can personalize and energize any plastic element in your home. Coordinate a child's patio set using a dramatic shade of paint. Use it on outdoor pots, utility covers, and more to extend the theme.

▶ *Brighten up the yard:* Plastic furniture and fences, shutters, mailboxes, hose boxes, yard ornaments, and other outdoor items are abused by the wind, the sun, and the rain, which leave them faded and discolored. Revive them with a dash of color. ■

PROJECT: CONTAGIOUS CONTAINER GARDEN

Difficulty level: ⊤

Andrea's Choice:
A Garden Tower

Looking for a new way to display the fruits of your labor—literally? Try Nancy Jane's Stacking Planters. They are specifically designed in such a manner that, when stacked, they produce a column of multiple pots that may be suspended in a hanging position or just left freestanding. Enjoy the freshness of leaf lettuce and miniature tomatoes where you never thought you had the room before. Admire the beauty of cascading ferns, wave petunias, portulacas, and many more. (Visit www.stackingpots.com.)

Container gardening is the latest craze, and if you're not one of the more than 90 million households that participate in some type of indoor or outdoor gardening activity, now is a great time to start. Container gardening is popular among all ages and lifestyles for a variety of reasons: it allows anyone to garden anywhere, even in an apartment or home with limited space; it allows you to garden indoors or out, regardless of climate; it's easier on the body than typical gardening; and it's less time consuming and more efficient. Containers can be used as centerpieces, herb gardens, or even as spots of color within other flower beds and gardens. Plants can be grouped by color or fragrance, and pots can be rotated to show the best blooms. You're limited only by your imagination!

You will need:

✓ Garden container(s)
✓ Soil
✓ Plant
✓ Gardening gloves (optional)
✓ Potting soil
✓ Watering can (or hose)

1. CHOOSE YOUR POTS. The key to success is selecting the right pot for the right job. Clay, wood, plastic, and concrete are all materials that are used outdoors. Heavy-duty polypropylene with UV inhibitors to resist fading and cracking offers durability, design, and not a lot of extra weight, which makes it a good choice for outdoors and for hanging. Ceramic and metal are often used, but primarily indoors. Self-watering pots feature different types of systems to wick and/or redirect the water and can reduce the frequency that your container garden needs watering.

Hanging baskets are often made from the previously mentioned materials or wire. Wire hangers tend to dry out more quickly and need to be watered often. When selecting a pot for outside use, look for colors that complement your landscaping and the exterior of your home.

2. CREATE A DRAIN HOLE. After choosing the type of planter you want, consider drainage. The pot should have holes. If it doesn't, you'll need to create them. Many pots have holes marked in the bottom. You can easily drill or punch through them. Some clay pots may require a masonry drill bit to make the proper hole. (Caution: be prepared to break a few pots as you learn how to drill through clay without damaging it). You can use newspaper to prevent the soil from pouring out the holes. Be sure to use a saucer under the pot to catch and hold any excess water. If you are dealing with a very large container, look for one that has a tray with wheels. It's easier on both your back and your movable garden.

3. CHOOSE THE PLANTS. The size of the planter will be determined by what you are planting, or the reverse can be true. If you have an abundance of small pots, be sure to choose plants that stay small—or plan to do frequent repotting. You might want to choose a color scheme, a mix of varying plants and heights, or a particular flower or scent that is your favorite. Consider whether the plants can tolerate sun, do well in partial sun, or prefer shade. It's best to group together plants that like the same conditions. You can also plant an herb garden or even vegetables in a container. Just be sure that the container has space large enough to allow for the plant's root growth.

4. MIX THE POTTING SOIL. Now that you're ready to plant, choose a good soil mix: one that is not too heavy and is easy to work with. Mix in a water retention medium (a special polymer that helps to hold in water), available at most garden centers or nurseries, to help maintain the moisture. Fill the pot up to 1 inch from the rim, as there will be some settling. Then get planting!

5. MAINTAIN YOUR PLANTS. Don't be afraid to feed your potted plants with fertilizer. Slow release or liquid soluble fertilizers are best absorbed. Follow the directions on the packaging.

Be sure to keep an eye on the temperature and watch out for extremes in either direction. Plants in containers can freeze or overheat more quickly than bedded plants. Keep them looking healthy by pruning and deadheading them regularly. This will also help keep them from getting too long and leggy. Place the containers in spots that receive enough light and rotate them often. ■

Andrea's Choice:
A Lighted Hanging Basket

Display any hanging basket, wind chimes, or small objet d'art from a unique lighted tulip that connects to a Malibu low-voltage lighting system. Seven watts of power help provide nighttime safety and romance around your pool, walkway, or yard. The all-metal construction and delicate, curving light will last for many seasons. Use singly or in groups to create a lighted garden path to paradise. (Visit www.intermatic.com.)

PROJECT: FLOWER BED FRENZY

Level of difficulty: $T T T T$

If you love to get your hands dirty in the garden, you'll love this project. Building a flower bed is an enjoyable process with lasting rewards. Just follow these simple steps and you will have blooms in no time.

You will need:

- ✓ Rope, garden hose, or garden stakes with kitchen twine
- ✓ Trowel
- ✓ Shovel or spade
- ✓ Cardboard and newspaper (if you choose the second option in step 2)
- ✓ Compost or enriched soil
- ✓ Choice of flexible plastic or metal edging
- ✓ Peat moss
- ✓ Fertilizer
- ✓ Mulch
- ✓ Tiller

1. DETERMINE THE SHAPE OF YOUR FLOWER BED. Mark the shape of the flower bed with rope, a garden hose, or anything flexible enough to keep its shape. Or tap a wooden or metal stake into the ground at each curve or corner of the flower bed and wind kitchen twine around each stake.

2. START DIGGING. At this point, you can either dig up the top layer of sod and topsoil or you can lay down layers of cardboard, paper, and compost so that the sod naturally decays within a few months. Either way, the goal is to clear out the bed and enrich the soil. Let's look at the two ways we can do this.

> ▶ Cut the sod out with a shovel or spade, about 1 inch below the topsoil, and move it to another section of the yard. The sod can be used to cover bare areas or left to decay and mulch. Clear the bed of rocks and branches and of any stray roots and grass. Turn up the soil to aerate it. Ideally, your soil will be loose up to 1 to 2 trowel blades deep. Turn compost into the soil with a tiller.

► If you can plan to wait a few months before planting, another way to prepare the bed is to cut cardboard out in the shape of the cordoned-off area. Place it on top of the grass and wet it down thoroughly. On top of the cardboard, lay several sheets of newspaper. Cover the newspaper with compost or with enriched soil from a nursery up to about ½-foot high. If you do this now, in 2 to 4 months, the bed will be ready to aerate and plant. At that point, follow the same instructions as above.

3. BEGIN EDGING. To prevent grass from growing in the bed, line the edge of the bed with flexible plastic or metal edging. Edging pieces, which come in a variety of colors and shapes, can usually be hammered into the ground. You may choose to liven up the edge of your flower beds even further by creating a border of bricks, concrete pavers, or wooden beams.

4. ADD ORGANIC MATTER. Before planting, thoroughly blend the soil with peat moss and fertilizer or other recommended organic matter. You may want to mix in some moisture retention medium as well.

5. GET PLANTING. Now it's time to bed the plants. Determine the placement of your plants by referring to the tag that is supplied with each variety or by asking for advice at your local garden center or plant retailer. Place the plants into the correct size hole and press them firmly into place.

6. COVER THE BED WITH MULCH. After your plants are in place, top the bed off with a layer of mulch. Shredded bark is a good choice for a mulch because it is both decorative and functional; it helps to retain moisture and keep the beds clean. ■

Quick Tip:
Less Is More

My friend Fran Sorin, author of *Digging Deep*, offers the following advice to budding gardeners: "My rule of thumb when it comes to gardening tools is 'less is more.' I am a firm believer in buying only the tools that I need and taking my time in selecting quality ones that feel comfortable in my hands. If you treat your tools with care, they will be your lifelong friends."

Has your yard seen better days? Do you long for a tranquil and serene haven, a private retreat from the noise and bustle of a busy lifestyle? Read along as we transform your botanical dreams into a "plantiful" paradise.

You will need:
- ✓ Plants
- ✓ Spade or shovel
- ✓ Small rake
- ✓ Tiller
- ✓ Organic matter
- ✓ Hedge trimmer
- ✓ Trowel
- ✓ Flagstone
- ✓ Granite mixture
- ✓ Bags of sand
- ✓ Engraved bricks or stones
- ✓ Misc. garden decor

1. LAY OUT A DESIGN. Begin by sketching out a plan of the whole project, taking into account your family's needs, desires, and entertaining style. One way to minimize expenses is to utilize as much of the existing materials as possible, so take stock of what you have that can be repaired or salvaged.

2. CONSIDER MAJOR PURCHASES. Is there a special something that can become the focal point of your new garden paradise? Can you afford it? If you are considering a hot tub or even a swimming pool, now is the time to determine such necessities as space, electrical source, and water usage. Even if you're not yet ready to make the big splurge, plan for it now if you know it's just a matter of time. For instance, if the spa is in next year's budget, now is the time to lay a Pavestone or concrete pad for it so that you won't have to damage surrounding plants at a later date. Use it as a minibistro patio until the spa is installed.

Quick Tip: Get Professional Help

On my last yard renovation, I decided to do something that I had never done before. I hired a landscape designer to help plan the new space. Chris Van Horn of LandCreations in Dallas laid out a flowing landscape, utilizing the curves of my yard's native topography and placement of the home. He recommended materials and plants that would minimize upkeep for my busy family. Natural stones were used in many areas to develop an English countryside appearance, along with seemingly random plant beds to enhance the rustic effect. I could not be happier with the results.

Andrea's Choice: Do-It-Yourself Spa

If your backyard was not originally wired for a hot tub, it can be quite costly to have 220 volts installed to accommodate the average model. I had the same problem in my own yard, so I

→

3. PREPARE THE SITE. Use a tiller to help irrigate the soil and blend in organic matter. (See the project on preparing flower beds on page 256 for more information.) Also, since your home's gutters will help to irrigate the new plant beds, you should do any necessary rerouting before delicate foliage is in place. Take the time to trim back any overgrown tree limbs to allow more sunlight to penetrate the yard, which will foster plant growth and prevent future damage to your roof and gutters.

Now is also the time to repair any broken or damaged concrete, pavers, brickwork, rotted landscape timbers, or any other elements that could affect the garden atmosphere. Also, check to be sure that your sprinkler system is working properly and make any necessary repairs. If you don't have a sprinkler system, now might be a good time to have one installed.

4. CHOOSE YOUR NEW PLANTS. Here comes the fun part. Study plant and seed catalogs to educate yourself. Then visit some local nurseries and talk to the staff. Usually, they can advise you on which plants will thrive in your area and the varieties that suit your particular yard. Take care to complement the style of your home and to maximize sunny and shaded areas. Choose low-maintenance perennials (plants that live for several growing seasons) that can become a permanent part of the new landscape as well as colorful annuals (plants that only live for one growing season) that will create some accent beds. Although annual plants last only one year, their color displays make them well worth the investment. If you want lots of color, but still want plants that will come back next season, buy perennials at the nursery that are already in bloom. With the looming threat of drought in many areas, consider plants that can survive and even thrive during low-water conditions.

5. MIX AND MATCH YOUR PLANTS. In nature, random flora and fauna work together to create a harmony that is difficult to match. However, by interlacing a myriad of plant species, you can imitate nature's handiwork. Try to choose a blend of colors and textures that complements your home, placing shorter foliage in front of taller-growth plants. Also group your beds by their watering requirements and need for sunlight and shade.

opted for a do-it-yourself spa, manufactured by ThermoSpas. It can be ordered with a simple 110-volt plug, eliminating the need for expensive wiring. I only had to add a GFCI (ground fault circuit interrupter) for safety's sake. Plus, although the spa appears to be a permanent fixture, I'll be able to take it with me when I move. My model accommodates five adults and includes a built-in cooler and drink holders.

Quick Tip:
Perfect Plants

Garden designer Chris Van Horn offers the following advice for creating your own botanical paradise: "Start with good plants. Obtaining plant material that is healthy and full can make the difference between a poor landscape and a great one." Chris adds, "In times of drought, plants which are in one gallon or larger containers can withstand less watering than plants that are purchased in flats, so they are often worth the extra investment. The larger root ball holds moisture longer so your chances of a strong start are better. Smaller starter vegetation may need watering two or three times per day, which may conflict with watering restrictions in your area."

6. ADD SERENITY ACCENTS. When you've had a hard day, who doesn't dream of an escape from life's tension and stress? What could be better than a serenity garden in your own backyard? To finalize your botanical paradise, ring your garden with bricks and stones engraved with words that hold special meaning to you and your family—Love, Wisdom, Faith, and so on.

Try a pair of etched benches placed in a semicircle to form a cozy spot for meditation and relaxation. Add a stone or copper fountain, some bird feeders, and wind chimes to provide a delicate melody for you and any guests who visit your serenity garden. ■

Quick Tip:
Fun-tastic Flagstones

Looking for a long-lasting solution for filling a rough or oddly shaped area in your yard? Try laying down flagstones on a bed of decomposed granite. Choose an assortment of stones that can be fit together like a puzzle on top of approximately 3 inches of granite mixture (available at most garden suppliers and home centers). The granite, like a coarse sand and gravel mixture, will eventually harden into a concretelike mortar between the stones. Flagstones and granite are great for walkways, too.

Serve up an entrée of flowers in your backyard and you'll soon discover garden pests and guests dropping in for a buffet of garden treats. Learn how to distinguish the marauding insects from the allies and discover which plants will attract more friendly guests to your garden.

To the squeamish, the garden is full of "creepy crawlers," but it can be a relaxing place full of discovery and beauty that attracts butterflies, ladybugs, dragonflies, and myriads of other helpful insects. Helpful insects eat mosquitoes and other pests and aid in pollination. Have fun creating a buffet of flowers that is a feast not only for the bees and butterflies, but also for the eyes. And yes, at times there are "creepy crawlers," but with the right insect allies in the garden, a delicate and harmonious balance can be achieved.

You will need:

- ✓ Zinnias
- ✓ Pentas
- ✓ Butterfly bush
- ✓ Lavender
- ✓ Mexican heather
- ✓ Shasta daisies
- ✓ Ladybugs
- ✓ Praying mantises
- ✓ Water sprayer
- ✓ Bird feeder
- ✓ Birdbath
- ✓ Plants

1. CHOOSE THE PLANTS. Everyone can appreciate the delicate beauty of a butterfly as it flutters through the garden. But not everyone knows how easy it is to create a garden oasis that will attract butterflies. There are a variety of flowering plants that are as self-sufficient as a pet rock and yield a lot more pleasure. This is especially helpful as water restrictions have become stringent in many cities around the country.

Quick Tip:
Magic Moss

One of the most beautiful features of a garden makeover can be an assortment of mossy boulders to dot the landscape. Want to grow moss in your own yard? Start with a rock that has moss or lichen on it, which you can buy at most stone yards. Try to find stone that is from your region so that the moss is accustomed to the climate there. Place the stone in a cool, shady, rocky spot. Drizzle the moss regularly with buttermilk, which encourages growth, and watch the moss spread to nearby rocks and ground.

Pick Your Plants!

Taking your budget, gardening experience, and your plans for the garden into consideration, you can choose from a variety of butterfly-attracting plants.

ANNUALS

▶ *Zinnias:* You'll find the dwarf and tall varieties of zinnias in pink, yellow, orange, and fuchsia at your local nursery. Zinnias are annuals, which means they will die when the weather gets cold, but they reseed profusely, so new flowers will spring up year after year. The dwarf version tends to get bushy in a manageable way and does well in controlling weeds by literally squeezing them out. The larger version grows taller and is more compact. Although zinnias will occasionally attract caterpillars that can eat some plants, they are for the most part a carefree, drought-tolerant, sun-loving plant, perfect for the beginning butterfly gardener.

▶ *Pentas:* A butterfly favorite, pentas feature clusters of star-shaped blooms all season. Blooms come in white, pale pink, and fuchsia. They will die with the first freeze, and so you'll need to purchase new flowers each year, but they are worth the expense in attracting butterflies. They will also attract caterpillars, but luckily caterpillars are easy to locate and remove.

PERENNIALS

▶ *Butterfly bush:* With a name like butterfly bush, how can a butterfly gardener resist? True to its name, the butterfly bush will attract countless butterfly visitors to the garden. Butterfly bush is easy to grow and difficult to kill. It features clusters of sweet fragrant blooms in purple, pink, lavender, blue, white, and orange.

▶ *Shasta daisies:* Another of my favorites—they can grow almost anywhere and thrive even with minimal care. Butterflies love Shastas, plus they make nice cut bouquets for your home. The plants burst with white flowers in masses of 3-inch blooms with a yellow center. Each plant can grow up to 3 feet tall and 3 feet in width.

2. BRING ON THE BEES. Bees are easily attracted to a garden ripe with blooms, and they are fascinating to watch. However, be wary if you have young children or family members that are allergic to bees. Lavender is a perennial that can be enjoyed yearlong, with plumes of purple flowers that attract bees in the spring and summer. Mexican heather will reach its prime in the summer, attracting countless bees to its tiny purple flowers. Both plants require virtually no care and do well with little watering.

3. WELCOME LADYBUG WARRIORS. Ladybugs are welcome guests to any garden, as they feed tirelessly on plant-destroying aphids. You can purchase live ladybugs for your garden at specialty nurseries and garden centers. Keep in mind that it's impossible to make them stay in your garden once they're released, but many will stick around if you have enough of a food source to entice them. Aphids beware!

4. PRAY FOR MANTIS. The praying mantis is one of your best allies in your garden because it is a predator of many garden pests. It can be difficult to spot, as it often resembles the foliage. The praying mantis eats many other insects, including grasshoppers, beetles, flies, and moths. Mantis eggs can be purchased at your local garden center or specialty catalogs.

5. DRAW IN DRAGONFLIES. A welcome predator in the garden, dragonflies are attracted to water sources such as ponds, lakes, and streams. They eat mosquitoes, flies, and butterflies, and can be found perching on branches or stems.

6. WARD OFF THE APHIDS. Aphids are tiny insects that suck the sap out of foliage. They are generally yellow, green, white, or black and move very slowly. You'll find them on the underside of leaves or along the stems on vines. In addition to causing leaves to wilt, they can spread viruses. You can remove them by spraying the foliage of the plant vigorously with a strong water sprayer, or spray the insects that you find on the plants with a mixture of soap and water, but you'll need to spray the plants on a regular basis. Aphids will excrete a honey dew that attracts ants; in fact, the two tend to live together harmoniously.

7. WATCH OUT FOR GOBS OF GRASSHOPPERS. A familiar visitor in your lawn, the grasshopper is known to inflict damage by chewing on the leafy foliage of grass as well as plants. Spiders and birds are their common natural predators. Place a bird feeder and birdbath to attract birds to your garden.

8. CATER TO CATERPILLARS. Without the caterpillar, there would be no butterfly. But don't let this fact make you turn a blind eye to your plant leaves and tender flower buds that are steadily being nibbled away. Leafy plants such as chard and ornamental kale serve as fast-food neon signs for caterpillars. You'll recognize the holes eaten through the leaves. Hibiscus is another caterpillar favorite. They will eat holes through the little buds, and then when the buds finally bloom, you'll see holes through the petals. Instead of using insecticides on plants in your vegetable garden, examine the plants on a regular basis to manually remove the caterpillars.

9. SHAKE OFF SLIMY SLUGS AND SNAILS. Slugs and snails inflict damage to a garden by eating foliage, flowers, and even fruits. They tend to be attracted to young, tender growth, and you can often find the culprits down at the base of a plant. You can also distinguish their damage by the silvery trail they leave behind. You'll find them in moist, shady parts of the garden, sheltered under weedy areas or hidden under ground cover. Heavy rainfall and overwatering will encourage them to flourish while dry, cold weather makes them inactive. You can gather them by hand and discard them. ■

Is your grass a little patchy? Whether it's from one-too-many hot days, drought, or disease, many lawns suffer from bald spots. But there is a simple way to patch up your lawn to perfection.

You will need:
- ✓ Sod
- ✓ Knife
- ✓ Rake
- ✓ Shovel
- ✓ Trowel

1. **IDENTIFY AREAS AROUND YOUR YARD THAT NEED A PATCH JOB.**

2. **REMOVE BAD SECTIONS OF YOUR LAWN.** Using your shovel and trowel, dig up the old, dead, or disease-ridden sections of grass. Even if an area is already bare, it's not a bad idea to turn the soil and make sure that it is completely clear of residual grass and weeds.

3. **RAKE OVER THE AREAS TO SMOOTH OUT THE SURFACE.**

4. **PREPARE THE SOD PATCHES.** Cut pieces of sod that are the same sizes and shapes as the bare areas and make sure they fit snugly. Press down on each patch with your foot to make sure they settle into the soil.

5. **WATER THE SOD PATCHES.** Soak the patches with water and keep up a good watering regimen until the new grass has been completely established and has a good chance of surviving and blending in with the rest of the lawn. ■

Three Tips to Lawn Success

It is a whole lot easier to have a great looking lawn than most people realize. Here are three foolproof tips from my buddy Ashton Ritchie, the spokesperson for the Scotts Miracle-Gro folks.

1. Mow your grass taller. By adjusting your mower height to the highest setting, you will help your lawn grow deeper roots to match the increased leaf growth. A taller lawn will be a better competitor against creeping weeds and weed seedlings. And your lawn will be better able to withstand hot, dry weather.

2. Only water when your lawn really needs it, but water long enough so your soil gets moisture down deep. Lawns need about 1 inch of water a week from rainfall or watering. Without this water, the grass will stop growing and go into a brown, dormant state. If you must water your lawn regularly, keep these tips in mind: When you can leave footprints on your lawn, this means it could use some water. Run your sprinklers long enough to put down a half inch of water twice a week so that your lawn will get the 1 inch of water per week that it needs. To determine how long to run your sprinklers, do this simple test: Place an ice tea glass on the lawn, run your sprinkler for half an hour, then measure how much water you have in the glass. This will help you calculate how long to run your sprinklers to get half an inch of water. This deep watering will encourage your lawn to grow deep roots.

3. Feed your grass. Aside from the basics of mowing and watering, the single most important thing you can do for your lawn is to provide proper nutrition by fertilizing. One or two feedings a year make a marked improvement; however, the difference between a so-so lawn and a truly beautiful lawn can be seen with four or five feedings a year. Different brands of fertilizer vary widely in effectiveness, even if they have the same nitrogen-phosphorus-potassium (N-P-K) numbers on the bag, so get a brand you can trust, like Scotts or Vigoro. Ask your lawn care dealer for products that work well in your area. Follow the schedule on the back of the package so that you are using the right product at the right time of year to keep your lawn immaculate.

That's all there is to it. Your grass will thank you and your neighbors will hound you for advice when you mow tall, water deeply, and follow an annual feeding schedule of four or five feedings.
(Resource: Scotts Company)

With the right mixture of low-voltage and sun-powered solar lighting, the fun doesn't have to stop when the sun goes down. No matter your budget or do-it-yourself skills, anyone can create a great atmosphere around the home with simple, cost-effective, easy-to-install, and energy-efficient outdoor lighting. Outdoor lighting differs from indoor lighting in that it is water resistant and protected from the elements. New technologies make installation safer and quicker than ever.

Outdoor lighting is available in three major types.

▶ Sun-powered solar-accent lighting, which uses a specially designed solar collection panel to convert sunlight into electrical power, providing up to 15 hours of light when fully charged

▶ Low-voltage lighting, which runs directly from a transformer and plugs into a main socket

▶ Hardwired, 120-volt outdoor lighting, which is part of your home's standard electrical system

Choosing Between Solar, Low Voltage, and Hardwired

Installing outdoor lights is usually a very simple task. Solar lighting couldn't be easier. The only requirement is to ensure that the solar panel receives direct sunlight. New technologies in solar panels even allow for remote placement approximately 20 feet from the light itself. This application is ideal for lighting a remote tree or a statue, for example, where underground wiring is not practical. Solar lighting is not as bright as low-voltage and hardwired, in most cases.

Low-voltage lights are also simple to install and extremely safe. Because most systems require only 12 volts of power, there is no special electrical expertise required. I designed and installed a low-voltage system around my own home over a Saturday afternoon. It was quick, easy, and fun.

Since low-voltage lights use the same principle as model trains, reducing the regular household electrical current (120 volts) to a safe 12 volts, they're great for use around children and pets. Plus, they're far more economical to operate than ordinary 120-volt lighting fixtures. In fact, a typical six-light set uses less electricity than a single 75-watt bulb.

If you need bright light for security purposes, hardwired fixtures are the best choice, but they use more energy than low voltage. One way to save kilowatts and still provide security is to replace standard outdoor light fixtures with motion-sensor lighting, which is perfect for areas where constant light is not needed.

By using a blend of 120-volt hardwired, low-voltage, and solar-accent lighting, you can create a beautiful landscape day and night, making your home and grounds more attractive and secure.

1. PLAN YOUR "LIGHTSCAPE." Create a drawing of your home and lay out the general elements you want to light. Include walkways, steps, driveways, patios, landscaping, gardens, decks, and other outdoor elements. Ask yourself the following questions:

▶ What are the most attractive features of your yard?

▶ Which areas need to be lit for security?

▶ Which areas need to be lit for safety?

2. DETERMINE THE PLACEMENT OF YOUR LIGHTING. Follow your own tastes and needs to mix and match different types of lighting to create the perfect "lightscape." The first step is to understand the different types of lighting techniques and their benefits, including:

▶ *Downlighting:* Lights are placed above an object or area and aimed downward to imitate natural light. Downlighting is often used to provide security to an area such as along walkways and steps, outline driveways, mark garden paths and flower beds, and accent patios and decks. Fixtures of this type may include flood- or spotlights.

▶ *Backlighting:* Often used for security, backlighting is usually placed to cast a silhouette on a wall or directed onto a surface behind the object that is to be lit. The best uses for backlighting include accenting trees and bushes, illuminating walls and fences, and lighting up a home's exterior.

▶ *Uplighting:* Lights are placed at ground level and are aimed upward to highlight focal points in the landscape. Uplighting can beautify specific areas and is best used to create a dramatic focal point, highlight small trees and shrubs, and illuminate fountains and garden statuary.

3. SELECT YOUR LIGHTING FIXTURES. Consider the different types of low-voltage and solar-lighting available. Here are a few of the most popular.

▶ *Floodlights:* These lights literally flood an area with light. They are often used to accent shrubbery and large trees. They are also useful to illuminate fences and walls and for security purposes.

▶ *Walk lights:* These are usually taller fixtures that allow light to disperse over a large area to provide more illumination to surrounding surfaces. They can be useful to light up pathways, gardens, and entryways.

▶ *Surface/deck lights:* Surface and deck lights are a nice way to keep your pool and deck area well lit and safe for night use. These lights can mount directly onto the surfaces of walls, fences, decks, and gazebos. They help to direct foot traffic around steps, benches, and railings.

▶ *Tier lights:* Tiers and shades direct light downward to minimize glare. Tier lights are ideal for lighting walkways and steps.

▶ *Low-profile lights:* If you want the light to blend in with your garden or illuminate light closer to the ground, try low-profile lights. These styles of lights are perfect for landscape borders and driveways.

4. DETERMINE YOUR POWER REQUIREMENTS. Determine the type of power needed for your lights. If you are installing lights in a location that does not have electrical power nearby, solar lights are a good option, because they can be installed anywhere. For other areas, locate the nearest power outlet. Consider installing a weatherproof cover to keep rain and snow out of the outlet.

Power packs are designed to provide safe low-voltage power to your light fixtures. They are available in sizes up to 900 watts, so you can select the power pack that is right for your installation or expand your existing system. When installing low-voltage lights, add up the individual bulb wattages of all the fixtures. Use the total wattage to select a power pack with enough power to properly light all of your fixtures. Ask your lighting dealer for assistance if you are unsure.

5. LOCATE THE POWER PACK. Once you have selected the right unit, connect the power pack at least 1 foot above ground. Then check the lighting fixture positions in your lighting plan and determine the length of cable needed to connect the fixtures to the power source. Keep cable runs as short as possible from the power pack—around 10 to 20 feet, if possible.

6. INSTALL THE LIGHTING FIXTURES. Begin installing solar lights first, since they do not require receptacles or transformers. To install low-voltage lights, locate the power pack and attach the low-voltage cables. Turn the power pack on. Lay out the cable and attach individual light fixtures to it with the power on. Most low-voltage systems install with a simple clip that connects into the main wire.

Install the fixtures into the ground or on surfaces according to the instructions. Most outdoor lighting comes with an easy-to-use ground stake.

7. FINISH UP. Check all the lights to ensure each fixture works properly. If you are pleased with the layout and position of the fixtures, hide the exposed cable with mulch, dirt, rocks, or leaves. They only need to be an inch or so underground. Then relax and enjoy your new lighting system!
(Resource: Malibu by Intermatic/www.intermatic.com) ■

resource guide

Acoustic Ceiling Products, LLC
Maker of a nifty faux tin product for walls,
    backsplashes, and ceilings.
www.acpideas.com
800-434-3750

AirAdvice, Inc.
Resource for indoor air quality testing.
www.airadvice.com
866-247-4800

Air Conditioning Contractors of America
Trade organization for heating and air-
    conditioning pros.
www.ACCA.org/consumer

Amerimax Home Products, Inc.
Manufacturers of gutters and parts for
    gutter repair.
www.Amerimax.com
800-347-2586

Arborilogical Services
Professional tree experts in
    Dallas/Ft. Worth area.
www.aborilogical.com
972-442-1524

Aspen Shops, LLC
Distributors of Un-Do, an adhesive removal
    product.
www.AspenShopsOnline.com
877-834-8541

Benjamin Franklin Plumbing
A franchise grouping of plumbers.
www.benjaminfranklin plumbing.com
866-423-6669

Bemis Manufacturing Company
Manufacturers of toilet seats and parts
www.bemismfg.com
800-558-7651

Better Business Bureau
Watchdog organization of US businesses.
www.BBB.org
703-276-0100

Better Living Products International Inc.
Manufacturers of soap dispensers and
    organizers for bathrooms.
www.dispenser.com
800-487-3300

Blaine Window Hardware, Inc.
Makers and distributors of parts for
windows, old and new.
www.BlaineWindow.com
800-678-1919

BonaKemi USA, Inc.
Makers of high-quality floor finishing
products.
www.bonakemi.com
800-574-4674

Bramton Company
Makers of Simple Solution, a product that
helps neutralize pet odors.
www.simplesolution.com
800-272-6336

Briwax International, Inc.
Importers of Briwax and other fine wood
care products.
www.briwax.com
800-527-4929

BuildBiz, Inc.
www.designbiz.com
800-925-1607

Centers for Disease Control and Prevention
(CDC)
www.cdc.gov

Clutter Queen, Inc.
Jennifer Humes, the ultimate organizer
www.ClutterQueen.com
214-906-9648

Consentino USA
Makers of Silestone.
www.silestoneusa.com
800-291-1311

ConservCo Water Conservation Products, LLC
Manufacturers of water-saving products
like the Drip Stop valve.
www.DripStop.com
775-747-3340

Consumers Union of USA, Inc.
The folks who write and distribute
Consumer Reports magazine.
www.ConsumerReports.com
800-333-0663

Core Distribution, Inc.
www.Core-Distribution.com
Makers of Xtend & Climb Telescoping
Ladder.
612-330-9915

CPFilms Inc.
The window film experts.
www.GilaFilms.com
800-528-4481

CSS Global
Caulk-mate is a nifty product that helps
make a smooth caulk line.
www.caulkmate.net
877-228-5539

Dwight and Church, Inc.
The folks who make baking soda.
www.armandhammer.com
800-524-1328

Efficient Windows Collaborative
www.EfficientWindows.org
202-530-2254

E Z Faux Décor
Makers of stainless film and other
decorative films.
www.ezfauxdecor.com
913-451-0977

First Alert
Safety products from smoke alarms to fire
    extinguishers.
www.firstalert.com
800-323-9005

Fluidmaster USA
Parts and advice for repairing toilets and
    more.
www.fluidmaster.com
949-728-2000

Foundation Repair Association, Inc.
www.FoundationRepair.org
866-561-3724

Gerard Roofing Technologies
Manufacturers of stone-coated, steel roofs.
www.GerardUSA.com
800-841-3213

Gloucester Publishing
My friends who publish *Old House Interiors*
    magazine.
www.OldHouseInteriors.com
800-462-0211

GutterMaxx, LP
Hooded gutters
www.guttermaxx.com
800-595-1055

Great Neck Saw
Makers of every kind of hand tool under
    the sun.
www.greatnecktools.com
800-457-0600

Henkel Corporation
Glue, tape, and epoxy fillers.
www.stickwithpl.com
800-999-8920

Hinge-It Corp.
A nifty space-saving hook that fits right on
    a door hinge.
www.hingeit.com
800-284-4643

Home Buyer Publications/Active Interest
    Media
The folks who publish *Old House Journal*
    magazine.
www.OldHouseJournal.com

House Doctors, Inc.
Need a handyman? These fellows can help
    you.
www.HouseDoctors.com

IdeaStix, Inc.
Self-stick wall, tile and switchplate décor.
www.ideastix.com
310-530-9965

Insinkerator
The manufacturers of the best darn
    disposals around.
www.insinkerator.com
800-558-5700

Intermatic, Inc.
My good buddies who make Malibu
    outdoor lighting products.
www.intermatic.com
815-675-7000

Internet Brands: Homes Division
A wonderful online resource for DIY
    projects and products of all kinds.
www.DoItYourself.com
800-692-2200

JELMAR
Makers of Tarnex, CLR and other cleaning
    products.
www.jelmar.com
800-323-5497

Krylon
Spray paint and finish experts.
www.krylon.com
800-457-9566

Lennox Comfort Systems
Leaders in air-conditioning and heating
systems for homes and businesses.
www.lennox.com/residential
800-953-6669

Magic American Products
Makers of GooGone. No home should be
without it.
www.googone.com
800-321-6330

Mark Clement
A good friend, carpenter, and author.
www.TheCarpentersNotebook.com
info@centerlinemedia.com

McCall Pattern Company
Instant, self-adhesive wall décor.
www.wallies.com
800-255-2762

**Millenium International Development
Corporation**
Easy-to-use edging to spruce-up plain
mirrors.
www.MirrEdge.com
800-757-2990

MNG Hardware, LLC
Beautiful decorative hardware.
www.mnghardware.com
877-598-8889

Moen Incorporated
Faucet fanatics. Check out their new
models.
www.Moen.com
800-289-6636

Motsenbocker's Lift Off, Inc.
Makers of several formulas of stain
removers.
www.LiftOffInc.com
858-581-0222

**National Association of the Remodeling
Industry**
Looking for a remodeler. Contact NARI for
a complete list in your area.
www.NARI.org
800-611-6274

National Sanitation Foundation (NSF)
www.nsf.org
800-673-6275

National Trust for Historic Preservation
Publishers of *Preservation* magazine and
leaders in historic preservation in the
country.
www.NationalTrust.org

N J Supply Ltd.
Unique stacking pots for container
gardening.
www.stack-a-pots.com
nancy@stackingpots.com

Nostalgic Warehouse
My former company. The best reproduction
hardware around.
www.nostalgicwarehouse.com
800-522-7336

Pavestone®
www.pavestone.com
800-580-7283

QUIKRETE® Companies
www.Quikrete.com
800-282-5828

RainChains.com
An alternative to downspouts.
www.RainChains.com
888-480-7246

Reiker Room Conditioners
Celing fans that help to heat too.
www.buyreiker.com
866-473-4537

RepairClinic.com
An online resource for appliance parts and
free advice.
www.RepairClinic.com
800-269-2609

Rohm and Haas Paint Quality Institute
Find out about paint techniques and
decorating ideas at this unique Web site.
www.paintquality.com

Rust-Oleum Corporation
Makers of spray paint and pain décor kits.
www.Rustoleum.com
800-323-3584

SafeDrainCleaner.com
Makers of Bio-Clean, a natural drain
cleaner.
www.safedraincleaner.com
978-456-3848

Safety Quick Light
An easier way to install light fixtures.
www.safetyquicklight.com
770-754-4711

Samuel Heath & Sons Plc
Some of the best accessory hardware in the
world.
www.samuel-heath.com

Schlage Locks
The standard of the industry for home and
business door locks.
www.schlage.com
800-847-1864

Scotts Lawn and Garden
Using technology to make a greener world.
www.scotts.com
888-270-3714

Scripps Networks, Inc.
The folks who run HGTV and the DIY
Network.
www.diynetwork.com
800-311-3435

SDS Corporation
Makers of Crete Sheet, an easier way to mix
concrete.
www.cretesheet.com
866-571-7749

Sod Solutions
Developers of new strains of grasses for
southern homes.
www.sodsolutions.com
843-849-1288

Solatube
Makers of Solatube, tubuler daylighting
device.
www.Solatube.com
888-765-2882

Stiletto Tools Inc.
Crazy, titanium hammers.
www.StilettoTools.com
800-987-1849

Super Glue Corporation
Innovators in glues and epoxies.
www.SuperglueCorp.com
800-538-3091

Swann Communications
   USA Inc.
Security products for homes and
   businesses.
www.SwannUSA.com
877-274-3695

ThermoSpas
Turn your backyard into a health spa with a
   Thermspa hot tub.
www.ThermoSpas.com
866-702-9200

This Old House magazine
www.ThisOldHouse.com
800-898-7237

Thomas' Kitchen Art, Inc.
Makers of liquid stainless steel.
www.liquidstainlesssteel.com
800-650-5699

Thompson's Company
The folks who make Thompson's Water
   Seal.
www.thompsonsonline.com
800-367-6297

U S Department of Energy
www.eere.energy.gov
800-342-5363

US EPA
www.EnergyStar.gov
888-782-7937

Van Dyke's Restorers
A fantastic source for builders' and
   restoration hardware. Call for a free
   catalog.
www.vandykes.com
800-787-3355

Vermont Soapstone Company
Suppliers of soapstone countertops and
   other products to homeowners and
   builders.
www.VermontSoapstone.com
802-263-5404

Wallpaper Council
Online resource for wallpapering tips and
   ideas.
www.wallcoverings.org

Warrantech Corporation
Underwriters of home warranties.
www.warrantech.com
800-833-8801

Watermiser Broom
A super-useful patio cleaning device.
www.watermiser.com
877-744-9944

acknowledgments

This book is much like my radio show in that it has taken many folks to bring it to fruition. I am so fortunate to have a wonderful family and an extended network of dear friends who really care about me and visa versa. Almost everyone whom I know contributed something to this effort. Amy Legg and Ellen Locy spurred me to get this book started and Bill Strode helped me finish it. Remember those caning pics that you drew at the last minute, Bill? My son, Frank, was my rock during this last year, along with older siblings, Sally and Toni. My dad and mom who not only have loved and supported me since I was born but also fed Frank and me almost every night for months on end while I typed into the wee hours editing and rewriting. They never wavered in their love for us even during some trying moments. And what would I have done without Judy Parks, my right hand, friend, confidant, editor and partner? She listened to me as I triumphed and toiled all year, as she has done for fifteen years. I hope we have many more projects in our future.

So many more people were key to this book's completion; Kimyla Stegall who assisted with sources and support any time that I asked and many times when I didn't. My sister, Kate, who gave up her summer vacation to help format and brainstorm in the early days and all along this path. My other siblings and family members who cheered me on even when I was testy from fatigue or stressed during this process. Rob Courter and Keith Lowery who took some of the load off of me—and Keith also contributed to hardware installation tips and critiqued the whole hardware chapter. Robyn Short and Dianna Smoljan who ferreted out interested contributors and art insertions. Denise Holguin and Alicia Holston who generously supplied information. My friend, Doug Kellum, whose suggestions gave life to my introduction when writer's block had gripped me. Ron Schaer and Caroline Rich-ardson for their decor advice and experience. Ed Del Grande, aka Ed the Plumber, for his wonderful inroduction. Karl Champley whose Aussie style made many of the sections more fun. Mark Clemens, author of *The Carpenter's Notebook,* for his propensity to always say "yes" when I asked for help or input. Norm Alston who made sure that I kept one foot in the past as I walked into the future. Many others who are mentioned in these pages were a tremendous help as well as my radio show listeners—who often submitted ideas or suggestions for tips and topics.

I want to thank my agent, Judith Weber, and the wonderful Natalie Dupre for recommending her to me. I also wish to applaud my two editors at Collins Pub-lishers: Anna Bliss and Laura Dozier. They were patient, thorough, and a delight to work with.

I also want to express my sincere appreciation to the dozens of companies and manufacturers who generously gave information, photos and suggestions to en-hance many of the technical sections and projects. Please forgive me if I leave anyone out, but in particular, the folks at www.DoItYourself.com, www.Repair-Clinic.com, Lennox, Krylon, Great Neck Tools, Black and Decker, Superglue, Owens Corning, Moen, Fluidmaster, Ace Hardware, Home Depot, Malibu, Tony Termini of DripStop, First Alert, Ashton Ritchie and Scott's Lawn and Garden, Briwax, Schlage, Quikrete, Insinkerator, Amerimax, GutterMaxx, Thermatru Doors, Arboroligical Services, MD, Square D, GE, Dap, Gila, Reiker, and so many more—most of whom are identified within the body of the book.

index

compactors. *See* trash compactors

composition shingles, 228

compost, 175

Concrete Care Cleaner & Degreaser, 249

concrete caulks, 166

concrete coatings, 248–50

concrete floors, painting, 101–2

concrete forms, 245, 247

concrete foundations, 234–36
  common causes of shifting, 235
  common signs of damaged, 234
  preventive maintenance tips, 235–36

concrete staining, 249–50

concrete walkways, 245–47

Concrobium Mold Control, 15

ConservCo, 175

construction adhesives, 13

Consumer Reports, 34, 71

container gardens, 254–55

contractors, 23–25

convection ovens, 35

cooktops, 34–35
  tune-up tips, 41–42
  and work triangle, 29–31

cooling systems. *See also* air conditioners
  energy-saving tips, 163–65, 171–72, 181
  maintenance tips, 206

cordless drills, 3–4

cordless power saws, 4

corners, applying wallpaper to, 110–11

cost vs. value of home improvements, 19–20

countertops
  kitchen, 30
  tile, regrouting, 75–76

crayon marks, removing, 56

Crescent wrenches, 5

cross-threaded screws, 130

curb appeal, 243–44

damaged wood or metal,

repairing with epoxy filler, 196–97

DAP's Dynaflex 230, 167

dead-bolt locks, installing, 120–23

decal designs, for furniture, 137

deck care, 218–24
  cleaning, 219–21
  waterproofing, 218–19, 221–24

deck coatings, 221–24

deck lights, 269

Decorating Assistant, 87

decorating furniture, 137

decorating ideas, 81–113. *See also* painting; wallpapers
  choosing new paint color, 88–90
  creating design inspiration file, 85–87
  MTM (money, time, and methods), 82–84
  quick transformations, 88

decorative hardware, 131–32

decorative painting ideas, 96–98

decorators/designers, professional, 83–84

defrosting freezers, 39–40, 169

dehumidifiers, maintenance tips, 207

Dellutri, Laura, 41

Designs in Nature, wainscot kits, 60

Digging Deep (Sorin), 257

dimmers, for lights, 163

dishwashers, 36
  energy-saving tips, 170, 174
  tune-up tips, 42–43

dishwashing detergents, for stain removal, 15

Dispenser Plus Shower Basket, 64

disposals. *See* garbage disposals

distressing furniture, 137

dogs
  and air quality, 203–4
  stains and odors, products for

removing, 18

do-it-yourselfers, tips from Karl Champley for, 22–23

Donovan, Dave, 44

doors
  curb appeal of, 243–44
  hardware. *See* door hardware
  sagging, fixing, 125–26
  screens, replacing, 193–94
  weather-stripping, 160, 168

doorbells, 131
  replacing, 133

door chains, 128

door guards, 128

door hardware, 115–33
  fixing sagging doors, 125–26
  fixing wobbly doorknobs, 127
  functional and decorative, 131–32
  installing dead-bolt locks, 120–23
  installing security hardware, 128
  professionally refinishing, 123
  replacing doorbells, 133
  selecting new, 117–19
  unsticking sticky locks, 124

doorknobs, 115–19
  fixing wobbly, 127
  measuring existing, 117
  professionally refinishing, 123
  types of, 117–18

door locks. *See* locks

doorstops, 131–32

door sweeps, 160, 168

door viewers, 128

double-cylinder dead bolts, 128

downlighting outdoors, 268

down products, 204

downspout systems, 231, 232

drafty ductwork, 163

drafty windows and doors, 160, 194–95

dragonflies, 263

remodeling, 19–22
  bathroom plans, 60–61
  kitchen plans, 28–31
  MTM (money, time, and
    methods), 82–84
repair kits, basic home, 7–8
repairs. *See specific repairs*
replacement parts, for
    furniture, 136
repointing brick joints, 237–39
reproduction products, 21,
    32, 119
resource guide, 271–76
Restor-A-Finish, 48, 150
retro hardware, 21, 32
Richardson, Carolyn, 89–90
Ritchie, Ashton, 265–66
rollers, 94–95
  cleaning, 97
roofs (roofing), 226–29
  choosing, tips for, 227–28
  gutters and drainage, 230–
    33
  types of materials, 228–29
    room dividers, wallpapered,
    112–13
rope caulks, 167
rubber grips, 2
rubber mallets, 3
rust
  in dishwashers, 41
  in gutters, 232
  stains, 17
Rust-Oleum paints, 44
R-value of insulation, 178–79

safety at home, 9–11. *See also*
    carbon monoxide detectors;
    electrical safety; smoke
    alarms
  ladders, 10–11
safety glasses, 9, 12
Safety Quick Lights, 268
Sagan, Carl, 27
sagging doors, fixing, 125–26
Saint-Gobain Technical
    Fabrics, 193
salvage items, 21, 32, 119
Samuel Heath, 66
sanding blocks, 94

sandpaper, 94
saws, 4
Schaer, Ron, 84, 88
scratch-and-dent stores, 83
screen doors or windows,
    replacing, 193–94
screwdrivers, 3
sealants, 165–67
sealers (primers), 95, 249
sealing house leaks, 159–62,
    163. *See also* insulation
seam rollers, 109
seasonal energy efficiency ratio
    (SEER), 164
security hardware, installing,
    128
  dead-bolt locks, 120–23
self-defrosting refrigerators/
    freezers, 40
serenity gardens, 258–60
shasta daisies, 262
sheen striping, 96–97, 98
shifting foundations, common
    causes of, 235
shims, 126
shingles, 228–29
shopping for items, 86–87
  money-saving tips, 83
shower baskets, 64
shower curtains, 59
showerheads
  clogged, vinegar for, 79
  low-flow, 175
shower tiles, regrouting, 75–76
shrubs, 162, 224–25
silicone-based caulks, 166
Simple Solution, 18
single-pane windows, 161–62
sinks
  bathroom, 67
    refinishing with epoxy,
    77–79
  kitchen
    cleaning tips, 55–56
    work triangle and, 29–31
skill level, 82–84
skylights, 32
slate roofs, 226, 229
sledgehammers, 3
slip-joint pliers, 5

slugs, 264
smoke alarms, 197–99
  maintenance tips, 199
  placement of, 198
  power for, 197–98
  types of sensors in, 198
snails, 264
Sod Solutions, 266
SoftMetal decorative films, 35,
    38–39
solar heat gain coefficient
    (SHGC), 161
solar-powered lights, 163,
    267–68
solar water-heating systems,
    171
solar window screens, 162
Solatubes, 32
Sorin, Fran, 257
space, evaluating your, 85–86
spas, do-it-yourself, 258–59
"special" tools for furniture
    kits, storing, 10
spray-on radiant barriers, 179
spray-on strippers, 148–49
Square D, 210
Stacking Planters, 254
staining cane chairs, 146
staining concrete, 249–50
staining wood, 151–54
stainless-steel appliances, 33
stainless steel, faux, 35, 38–39
stain-removing solutions,
    14–18
  bloodstains, 17
  candle wax, 17
  carpet and upholstery, 17–
    18
  fruit stains, 18
  general tips, 14–15
  grass stains, 16
  oil, grease, and lipstick on
    clothes, 15–16
  paint stains, 16–17
  pet stains and odors, 18
  rust, 17
  tile grout, 72–74
  wood, 150
stamping decorative patterns
    in concrete, 246, 249